More Strategies for EDUCATING EVERYBODY'S CHILDREN

ROBERT W. COLE, EDITOR

ASCD

Association for Supervision and Curriculum Development
Alexandria, Virginia USA

Association for Supervision and Curriculum Development
1703 N. Beauregard St. • Alexandria, VA 22311-1714 USA
Telephone: 1-800-933-2723 or 703-578-9600 • Fax: 703-575-5400
Web site: http://www.ascd.org • E-mail: member@ascd.org

Printed in the United States of America.

ASCD Product No. 100229
s1/2001
ASCD member price: $21.95   nonmember price: $25.95

Library of Congress Cataloging-in-Publication Data

More strategies for educating everybody's children / Robert W. Cole,
editor.
     p. cm.
Companion vol. to: Educating everybody's children, c1995.
Includes bibliographical references (p.) and index.
    ISBN 0-87120-501-7
   1. Education—United States—Experimental methods. 2. Educational
equalization—United States. I. Cole, Robert W., 1945– II. ASCD
Improving Student Achievement Research Panel. Educating everybody's
children. III. Title.
    LB1027.3 .M67   2001
    371.3—dc21   00-012067

07 06 05 04 03 02 01   10 9 8 7 6 5 4 3 2 1

More Strategies for
EDUCATING EVERYBODY'S CHILDREN

FOREWORD

We may be facing the first time in history that the success—perhaps even the survival—of nations and of people has been so tightly bound to their ability to learn. Our own future depends now, as never before, on our ability to teach.

At the beginning of the 21st century, schools around the world are being asked to develop a far wider range of human potential to realize the staggering variety of individuals' intelligence. It is time that we begin thinking about this place called "school" in terms of children and learning. It is past time for us as education leaders to transform rhetoric and good intentions into action and results. It is not about what we can do but rather about what we *get done*.

The "millennium generation" is more diverse than any that preceded it; demographics suggest that this diversity will become increasingly pronounced. The challenge of this millennium is the advancement of a new kind of teaching, one that is very different from what we have known for most of the last century. We need to understand how to teach in ways that respond to students' unique starting points, and then carefully build a supporting framework aimed at increasing all students' achievement.

Increasing the achievement levels of *all* students in our schools is a critical moral imperative, an economic necessity, and a demand that grows out of our democratic ideals. We must take the lead in creating a culture and climate for improved learning for all students while ensuring that schools remain the vital nursemaid of democracy. Teaching and learning, at all levels, should inescapably expand the choices of how our children will seek to live their lives. Now, as we call ourselves to task for our democratic ideals, we expect schools to educate a much broader population for a swiftly changing global society.

What is the message for teachers and education leaders? Successful preparation of our young people for the 21st century requires new models and understanding of how we learn and develop independence—and the involvement of the entire community. It means we must grasp the power to shape and take control of our own destinies.

I hope you will honor the words of Alberto Granada, a young student from Columbia, as you accept the challenge of educating everybody's children: "A free world is one where every child has the key to a school."

GENE R. CARTER
Executive Director and Chief
 Executive Officer
Association for Supervision and
Curriculum Development (ASCD)

PREFACE

This book is a project of passion. Just like its predecessor, *Educating Everybody's Children: Diverse Teaching Strategies for Diverse Learners*, this second verse of the same haunting refrain aims simply to help those children who need our help the most. It is motivated by the certain knowledge that we know far more than we have found the will to do in our classrooms. Here in this volume, just as before, the Association for Supervision and Curriculum Development (ASCD) makes available to practitioners a rich array of proven practices that bring research to vivid life for those whose lives desperately need enriching.

In 1995, ASCD worked to draw together the most current knowledge about how to teach culturally and linguistically diverse youngsters. The result was *Educating Everybody's Children*. The simple premise of that landmark work was that young people's dual heritages of culture and language directly affect their performance—in school and in life—more than their socioeconomic status, ethnicity, or gender. That powerful, eminently practical book described how teachers can effectively put to use our exhaustive (and vastly underused) knowledge base in any classroom setting.

We are proud to have worked together—as editor and project director—to produce *Educating Everybody's Children* and delighted to bring its sequel to life. As professionals who have worked in the field of education for our entire careers, we cannot help but observe that the U.S. public has largely grown numb to the daily headlines, telling us again and again that "some" kids aren't achieving in school. In the United States today, nearly a million and a half public school students are not meeting state standards in core academic subjects (*USA Today*, March 4, 1999). Who are these children? In shockingly disproportionate numbers, they attend schools that serve a high percentage of students of color and children who live in poverty. Any number of reliable indicators of progress inform us that their education has been inadequate. Expert witnesses proffer a thoroughly reasonable litany of explanations for why so many of these children—our children, children of the United States—are not achieving: their parents' income, the difficulty of learning standard English, drugs, violence, abuse. But a core question remains to haunt us: Have we written off certain youngsters because of their demographic and socioeconomic characteristics? Are legions of our children doomed because of who they are and where they live?

"Poor children need the best possible schooling to give them a fighting chance to lift themselves out of poverty," read the preface of the predecessor to this book (Cole, 1995). Typically, those students who are most academically and socially challenged perform less well than their peers. And there we see implied our greatest educational challenge in the years ahead: How can we prepare teachers for the rigors and demands of teaching, and also broaden their repertoire of teaching strategies so that more students succeed?

With that challenge in mind, the authors of *Educating Everybody's Children* identified the most powerful teaching strategies for increasing students' performance—all students' performance—in reading, writing, oral communication, and mathematics. Chapter 3, "A Baker's Dozen," offered a set of universal teaching approaches that support high-quality instruction in all content areas and on every grade level. Not only do these universal strategies dramatically improve performance, but they are highly adaptable, proven with students of diverse backgrounds and wide-ranging abilities.

This deep commitment to high-quality instruction for culturally and linguistically diverse youngsters is grounded, too, in a conviction that excellent education capitalizes on each child's strengths and preferences. If we are to capitalize on each child's strengths, then we must surely regard every child's cultural and linguistic heritage as a valuable resource rather than a deficit to be overcome. As Lisa Delpit observed, "Culture doesn't help you teach somebody. Start off with what is, to the best of your knowledge, good teaching. If you run into problems, then culture is one of the explanations that you look into to solve a problem." (*Education Week*, March 13, 1996, p. 43)

In the years since *Educating Everybody's Children* was released, educators around the world have reported that its multitude of strategies have helped them better understand and accommodate the academic needs of diverse learners. Thus encouraged, ASCD turned its attention to extending the scope of the work to provide educators at all levels with further assistance. This book is the result of that effort.

In this volume, the authors identify and describe the most effective teaching approaches for helping students learn history, civics, geography, and science. Coupled with the content-specific strategies outlined in *Educating Everybody's Children*, the two books now address the best practices in all the content areas regularly measured by the National Assessment of Education Progress (NAEP).

More Strategies for Educating Everybody's Children extends our notion of diversity by examining other populations that have been underserved by schools, including homeless and immigrant youngsters. To clarify misconceptions about these young people, we asked the authors to profile the conditions under which these students attend school, the effect of their life conditions on their schooling experience, the ways we might best promote resilient

behaviors in these children, and the most effective research-based teaching strategies for enhancing their performance. Because of the special challenges these young people face, our authors describe the support services needed to help them achieve at the level of their peers.

We hope—we *believe*—that the ideas and recommendations contained herein will give school people both knowledge and renewed hope. Research shows plainly, repeatedly, that teachers who succeed at bringing diverse learners to high levels of achievement possess a wide array of research-based teaching and learning strategies. And that is the single most important message delivered in both volumes: As our students become more and more diverse, so must our ways of teaching them. It is the quality of instruction, not a youngster's life circumstances, that determines performance in school.

All too often, the young people in our classrooms live lives on the ragged edges of viability. Homelessness, discrimination, starvation, abuse—the everyday conditions of their lives defy our convenient attempts to compartmentalize their experiences and our prescriptions for dealing with them. Too often, they and the barely subsistent families—if they have families at all—from which they come are voiceless. We have the Promethean power to give them a voice, to give them power, to give them the keys to a better life. Those keys may be found in the pages of this book. Use it wisely and well, please.

ROBERT W. COLE
HELENÉ HODGES

BIBLIOGRAPHY

Cole, R. W. (1995). *Educationg everybody's children: Diverse teaching strategies for diverse learners.* Alexandria, VA: Association for Supervision and Curriculum Development.

Henry, T. (1999, March 4). Three R's, 11 lawsuits. *USA Today*, pp. 19–20.

Viadero, D. (1996, March 13). Lisa Delpit says teachers must value students' cultural strengths. *Education Week*, p. 43.

1

Overcoming a Pedagogy of Poverty

Helené Hodges

In 1999, UNESCO declared that every child has the right to high-quality educational experiences. Unfortunately, an enormous gap yawns between that high-minded declaration and the reality of schooling for too many of our children. The good news is that world-wide efforts continue in the effort to educate *everybody's* children. The bad news, of course, is that so much remains to be accomplished—especially for students with diverse learning needs.

Research shows an ever-widening gap between the academic performance of children living in poverty and children in more fortunate circumstances. Researchers are examining the barriers that some children face in our schools—barriers too often grounded in class and race—that systematically exclude them from any chance of success in school and in society. Somehow, they imply, we find it dangerously easy to view some children as little more than the sum of their socioeconomic or demographic statistics. Despite the steep odds against certain young people, the barriers they face every day can be—have been—successfully overcome with the application of a rich knowledge base of best teaching and learning practices.

A Pedagogy of Poverty

It is no mystery why some children fail. Our educational system was designed in the early 1900s as a convenient means of sorting and labeling young people. Labels brand and stifle children rather than encouraging them to succeed. Labels identify some children as being less worthy of high-quality school experiences.

The result of such systemic labeling is what Martin Haberman (1991) called a "pedagogy of poverty" (pp. 290–294), in which low-level tasks become the norm for the less fortunate. Haberman identified the heart of this all-too-common approach to instruction as a set of activities that certain teachers use "to the exclusion of nearly everything else." These tasks include "giving information, asking questions, giving directions, making assignments, monitoring seat work, reviewing assignments, giving tests, reviewing tests, assigning homework, reviewing homework, settling disputes, publishing noncompliance, marking papers, and giving grades" (Haberman, 1991, p. 291).

Every one of these activities can be beneficial, admits Haberman. But, he notes, "[t]aken together and performed to the systematic exclusion of other acts, they have become the pedagogical coin of the realm in urban schools. They constitute the pedagogy of poverty—not merely what teachers do and what youngsters expect, but, for different reasons, what parents, the community, and the general public assume teaching to be" (Haberman, 1991, p. 291).

As Eleanor Dougherty and Patte Barth (1997) have observed, "Poor and minority children are systematically bludgeoned into low academic performance with a steady dose of low-level, boring, if not downright silly assignments and curricula" (pp. 40 & 44). In such settings, children are not taught how to think critically and thus are unable to use what they already know to help them understand their world. The willful failure to provide a high-quality education can be a death sentence. Yet we allow some youngsters to languish in such settings all the way through school. A pedagogy of poverty contradicts what we have learned of best teaching and learning practices; it is a subtle, pernicious form of racism.

The assignments in the three paragraphs that follow were given to groups of elementary, middle, and high school students. Do these assignments underestimate students' intelligence?

A class of 4th graders is asked to read a poem about pizza. The eight lines describe the variety of toppings, from mushrooms to anchovies, that go on a pizza. The students spend considerable time copying each line of the poem into a book they have made by hand, and decorating the book with lots of color. Each student then writes one sentence about what kind of pizza he or she likes best. This activity is intended as an exercise in critical writing.

In another city, 8th graders are studying a social studies chapter on colonialism. The teacher wants to give them an assignment that will build their reading comprehension and vocabulary based on new terms used in this chapter. She does not ask them to write their own definitions. Instead, they're asked to copy the definitions for the 12 words from the chapter's glossary. These 13-year-olds and 14-year-olds are then required to draw a picture for each word. The words on the list include deism and smuggling.

11th graders in a . . . social studies class were assigned a major project on a famous person of their choice. Each student was to spend an entire month studying one historical figure in depth. So far, so good. Yet the culminating task, intended to show the results of the students' study, was this: "Photocopy a picture of the person you selected and glue it in the center of the posterboard. Then, decorate the poster board. When you have finished, write one or two sentences in each of the four corners summarizing what you have learned about the historical figure." The poster was the final grade for this five-week unit. Students who turned one in got an A or B. A typical project consisted of a picture and five disconnected sentences (Dougherty & Barth, 1997, p. 40).

These students—children of color who attend high-poverty urban schools—are taught by teachers who "often do not realize that they are setting such low expectations" (Dougherty & Barth, 1997, p. 40). Like teachers in many diverse settings, they have few opportunities to interact with their fellow teachers or to pursue enriched professional development opportunities—opportunities that should be a part of the professional experience of all teachers, regardless of where or whom they teach.

Teaching and learning are complex processes, best supported by research-based practices. These practices cannot be learned and implemented in a vacuum. They must be learned and used within the context of high-quality professional development experiences.

Naturally, all teachers do not intentionally deliver poor instruction. Some most certainly *are* guilty of doing so, however, and we cannot continue to avoid the subject as if it does not exist. Children simply cannot learn when they are intellectually starved. Dougherty and Barth (1997) believe that "Schools would be far better off ensuring that every activity in every classroom challenges students and guides them toward achieving mastery of core academic content and skills. The best way to do this is by making every assignment worth doing" (p. 40). But more often than not—particularly in the case of diverse learners—every assignment is *not* worth doing.

This unrelenting exposure to a pedagogy of poverty continues to be a pervasive problem in high-poverty schools. Mary Metz (1998–99) found glaring differences in the educational experiences offered to youngsters in high-poverty areas:

When analyzing the differences in teachers' work in . . . schools across communities differing in social class . . . everything was different . . . the teachers' concerns, and, most strikingly, the rhythm and content of classes—even when they had the same title and used the same textbook. American schools are supposed to be similar, in order to provide equal opportunity to all children. . . . There are, increasingly, . . . distressing circumstances that hinder education in schools in poverty areas, especially those in central cities. These differences between schools [differing in social class] are informal and unofficial, however. These differences in student achievement . . . and the differing expectations that teachers . . . hold for their future accomplishments powerfully affect . . . teachers'. . . motivation to pour resources into academic effort. It is painful and politically delicate to look too closely at the separation among schools created by housing and school district lines in metropolitan areas. To look too closely, to admit that this separation has profound educational consequences, is to admit that we are not offering equality of opportunity to the nation's children (p. 6).

Although the differences Metz describes fall along income lines, it is important to note that they also fall along color lines. When it comes to academic achievement, a disproportionate number of youngsters with black, brown, or red skin finish at the bottom. Racism permits some youngsters access to the very best that U.S. society has to offer, while barring others from an equal chance for success in life. Changing this nation's deeply entrenched attitudes toward children of color will take courage—and time.

Can we hope to change the outlook of an entire nation, working person by person? One thing is certain: We can work to ensure that each student—regardless of background and racial characteristics—receives a high-quality education. The most vital fact we have learned as a result of the education reform movement is this: *Student achievement stands or falls on the motivation and skills of teachers.* We can begin by certifying that all teachers are capable of delivering a standards-based curriculum that describes what all students should know and be able to do by the time they reach specified grade levels. Then we must ensure that these standards are delivered by means of a "pedagogy of plenty." By these two acts alone we can guarantee that all schools will be ready and able to educate everybody's children.

A PEDAGOGY OF PLENTY: THE SOLUTION TO THE ACHIEVEMENT GAP

Just as we can identify reasons why some of our children are doomed to failure, we can also identify concrete solutions that offer all youngsters greater opportunity to succeed in school. These solutions constitute a pedagogy of plenty.

A pedagogy of plenty is, quite simply, teaching at its best. We are constantly translating a vast knowledge base of proven, research-based strategies into daily classroom practice. This book and its predecessor, *Educating Everybody's Children*, are two powerful results of translating research into immediately usable ideas.

When we use all that we have learned to help children transcend their social setting, then we help them to grow, to reach their highest potential, and in the process to acquire a range of resilient behaviors that lead to success— not only in school, but in life. What, for instance, might all children attempt if they knew they could not fail? That is exactly what high-quality schooling affords all students— the ability to reach new heights, to believe that they are going to be somebody. We know that the stronger children's self-esteem, the likelier they are to capitalize on their

strengths. That is why some children do well despite the many obstacles in their lives.

So what does a pedagogy of plenty look like? The hallmark of high-quality teaching includes the use of universally sound teaching practices that provide youngsters many avenues for academic success. They are powerful ways of teaching that benefit all students, but are particularly appropriate for diverse learners. A pedagogy of plenty, or good teaching, is going on when children are

• Offered authentic tasks within a meaning-driven curriculum. Authentic tasks offer students real purposes for reading, writing, speaking, and doing mathematics and real audiences for their work.

• Provided with a literacy-rich learning environment offering a wide variety of high-quality resources.

• Helped to make connections between what they learn in school and their day-to-day experiences in their homes, community, and culture.

• Exposed to resources that offer experiential, problem-based, active learning opportunities.

• Engaged in a variety of social configurations in cooperative and collaborative learning groups, working on issues and problems of deep concern to them.

• Exposed to an inquiry-based approach to instruction that makes *meaning*, not just getting the right answer, the essence of instruction.

• Engaged in substantive dialogue, discussion, debate, and conversation to help them to learn, understand, make informed judgments about, and apply the substance of a content area.

• Allowed to have their home and community culture, language heritage, and experiences acknowledged and incorporated into their schooling.

• Presented with cognitive and metacognitive problems within the context of purposeful activities.

When we speak of accommodating the needs of diverse learners, it is imperative that we describe how we will alter instruction to improve learning and why we choose the strategies we do. Teachers who succeed in bringing diverse learners to high levels of achievement have a high degree of expertise in, and knowledge of, subject-specific learning practices. Yet they also recognize the critical importance of using a set of universal teaching and learning practices that have been proven to improve achievement for all students while building on diverse youngsters' varying backgrounds, experiences, and perspectives. These universal research-based approaches help

FROM THE PROJECT TO HARVARD

SONJA LUTZ

There was no doubt that she knew about violence. After all, she lived in the project. In 8th grade, she wrote:

> The civic center
> prom,
> everyone dancing. I turned,
> yelled, "No!"
> a flash of light
> and it was over.

The project is crowded with tiny, dilapidated houses and drooping apartment buildings from which boom boxes blare into the night. At dawn, field workers mingle in front of the local convenience store, waiting for the gray farm buses to transport them to back-breaking work in the fields. By day, old men push grocery carts to collect cast-off items. By night, young girls stand on the streets in tight dresses to look for business. Life in the project is not safe, not easy. Yet we teachers never connected her with the project. She was a star. Cheerleader, state science fair winner, valedictorian, advanced placement student—she had it all. She was even beautiful: tall and slender (she let everyone know she was a size 3), with skin the color of a satiny chestnut. I loved to teach her. We all did.

While many of her peers used poverty as an excuse for why they couldn't succeed, she succeeded. She won essay contests, oratorical events, and Shakespeare recitation competitions. She was a class officer, member of the National Honor Society, and homecoming queen. She scored high on the SAT and ACT. Her exemplary work in class, coupled with a certain pride, set her apart from other students. In short, she rose so far above her peers that we never connected her with the project. We simply relished her success and wished that we had an entire classroom of students just like her.

Then one day during her senior year, she asked for a ride home. She needed to print out a page of an essay that was due for a competition, so I drove her to her house. As I waited in the living room of a tiny dark house with bars on the windows, she worked in a cramped space on the bar in the kitchen. Noise was everywhere—the television was blasting, people were talking loudly on the porch, neighbors were calling across the courtyard of an apartment building next door. She didn't hear anything. She was entirely focused on finishing the essay. As the word processor clicked away, I considered the obstacles this girl had hurdled throughout the years to become the light of our classes.

As valedictorian of her graduating class, she won a full scholarship to Harvard. She decided on medicine. "Why medicine?" I questioned. "You're so talented in language and literature." "Maybe I'll change," she replied, "but for now, I'm going into premed." There was no use discussing it further. She set her own goals always. It wasn't long, however, before I received an e-mail saying that she had switched majors. She was now going into law. "Good," I thought. "She'll make a fine lawyer."

I can only imagine what her next three years were like. I heard from her sporadically. At one point, she toyed with the idea of transferring schools to be closer to home. She never said, but I guessed she was unhappy. Another time, she wrote that she was thrilled to act as a big sister to a child in the ghetto. She seemed happy. By summertime, she needed a letter of recommendation for a job in the court system of New York. She had adjusted and was going full steam again.

Then last June, I received an impressive invitation to her graduation from college. As I ran my hand across the smooth leather announcement, I thought about the girl with the radiant smile who, determined to do everything right, was always the last to turn in her exams. I pictured her jumping high into the air on the football field. Then I remembered the dark, noisy house and the neighborhood where she had lived, and I was filled with the wonderment of it all. In 28 years of teaching, she was the only student I had ever taught to have graduated from Harvard.

I cried.

teachers support the successful implementation of content-specific strategies. More important, they are adaptable and proven to work with a wide variety of students of diverse backgrounds and widely ranging abilities.

Educating Everybody's Children identified these universal practices:

- Provide opportunities to work together.
- Use reality-based learning approaches.
- Encourage interdisciplinary teaching.
- Involve students actively.
- Analyze students' learning and reading styles.
- Actively model behaviors.
- Explore the fullest dimensions of thought.
- Use a multicultural teaching approach.
- Use alternative assessments.
- Promote home and school partnerships.
- Use accelerated learning techniques.
- Foster strategies in questioning.
- Emphasize brain-compatible instruction.

Since 1995, our continuing investigation of good teaching and learning practices has led to the identification of three additional practices, for a total of 16 universal teaching strategies. The three additional keys to bridging the achievement gap include practices that activate students' prior knowledge; that use a constructivist approach to teaching; and that design, organize, and manage instructionally effective classrooms. A brief description of each approach follows.

● **STRATEGY 1.1: ACTIVATE STUDENTS' PRIOR KNOWLEDGE. TO HELP STUDENTS INTEGRATE NEW KNOWLEDGE AND SKILLS WITH THEIR EXPERIENCES, FIND OUT WHAT STUDENTS ALREADY KNOW ABOUT A TOPIC BY ACTIVATING THEIR PRIOR KNOWLEDGE.**

Activating students' prior knowledge—through the use of schema theory, for example—helps youngsters integrate new knowledge and skills with their own experiences. By doing so, teachers acknowledge that all students, regardless of their background, bring a wealth of knowledge to learning. The kind and amount "of knowledge one has before encountering a given topic in a discipline affects how one constructs meaning," writes Gaea Leinhardt. "The impact of prior knowledge is not a matter of 'readiness,' component skills, or exhaustiveness; it is an issue of depth, interconnectedness, and access. Outcomes are determined jointly by what was known before and by the content of the instruction" (Leinhardt, 1992, pp. 51–56).

Consequently, it just makes sense for teachers to begin by learning what students already know about a topic, thus preventing youngsters from having to repeat what they already know or try to build on knowledge they do not yet possess. Connecting new knowledge to previous learning builds a strong foundation for future learning; it also gives teachers valuable opportunities to correct misperceptions. Modifying activities to suit learners' preferences helps them construct new understandings.

When tapping into students' prior knowledge, teachers recognize that the most effective means of learning is discovery, and the most effective means of teaching is modeling. Modeling by the teacher is one of many powerful tools for activating prior knowledge. Depending on the task, the teacher decides what prior knowledge needs to be activated and asks students to develop and answer questions that cause them to activate it. The teacher then proceeds to model appropriate questioning processes. Activating students' prior knowledge engages them more actively in learning, in generating their own questions, and in leading their own discussions.

Another strategy that effectively activates students' prior knowledge, allowing them to explore what they already know about a topic, is the K-W-L activity, first developed by Donna Ogle. This strategy asks students to identify what they already <u>K</u>now about a topic, <u>W</u>hat they would like to learn, and, at the conclusion of the unit, what they actually did <u>L</u>earn.

Teachers can encourage students to develop a list of questions they would like to answer. (Teacher modeling helps students form these questions.) Teachers can then assist students in clustering similar questions and in deciding which questions to answer by further explaining the content to be learned. The teacher and students design a plan to find the answer for each question. Allowing students to work in cooperative and collaborative groups is effective because such groups encourage students to share their answers and the rationale behind the answers. During the sharing, the teacher is given an opportunity to correct student misunderstandings.

In exploring new topics, students can experience a variety of active, experiential, or authentic assignments. Such assignments—for example, manipulating objects or concepts, engaging in product-oriented activities, and participating in real-life experiences that actively construct knowledge—allow youngsters to explore concepts in some depth and to make discoveries on their own. The opportunity to apply new learnings to real-life contexts that reflect the students' world helps them retain and effectively use new concepts and skills.

● **STRATEGY 1.2**: USE A CONSTRUCTIVIST APPROACH. FACILITATE LEARNING BY PROVIDING APPROPRIATE ACTIVITIES, QUESTIONS, AND CLASSROOM ENVIRONMENTS SO STUDENTS CAN CONSTRUCT THEIR OWN UNDERSTANDING OF CONCEPTS.

A great many of the approaches to teaching and learning that appear in *Educating Everybody's Children* and in this book challenge the traditional model of schooling, which demands that students receive knowledge solely from the teacher. In explaining the nature of the pedagogy of poverty, Martin Haberman notes that teachers and students are engaged in fundamentally different activities: Teachers teach and students learn. But what if teachers join students as fellow learners searching for answers to real-life problems or for ways to describe and generalize scientific phenomena?

Another way to create a pedagogy of plenty is to embrace a constructivist approach to teaching. Constructivism emphasizes an understanding of how and why students (and adults) learn; it provides a way to combine good teaching and learning practices. These practices include activating students' prior knowledge; providing a variety of active learning resources; using a variety of hands-on, minds-on activities; engaging youngsters in a variety of cooperative learning experiences; allowing students to formulate questions and discover concepts that can guide future learnings; asking students to think aloud while approaching a task; modeling powerful thinking strategies; and providing students with opportunities to apply new learnings within the context of real-life activities.

Such an instructional setting honors the importance of hands-on and "heads-on" experiences in learning. For students to learn to reason about their world, they must be constantly encouraged to ask questions and solve problems that have meaning to them. Teachers can provide a wide variety of activities to help students construct—and reconstruct—their new learning in their own terms, as they begin to realize that knowledge is created out of life experiences.

Constructivist theory suggests that the goal of schooling is not simply acquiring specific knowledge and expertise, but rather building understanding. Learning how to learn becomes the goal. Considered from a constructivist viewpoint, the learning environment is a laboratory that provides the tools to support learners in their quest for understanding. In this approach, teachers facilitate learning by providing appropriate activities such as modeling and questioning techniques in well-designed, well-organized, and well-managed classroom environments that allow students to construct their own understandings of concepts.

Constructivist teaching is best facilitated though the use of varied learning configurations. Providing students with opportunities to work in collaborative or small-group learning activities helps them to construct their own knowledge. Students have the opportunity to listen to other points of view, debate, discuss, and form insights into new ideas while working collaboratively with their peers. Such activities must also activate students' prior knowledge to help them develop questioning skills.

● **STRATEGY 1.3: ORGANIZE INSTRUCTIONALLY EFFECTIVE CLASSROOM ENVIRONMENTS. TEACHERS DESIGN, ORGANIZE, AND MANAGE ENVIRONMENTS THAT SUPPORT AND ENHANCE STUDENTS' LEARNING EXPERIENCES, AND, IN THE PROCESS, ACCELERATE YOUNGSTERS' ACADEMIC ACCOMPLISHMENTS.**

When the classroom environment encourages growth and development, students will respond. Instructionally effective environments offer youngsters a wide variety of powerful experiences, which include ways of interacting with and learning from one another in instructional areas that support experiential, problem-based, active learning. Creating such environments calls for the teacher to construct and allow cooperative, collaborative strategies.

Classroom design simply means arranging the room to make the best use of space and to create a comfortable learning climate—both physically and psychologically. Classroom management reflects the ways in which the teacher orchestrates high-quality instructional activities that help children take charge of their learning, and eliminate unwanted behavioral and discipline problems.

CLASSROOM DESIGN

Our school system was invented to provide a sit and learn process of education. In 1915, for instance, John Dewey reportedly described the difficulties he encountered during an exhaustive search for furniture "suitable from all points of view—artistic . . . and educational—to the needs

of children." According to the account, Dewey finally met one school-supply dealer who admitted, "I'm afraid we do not have what you want. You want something at which children may work; these are for listening."

Amazingly, little has changed in U.S. classrooms from Dewey's time. Regardless of individual differences, many, many children are still expected to sit on a hard seat, not move, and not speak—just listen and answer questions.

Research strongly supports the important role of environmental preferences in students' motivation and their ability to learn. The *quality* of the environment in which we live and work is vitally important. Individuals tend to respond to their physical environment first in terms of personal comfort. Harmony makes it easier to concentrate and remember information.

The proper use of space within a classroom generates student activity and learning. Room arrangement, for example, allows students to work at computer stations, engage in small-group work, engage in project-based learning, and use multimedia equipment beside individual or group activities. Appropriate classroom design empowers teachers to create instructional areas, such as learning and interest centers and media centers, that offer students varied learning opportunities, and accommodate individual learning needs and interests.

Well-designed classrooms display high levels of student cooperation, academic success, and task involvement. Teachers work to develop intrinsic motivation in students, which is essential to creating lifelong learners. Thus, effective classroom environments create multiple learning situations capable of addressing students' diverse characteristics to enhance their satisfaction and academic performance. Such classes are child centered; they meet young people's instructional needs by exposing them to a variety of highly motivating, stimulating, multi-level instructional activities.

Current research in the functioning of the brain confirms that we learn best in a rich, multisensory environment. We learn more about people by interacting with them in real-life contexts. We learn more meaningfully when we are fully immersed in the learning experience. Thus, we should provide students with active learning experiences that incorporate a wide variety of materials, including high-quality, well-written literature.

Powerful learning activities are most likely to occur in a highly organized learning environment. When orchestrating such a setting, it is important to keep in mind how instruction will be reinforced, reviewed, and enriched to extend youngsters' learning potential; how procedures for completing assignments, working, locating instructional resources, and acquiring assistance will be facilitated; and how students will evaluate their own performance and that of others.

CLASSROOM MANAGEMENT

Making a classroom an effective educational tool depends on creating not only a physically comfortable environment that supports instructional goals but one that is also emotionally, socially, psychologically, and physically safe. Classrooms should be places where a child can think, discover, grow, and ultimately learn to work independently and cooperatively in a group setting, developing self-discipline and self-esteem. At the heart of an emotionally safe learning environment is cooperation—among staff, students, and other stakeholders.

Cooperation leads to ownership, involvement, and great opportunities for student self-discipline, says Jerome Freiberg (1996, pp. 32–36)—but first must come *trust*. Students learn to trust through opportunities to take ownership and take responsibility for their own actions and those of others. Strategies to promote cooperation include establishing rules and regulations (with the assistance of students) for codes of behavior and conduct; talking about consequences of behavior; offering youngsters training in peer mediation and conflict resolution; creating rotating classroom management positions, with clearly outlined responsibilities; and helping youngsters develop norms of collaboration and social skills to enable them to work effectively in groups.

When children are truly engaged in learning and the approach to discipline is an active one, teachers do not have to waste valuable time dealing with disciplinary issues. When learning becomes less meaningful to students' lives, less interactive, or less stimulating, teachers increasingly need to control their students; in the process, they unwittingly create opportunities for undesirable student behaviors.

Teachers who try to impose too many rules, too much rigidity, and too many uniform activities quickly lose control. Teachers who can bring themselves to share power and confidence with their students gain more control. That is exactly why teachers should concentrate on creating conditions in which students can and will manage themselves.

MAKING BEST USE OF A PEDAGOGY OF PLENTY

Closely linked to learning a broad instructional repertoire is knowing how and when to implement these exemplary practices. To help practitioners systematically apply a range of powerful teaching practices, I've developed an organizing framework. The framework may be used to deliver both universal learning practices and content-specific teaching strategies. Practices founded in a common philosophical base—and best implemented in context with one another—are grouped together. By simultaneously implementing complementary strategies, teachers offer their students increased instructional support for learning how to learn.

By capitalizing on students' learning strengths and diagnosing how they learn best, teachers are in a better position to match appropriate instructional methods to students' instructional needs. Once teachers have begun to teach to youngsters' strengths, they can further increase students' interest, motivation, and engagement in learning by creating varied learning configurations that enable students to make connections for understanding.

This handy framework grew out of the thirteen universal teaching practices outlined in Chapter 3 of *Educating Everybody's Children,* and was enhanced by the three additional strategies outlined in this chapter. The strategy number refers to chapter 3 (*Educating Everybody's Children*) or to this chapter (1).

- *Capitalize on Students' Strengths*
  Strategy 3.5: Analyze students' learning and reading styles and multiple intelligences
  Strategy 3.13: Emphasize brain-compatible instruction

- *Match Instructional Methods to Students' Instructional Needs*
  Strategy 3.2: Use reality-based learning approaches
  Strategy 3.4: Involve students actively
  Strategy 3.6: Actively model behaviors
  Strategy 3.11: Use accelerated learning techniques

- *Increase Interest, Motivation, and Engagement*
  Strategy 3.12: Foster strategies in questioning
  Strategy 1.1: Use a constructivist approach
  Strategy 1.2: Activate students' prior knowledge

- *Create Varied Learning Configurations*
  Strategy 3.1: Provide opportunities to work together
  Strategy 1.2: Design, organize, and manage instructionally effective classrooms

- *Make Connections for Understanding*
  Strategy 3.3: Encourage interdisciplinary teaching
  Strategy 3.7: Explore the fullest dimensions of thought
  Strategy 3.8: Use a multicultural approach
  Strategy 3.9: Use alternative assessments
  Strategy 3.10: Promote home/school partnerships

This framework, which has been applied in several settings and with different content-specific teaching approaches, affords all practitioners an opportunity to effectively implement the knowledge base of best teaching and learning practices—with a focus on improving *all* students' performances.

MEETING THE NEEDS OF ALL CHILDREN

What does it take to meet the academic needs of all children? If we want our students to excel academically, we must prepare a qualified teaching force equipped with a wide array of teaching practices and approaches. Good teaching is a powerful tool that cultivates the kinds of resilient behaviors that diverse learners need to turn barriers into successes. And teachers play a key role in helping these young people realize their aspirations. Teachers are powerful change agents who can either escalate or limit the development of every child they touch.

As one wise ASCD member named Charles Harrington said, "Children are like wet cement: They're very impressionable. So be very careful while making the mold." We may never know how profoundly each of us touches the life of a child, but we do know that *Educating Everybody's Children* is everybody's business.

BIBLIOGRAPHY

Dougherty, E., & Barth, P. (1997, April 2). How to close the achievement gap. *Education Week*, 40, 44.

Freiberg, J. (1996, September). From tourists to citizens in the classroom. *Educational Leadership*, 32–36.

Haberman, M. (1991). The pedagogy of poverty versus good teaching. *Phi Delta Kappan*, 290–294.

Leinhardt, G. (1992, April). What research on learning tells us about teaching. *Educational Leadership*, 51–56.

Metz, M. (1998–1999, Winter). Community social class affects teachers' perspectives and practices. *WCER Highlights*, Wisconsin Center for Education Research, University of Wisconsin–Madison School of Education, 6.

2

DIVERSE TEACHING STRATEGIES FOR HOMELESS CHILDREN

EVELYN REED-VICTOR AND JAMES H. STRONGE

Every leader, parent, and citizen personally and collectively must commit to reclaim our nation's soul and give our children back their hope, their sense of security, their belief in America's fairness, and their ability to dream about, envisage, and work toward a future that is attainable and real.

—Marian Wright Edelman, cited in Children's Defense Fund, 1995, p. 4

One continuing challenge that faces the U.S. educational system is helping students from unstable learning environments achieve success. And when we consider students from unstable environments, no population of students is more challenged, and challenging, than those who are homeless.

The daily realities of homelessness place the education of these young people in constant jeopardy. Homeless students face economic deprivation, family loss or separation, insecurity, social and emotional instability, and general upheaval in their lives (Bassuk & Rosenberg, 1988; Nunez, 1994; Rafferty, 1995; Rafferty & Rollins, 1989; Quint, 1994; Shane, 1996; and Stronge, 1992, 1997). Against this backdrop, efforts to make education accessible and meaningful for homeless youngsters and their families are like swimming upstream against a swift current. These students deserve to be able to attend school and to succeed there—an opportunity paramount to breaking the hold of poverty and deprivation (Stronge, 1997, p. 14).

This chapter illuminates the problems that homeless students and their families face in achieving educational access and success, and then specifies teaching strategies that educators can use to provide a more stable, enriched learning environment for these students. Specifically, we will address the following questions to provide a backdrop for understanding the unique educational needs of homeless students:

- Who are the homeless?
- How extensive is homelessness in the United States?
- What problems affect the education of homeless children and youth?
- What emerging educational programs for the homeless appear to be working?

UNSTABLE LEARNING: THE EFFECT OF HOMELESSNESS ON EDUCATION

WHO ARE THE HOMELESS?

Defining homelessness would seem to be a simple task: "Either a person does or does not have a place to call home" (Stronge, 1992, p. 7). In fact, the definitions of homelessness vary widely (Stronge, 2000). Some definitions are quite literal—individuals living on the street or those living temporarily in homeless shelters (see, for example, Kaufman, 1984); more expansive definitions include all individuals who lack a fixed residence (see, for example, National Coalition for the Homeless, 1997).

The Stewart B. McKinney Homeless Assistance Act of 1987 (P.L., 100-77) defines a homeless person as one who (1) lacks a fixed, regular, and adequate nighttime residence or (2) lives in a shelter, an institution (other than a prison or other institutionalized facility), or a place not ordinarily used as a sleeping accommodation for human beings. Educators should keep this definition in mind when designing and delivering educational services to homeless students.

HOW EXTENSIVE IS HOMELESSNESS?

No accurate counts exist of homeless individuals in the United States. For a variety of reasons (e.g., transiency of the homeless, preference among the homeless to resist being identified), counting the homeless is an elusive task. In 1988, the National Alliance to End Homelessness estimated that figure at 736,000, with as many as 2.3 million in the homeless ranks over the course of a year. Using a slightly broader definition of homelessness, the National Coalition for the Homeless estimated in 1990 that there were at least 3 million homeless people in the United States.

Although similar challenges exist in identifying the number of school-age children and youth who are homeless, it is clear that their numbers are significant and appear to be increasing. Based on reports from the states and territories, in 1989 the U.S. Department of Education estimated that there were approximately 220,000 school-age children among the homeless population. By 1998 (the most recent period for which data are available), the department reported 608,000 homeless students.[1] These estimates tend not to reflect accurately the 56 percent of homeless students who do not stay in shelters. Moreover, children below school age are not included in the counts (Nunez, 1995), and homeless adolescents (often called runaways and throwaways) tend to be undercounted (Powers & Jaklitsch, 1992).

Homelessness is commonly thought of as an urban issue; however, approximately one-third of homeless people in the United States live in rural areas. The proportion of homeless families is higher in rural areas than in cities; in fact, single homeless women with children may be found in rural areas at double the urban rate (Vissing, 1996). In the last two decades, increased rates of young children living in poverty have been noted in the suburbs and within the white population (National Center for Children in Poverty, 1997).

[1.] In compliance with statutory requirements under the Stewart B. McKinney Act, states and territories conducted an "estimate" of homeless students in 2000. These data will be made available once they are aggregated by the U.S. Department of Education.

HOMELESS FAMILIES

Homelessness in the United States is growing, "composed of more families and children than ever before" and is what Nunez (1995) described as the "new American poverty" (p. 7). The characteristics of homeless families include the following:

• More than three-fourths of homeless families in one study were single-parent families headed by women (Bassuk & Rosenberg, 1988).

• The typical homeless family head-of-household is "a young, single woman without a high school diploma or substantial work experience" (Nunez, 1994, p. 14).

• Homeless mothers tend to be unmarried (91 percent), under age 25 (69 percent), and have children under age 6 (80 percent). Approximately 36 percent of homeless mothers are young women who have not graduated from high school (Nunez, 1997).

• The percentage of homeless families with children increased from 27 percent in 1985 to 38 percent in 1996 (James, Lopez, Murdock, Rouse, & Walker, 1997).

THE FEDERAL RESPONSE

In response to homelessness among school-age youngsters, Congress enacted the education portion of the Stewart B. McKinney Homeless Assistance Act in 1987 (P.L. 100-77), and subsequently, reauthorized the act twice—in 1990 (P.L. 101-645) and 1994 (P.L. 103-382).[2] The McKinney Act, the first comprehensive emergency aid program for homeless individuals in the United States, included requirements for the provision of a free, appropriate public education to homeless students of school age.

Whereas the initial legislation focused on requiring schools to allow access to school, more recent efforts have been intended to promote *success* (Helm, 1993). Barriers related to access include residency, guardianship, and student records. Once access is gained, barriers related to success in school include proper educational placement, provision of appropriate support services, and facilitation of students' social and emotional well-being (Stronge, 1993a). The 1990 amendments expanded congressional oversight from access to success (Helm, 1993; Stronge, 1993b, 1997).

[2.] The 1994 reauthorization is included in the Improving America's Schools Act of 1994, Title VII, Subtitle B.

THE BARRIERS TO EDUCATION

Several problems—some related to homelessness itself (e.g., financial barriers and transiency) and others associated with the organization of schools (e.g., residency requirements and transportation)—combine to create significant barriers to the education of homeless students (Stronge, 2000). Inconsistent attendance, frequent moving, poor parental and agency support, and barriers of access to education contribute to the "unstable learning" that many homeless students experience (Nunez, 1994, p. 62). Of particular concern as barriers to educational opportunity for homeless youngsters are legal issues, financial concerns, social and psychological issues, educational program concerns, and problems of educational performance.

LEGAL BARRIERS

Every state demands compulsory school attendance. Public education is both a duty imposed on students and their parents for the public good and their individual right as citizens. Before the McKinney Act, proof of residency was a significant barrier to enrollment; attempts to enroll homeless students sometimes resulted in litigation (Foscarinis & McCarthy, 2000; Rafferty, 1995; Stronge & Helm, 1991). Though compulsory attendance laws make good sense as public policy, these same laws can pose formidable barriers when applied to homeless students, delaying or even denying enrollment.

Despite the removal, generally, of residency as an enrollment barrier, other requirements related to enrollment (e.g., immunization and guardianship) are not so easily modified. Even when access to school is improved by removing residency barriers, "homeless students in different districts within the same state often have uneven access to educational services. State policies exempting homeless students from enrollment requirements do not eliminate barriers unless schools and districts are aware of and enforce these policies" (Anderson, Janger, & Panton, 1995, p. iii).

FINANCIAL CONCERNS

Financial constraints affect both schoolchildren and school districts. Homeless parents are often forced to concentrate on the most basic necessities: adequate food, proper clothing, and safe shelter. The inability to meet the costs associated with a "free" public education (such as fees, gym clothes, and supplies) can further impede progress.

SOCIAL AND PSYCHOLOGICAL ISSUES

Academic progress is certainly not our only concern when we face the challenge of educating homeless youth; we must also be concerned with students' social and emotional well-being. While academic success can break the grip of poverty, educators may not be able to focus on academic goals until they have met students' social and psychological needs (Anooshian, 2000). Children's personal reaction to homelessness—factors such as the length of time they have been without a home, the reason for their homelessness, and the availability of outside support systems—must be taken into account (Linehan, 1992). Areas of social and emotional support that may be needed include the following:

- Coping strategies for dealing with stress, crisis, and culture shock;
- Social role modeling and development of acceptable social skills; and
- Individual and group counseling services.

EDUCATIONAL PROGRAM CONCERNS

Educational records. Schools require records as a means of ensuring proper placement. States also require immunization records. Unfortunately, homeless students often lack these essential documents. Families who lose their homes and belongings, as well as youngsters living on their own, are frequently unable to produce academic and medical records.

Educational placement. Appropriate placement in educational programs is another area of concern. For example, homeless students often need special educational services. However, owing to the transient nature of homelessness, they may not stay in one school district long enough for their needs to be fully identified and evaluated so that they may be placed in the most appropriate program (Korinek, Walther-Thomas, & Laycock, 1992). Thus, when homeless students are enrolled in school, they may be underserved or inappropriately served.

EDUCATIONAL PERFORMANCE PROBLEMS

Many homeless students experience significant learning problems in school; their poor academic performance has been well documented (Bassuk & Rosenberg, 1988; Nunez, 1994). Moreover, homeless students have an exceptionally high dropout rate. Poor educational performance and participation, even in the short term, are major concerns. Because school failure is linked to subsequent poverty, teenage pregnancy, crime, substance abuse, and family violence (Children's Defense Fund, 1995), the long-term effects of inadequate education may well be the creation of a new generation of unstable families. Because the level of education achieved is the "single best predictor of later occupational attainment" (Entwisle, 1993), improving educational experiences for homeless children and youth is essential to their success.

CULTIVATING RESILIENCE

Concerted efforts by a host of public and private agencies—including the U.S. Congress, state education agencies, and local school districts and shelter providers—to assist homeless students and their families are beginning to yield dividends. One significant area of improvement is increased school attendance.

Anderson and colleagues (1995) found that the average school attendance rate for identified homeless students in elementary, middle, and high school was 86 percent. Compare this with earlier estimates of attendance rates of 69 percent for homeless students (U.S. Department of Education, 1989). Even when homeless students are enrolled in and attending school regularly, however, there is no guarantee of their success.

Building resilience in children by emphasizing constructive strategies that enhance individual, family, school, and community protective factors is a promising area of research (Reed-Victor, 2000; Reed-Victor & Stronge, 1997). The following section of this chapter explores resilience and likely pathways of success.

RESEARCH ABOUT RESILIENCE IN CHILDREN

Some individuals, regardless of their circumstances, seem able to bounce back from stress and adversity; they demonstrate resilience, or successful adaptation. Resilience is a dynamic process of change and adaptation, resulting from "the individual's unique strengths, capacities, vulnerabilities" in interaction with "the demands and opportunities of the environment" (Felsman, 1989, p. 79).

Studies of children in stressful circumstances—the violence of war, the instability of parental mental illness or substance abuse, the multiple dangers of street life—have identified the adaptability and competence of some children. These resilient children thrive and develop into

healthy adults, able to enjoy and contribute to their communities. Their competence is evident in their orientation toward achievement, school success, sociability, responsible behavior, and active involvement in school and community (Kimchi & Schaffner, 1990; Werner & Smith, 1982, 1992). These same studies also identified the supportive relationships and opportunities that have nurtured these children's positive development.

Resilient children and youth are not invulnerable to stress and crisis, but they are able to rebound from such experiences, demonstrating "the self-righting tendencies within the human organism" (Werner & Smith, 1982, p. 152). Several researchers have focused on the process of resilience (Haggerty, Sherrod, Garmezy, & Rutter, 1994; Werner & Smith, 1992), as well as the implications for school programs (Doll & Lyon, 1998; Pianta & Walsh, 1996; Wang & Gordon, 1994; Zimmerman & Arunkumar, 1994). While these pathways of success are complex (Liddle, 1994, p. 175), their collective stories provide a constructive framework for building more supportive educational programs (Hanson & Carta, 1995; Oxley, 1994).

WHAT CAN WE DO TO SUPPORT RESILIENCE?

Studies of resilience identify protective factors that moderate the effects of stress and promote adaptive responses (Zimmerman & Arunkumar, 1994). These protective factors reduce the negative effects of risks in multiple, interactive ways. For example, children exposed to the risks of homelessness and low parental self-esteem may be protected by their own problem-solving abilities and the caring support of their teachers. Protective factors include individual, family, school, and community characteristics that contribute to resilience (Werner & Smith, 1992). Though some factors cannot be addressed by schools, of course (e.g., birth order and individual physical characteristics), well-designed educational support can influence several protective factors.

Resilient children have developed coping skills, creativity, and a sense of humor. (Some individual characteristics that may serve as protective factors include cognitive ability; sociability; autonomy; special interests; positive self-concept; and age-appropriate sensory, motor, and perceptual skills.) In adolescence, resilience is particularly reflected in goal orientation, positive social behavior, and active involvement in community life. Resilient students demonstrate an internal locus of control through their self-confidence, responsible behavior, and internalized values.

Family factors. Significant adults play an important protective role by reliably supporting children's development of trust and acceptance of adults as resources. Adults also shape constructive paths through modeling behavior, creating access to knowledge, advocating for enlarged opportunities, teaching competence, and encouraging growth in facing challenges (Masten, 1994). The ability of families to provide an appropriate balance of high expectations, guidance, cohesiveness, and support for appropriate child or adolescent autonomy also promotes resilience.

School factors. Several studies of resilient adults mentioned teachers as significant role models of childhood (Kimchi & Schaffner, 1990, Werner & Smith, 1992). Teachers can be critical factors in students' academic and socioemotional development by providing responsive, supportive relationships; teaching problem solving; increasing access to knowledge; building on students' interests and experiences; and fostering talent (Masten, 1994). Schools provide further support through extracurricular activities, positive peer relationships, and links to special services (Oxley, 1994). Schools that support resilience implement various strategies to

• Increase the quality and continuity of student and teacher relationships.
• Facilitate student and family participation in school life.
• Increase the comprehensiveness and accessibility of services.
• Ease transitions for students and families across school levels.

Community factors. The larger community offers protective influences through increased opportunities for high-quality relationships with adults (e.g., religious leaders, coaches, counselors, and tutors), positive peer support, talent development, and access to special services (Kimchi & Schaffner, 1990; Masten, 1994; Werner & Smith, 1982). With community support, students can further develop the autonomy, social competence, problem-solving ability, and future focus that contribute to overall adaptability (Freiberg, 1994).

Many community-based programs also foster responsible behavior and real-life learning opportunities through service projects, recreational activities, and art productions (Heath & McLaughlin, 1994). When family, school, and community resources are integrated and focused on resilience, students have the opportunities and support to develop competence across these important and varied environments.

STRATEGIES FOR ENHANCING HOMELESS STUDENTS' ACADEMIC ACHIEVEMENT

How can teachers translate research findings about resilience and protective factors into classroom strategies that address the specific circumstances of homeless students? In the face of the challenges that homeless families and children encounter (which most educators can scarcely imagine), we must forge partnerships to develop positive long-term outcomes for young people. Masten (1994) outlined four principles that provide a foundation for identifying effective strategies.

1. Foster resilience through reducing risks.
2. Decrease children's stress.
3. Increase resources available to the child and family.
4. Mobilize all possible protective processes.

Given these guiding principles, strategies to promote the school success of homeless students include the following:

• Reducing barriers to school participation and the stress of school entry.
• Fostering staff and student awareness of the realities of homelessness.
• Increasing the supportiveness of adult and peer relationships.
• Maintaining high expectations for students' academic success.
• Building students' interests and aspirations.
• Individualizing educational and socioemotional supports.
• Creating links to families, shelters, and community resources.
• Building a safety net within the school through staff collaboration.

> The life stories of resilient youngsters now grown into adulthood teach us that competence, confidence, and caring can flourish, even under adverse circumstances, if children encounter people who provide them with the secure basis for the development of trust, autonomy, and initiative. Hope springs from odds successfully overcome, and each of us can share this gift of hope with a child—at home, in the classroom, on the playground, or in the neighborhood (Werner & Smith, 1992, p. 209).

The following section includes classroom strategies (for example, curriculum-based assessment, cooperative

RESOURCES FOR INFORMATION TO HELP HOMELESS STUDENTS

National Center for Homeless Education at SERVE
  (NCHE)
1100 West Market St., Suite 300
Greensboro, NC 27403
(336) 574-3891
http://www.serve.org/nche/index.html

Center for Homeless Education and Information,
  William Penn College
http://www.wmpenn.edu/PennWeb/LTP/LTP2.html

Emergency Food and Shelter
National Board Program
701 North Fairfax St., Suite 310
Alexandria, VA 22314-2064
(703) 706-9660
http://www.efsp.unitedway.org/efspnew/Pages/LROS.cfm

Homeless Shelters and Programs: Communications
  for a Sustainable Future
http://csf.Colorado.EDU/homeless/shelters/html

Homes for the Homeless, Institute on Children
  and Poverty
36 Cooper Square, 6th Floor
New York, NY 10003
(212) 529-5252
Fax: (212) 529-7698
E-mail: hn4061@handsnet.org
http://www.HomesfortheHomeless.com

Illinois's Opening Doors Program
Illinois State Board of Education
100 North First St.
Springfield, IL 62777-0001
(217) 782-3370
Fax: (217) 782-9224
Information Hotline: (800) 215-6379
http://www.lth3.k12.il.us/openingdoors

National Alliance to End Homelessness
1518 K St., N.W., Suite 206
Washington, DC 20005
(202) 638-1526
E-mail: naeh@naeh.org
http://www.naeh.org

National Coalition for the Homeless
1012 Fourteenth St., N.W., Suite 600
Washington, DC 20005-3410
(202) 737-6444
Fax: (202) 737-6445
E-mail: nch@ari.net
http://nch.ari.net

National Law Center on Homelessness and Poverty
1411 K St., N.W., Suite 1400
Washington, DC 20005
(202) 638-2535
Fax: (202) 628-2737
E-mail: info@nlchp.org
http://www.nlchp.org

National Student Campaign Against Hunger and Homelessness
233 N. Pleasant Ave.
Amherst, MA 01002
(413) 256-6417
Fax: (413) 256-6435
E-mail: nscah@aol.com
http://www.pirg.org/nscahh/

Pennsylvania Department of Education
Education for Homeless Children and Youth Program
Bureau of Community and Student Services
Division of Student and Safe School Services
333 Market St., 5th Floor
Harrisburg, PA 17126-0333
(717) 772-2813
Fax: (717) 783-6617
http://www.pde.psu.edu/homeless/esedhomech.html

The SHELTRS Project (Support for Homeless Education:
  Linking Technology Resources to Shelters)
http://www.tenet.edu/shelters

Project HOPE
The Virginia Education for Homeless Children and Youth
  Program
The College of William and Mary, School of Education
Box 8795
Williamsburg, VA 23187-8795
(757) 221-4002
Fax: (757) 221-2988
http://www.wm.edu/education/HOPE/Homeless.html

learning, problem-based instruction, and differentiation based on individual student profiles) that have proven to be effective in supporting the learning of many students. These strategies are especially important for homeless students as a means of supporting their access and success within the full range of learning opportunities that schools provide.

In addition, we have included strategies that stretch beyond the classroom to address the realities of homelessness and its effects on learning. Some strategies focus on the teacher's role as an advocate for additional supports and as a bridge to other learning opportunities. Other strategies address the physical and emotional realities of disrupted living and learning that homeless children experience each day—and bring with them into the classroom. Many of the strategies emphasize collaborative aspects of teaching and learning—within the classroom, the school, and the broader community. Increasingly, teachers and schools are working with shelter staff and community groups to provide enriched and well-coordinated supports for their students who are homeless. Such exemplary practices are included with each strategy.

● **STRATEGY 2.1:** **BUILD AWARENESS AND SENSITIVITY WITHIN THE SCHOOL COMMUNITY. STAFF AND STUDENTS LEARN ABOUT HOMELESSNESS TO BETTER UNDERSTAND THE LIVES OF STUDENTS WHO ARE HOMELESS AND CREATE A CARING CLASSROOM ENVIRONMENT.**

DISCUSSION

Homeless students and their families continue to be somewhat invisible within schools. Children and families are reluctant to identify themselves as being homeless, and many educators are simply unaware of the difficult circumstances in which such children live. One teacher wondered about the poorly fitting clothes one of her high school students wore, until another student told her that he was living on the street and taking clothes from unattended laundromats at night.

Even when students are identified as homeless, their enrollment in school is still frequently blocked by staff who are unaware of the McKinney Act's provisions regarding admissions policies. Staff development activities addressing such aspects of homelessness as the prevalence and effects of homelessness, legal requirements, available resources, and effective strategies are important supports to teachers and other staff members as they grow to understand and provide for homeless students.

Students need knowledge and guidance to understand the issue of homelessness. Without direct support, classmates may ridicule students who live in shelters or appear to be unkempt and generally out-of-step with their peers' lifestyle.

In a study of students' attitudes toward homelessness, Gibel (1996) found that students show marked preferences for students in living situations similar to their own, rather than for homeless or poor students. Homeless students try to conceal their circumstances from their peers. For example, a Maryland school secretary reported that students living in a shelter asked her to keep their book bags (which held all of their possessions) in the office during the school day—both to protect their possessions and to keep other students from discovering their homelessness.

Although it is essential to keep specific students' circumstances confidential, student attitudes may be changed by studying homelessness and developing positive responses within the community. Creating a supportive climate within the school and the classroom is an important step in fostering the academic success of homeless students.

CLASSROOM EXAMPLES

Amber Goodman and Lexi Walters, students at Loch Raven High School in Baltimore County, Maryland, developed Project 1000 to engage their classmates in responding to homelessness. Amber and Lexi developed vignettes about the diverse situations that may leave children, youth, and adults homeless. As Amber and Lexi read these stories, members of the audience took turns standing to represent the individuals in the stories. By creating awareness about the realities of homelessness, Amber and Lexi successfully engaged their peers in providing 1,200 personal toiletries kits to local shelters. Amber and Lexi also engaged district personnel in this experience as part of a staff development initiative.

Awareness-level projects can increase staff knowledge about the realities of homelessness, its impact on learning, the requirements of the McKinney Act, and the availability of school and community resources and specific classroom strategies. In Madison, Wisconsin, the Transitional

Education Program developed curriculum kits for teachers that included information about the local situation as well as suggested trade books, news articles, and learning activities (Anderson, Janger, & Panton, 1995). Teachers in Malden, Massachusetts, focused on specific teaching strategies for highly mobile students as well as their own roles as "attachment teachers" (Hightower, Nathanson, & Wimberly, 1997). Visits to local shelter programs have effectively increased staff understanding of the living environments and available resources for some homeless students and their families (Johnson, 1992).

Students have gained greater understanding of homelessness through specific social studies units, curriculum materials, and service learning projects. Study units and curricular guides are available for students at all levels; they include an emphasis on constructing more accurate, compassionate perspectives. *Faces of Homelessness* (Waddell, 1997) is a curriculum guide that examines the myths, causes, and effects of homelessness as well as potential action plans to help homeless people. Here are examples from that curriculum guide.

- Elementary classes discuss the basic question: "What would I do if I didn't have a home?" and include individual responses in their daily journals or develop a group response.
- Secondary students analyze the testimony of an adolescent about her life in urban hotels and discuss her dreams and problems.

Service learning strategies provide students with opportunities to study issues as they plan and carry out specific projects. Young students may become involved in regularly collecting books, clothing, and canned goods for neighborhood shelters. A collaborative project between the Cleveland Public Schools, AmeriCorps members, the Cleveland School for the Arts, and the Cleveland Playhouse resulted in a theater production, *Shelter*, and an accompanying art exhibit by high school students. Andrew Hamlet, chair of visual arts for the School of the Arts, described the results: "I have seen the students exhibiting profound expressions of compassion, understanding, respect, and support for . . . children who find themselves without a home" (Project ACT, 1997).

Compassionate educators and students can create caring learning environments that foster student resilience, but they must first become informed about the realities of homelessness. One Seattle teacher described the change that can occur from confronting the reality of homeless students' lives: " . . . leave the safety of school turf and cross that fine boundary line which separates school and neighborhood. . . . Once you have seen it, you cannot turn your back on it because it continues to influence every step you take" (Quint, 1994, p. 28).

RESOURCES

Anderson, Janger, & Panton, 1995; Baltimore County Public Schools, 1997; Black, 1994; Gibel, 1996; Gonzalez, 1992; Henderson, 1997; Hightower, Nathanson, & Wimberly, 1997; Johnson, 1992; Stronge, 1995; Tower, 1992; Vissing, Schroepfer, & Bloise, 1994; Waddell, 1997; Walther-Thomas, Korinek, McLaughlin, & Williams, 1996.

● **Strategy 2.2:** Develop a Coordinated School Support Plan. School staff—including teachers, administrators, secretaries, bus drivers, nurses, counselors, social workers, psychologists, and parent organization representatives—create plans for meeting the diverse needs of homeless students.

Discussion

In promoting access and success for homeless students, teachers collaborate with members of the school community to provide a broad spectrum of supports and accommodations in a coordinated and timely manner. Why a broad spectrum? Because it is certain that schools face the need to provide services for students with significant physical, emotional, and educational issues that challenge standard operating procedures and time lines. A comprehensive support plan ensures students' enrollment, records acquisition, transportation, expedited assessments, appropriate placements, and comprehensive services, as well as wide-ranging involvement with families and community agencies (Reed-Victor & Pelco, 1999; Williams & Korinek, 2000).

A coordinated plan is especially important in schools that experience a regular influx of homeless and other highly at-risk students. Staff members create such action plans by identifying homeless students' needs, effective support strategies, vital resources, and staff responsibilities. Implementing and monitoring these plans requires ongoing communication and feedback mechanisms (Gonzalez, 1992). Well-articulated contingency plans clarify staff roles and strategies to obtain necessary services, so that students can be integrated quickly into school life.

Existing collaborative structures (including student or teacher assistance teams, school councils, and strategic planning groups) may be used to support the development of this plan as well as the provision of services (Walther-Thomas, Korinek, McLaughlin, & Williams, 1996). Collaborative teams can promote student resilience by focusing on high expectations for student success, increased student and family participation, quality and continuity of relationships, and comprehensiveness of services (Reed-Victor & Stronge, 1997).

Student perceptions of staff support relate positively to their participation and performance in school (Battisch, Solomon, Kim, Watson, & Schaps, 1995). In this study of high-poverty schools that promoted a sense of community through shared values of belonging, autonomy, and competence, teacher morale was also high. These caring schools provided an important model for students in high-poverty circumstances—encouraging their involvement in school and their adoption of positive social values.

CLASSROOM EXAMPLES

Developing action plans can be a natural outgrowth of staff development activities. By exploring their neighborhood, the teachers and other staff members of B. F. Day Elementary School in Seattle faced the reality of homelessness. From this awareness grew a sense of ownership of the problem and the development of creative plans to reshape school programs to be more responsive to students and families (Quint, 1994). These plans were fueled by "a bond of morality, of good conscience, of purposeful interaction among the staff" (Quint, 1994, p. 28). From strong purpose and shared ownership grew comprehensive support programs for students and families. And teachers no longer felt isolated in addressing challenging issues.

In Baltimore County, Maryland, local shelter providers joined building-level teams of administrators, teachers, nurses, social workers, and counselors in exploring the needs of homeless students and developing goals for improving educational supports. To address potential enrollment barriers, school secretaries were involved in staff development to identify specific concerns and solutions. Supported by Title I and McKinney Act programs, staff development activities included presentations by researchers, policymakers, an effective school-based team, shelter providers, and a homeless parent.

Reviewing the pathways that students follow to gain access and success in school is a good starting place for a planning group; it clarifies the need for coordinated action.

School office staff are involved in the initial process of welcome and enrollment, and the counselor and nurse may request important records. Special transportation issues may need to be addressed. When one elementary school principal expressed his concern about maintaining the confidentiality of students' shelter residence to the school transportation department, the bus driver modified his route to pick up the shelter students first in the morning and return them last in the afternoon.

The child study team may identify the best placement for the students and organize expedited assessments. Social workers, in coordination with shelter providers, can identify family support programs. Parent organizations, service groups, or business partners may organize resources for emergency clothing and school supplies as well as volunteers for tutoring and mentoring. Teachers and specialists may work collaboratively to provide appropriate teaching and learning strategies for individual students, in team teaching or consultation arrangements (Gonzalez 1992; Walther-Thomas, Korinek, McLaughlin, & Williams, 1996).

RESOURCES

Battisch, Solomon, Kim, Watson, & Schaps, 1995; Gonzalez, 1992; Korinek, Walther-Thomas, & Laycock, 1992; Quint, 1994; Reed-Victor & Pelco, 1999; Reed-Victor & Stronge, 1997; Tower, 1992; Walther-Thomas, Korinek, McLaughlin, & Williams, 1996; Williams & Korinek, 2000.

● **STRATEGY 2.3:** SUPPORT STUDENTS' TRANSITION INTO THE NEW SCHOOL ENVIRONMENT. TEACHERS WELCOME AND ORIENT STUDENTS TO SCHOOL FACILITIES, CLASSROOM ROUTINES, FELLOW STUDENTS, AND STAFF. OTHER STAFF MEMBERS AND STUDENT PARTNERS ACTIVELY SUPPORT THIS PROCESS.

DISCUSSION

In a review of 100 programs that effectively prevented school failure and high-risk student behavior, Dryfoos (1990) identified program features that are also relevant to highly mobile students: significant support for students transitioning into new educational settings and follow-up to subsequent settings. Careful planning can create transitional supports for students and families as they move among classes, schools, educational levels, and agencies. Strategies that reduce bureaucratic stresses for students and families are essential in building student success (Mallory, 1995).

Schools can ease homeless students' entry by creating a welcoming process that includes modified enrollment procedures, buffering or bridging experiences, orientation to the classroom, and supportive relationships with staff and peers.

The effectiveness of transition strategies often depends on their fit with students' characteristics, intensity of needs, and previous experiences. If a transition is particularly stressful, establishing a buffer zone allows more time, space, and support for the student's adjustment to new expectations. Students benefit from a balance of well-articulated structure and necessary accommodations (Henderson 1997; Kling, Dunn, & Oakley, 1996).

Young homeless students rarely have the benefit of early childhood education; they may need more opportunities to air their frustrations, gain information about their new situation, and develop skills that lessen stress (Eddowes & Butcher, 2000). School transitions challenge the psychological and physical well-being of many adolescents, especially in the absence of support (Entwisle, 1993). This general concern multiplies for homeless youth, who may need significant sensitivity and support in relating to their peers and coping with the effects of erratic schooling (Penuel & Davey, 2000).

CLASSROOM EXAMPLES

The school counselor or social worker can maintain regular contact with shelters, review enrollment procedures with families, and prepare school staff for the arrival of homeless students. Clear enrollment procedures for students who may lack residency, immunization, and academic records bridge the first potential barrier to educational access.

Schools can create a "newcomers club" (Gonzalez, 1992) for all new members of the school community as a means of providing orientation to the school building, staff, routines, and resources. The principal can greet families and introduce the counselor, nurse, and other staff members involved in retrieving records and securing support services. Business partners and the PTA can provide welcome packs that include school supplies (e.g., T-shirt, plan book, folder, pencils, and student handbook) bearing the school's logo.

For some homeless students, the daily transition between chaotic living situations and the school environment may require additional attention. One solution is to create a transition space or dependable contact with a staff member to smooth the entry into school life.

Children who have spent the night in a shelter or on the street are often in a state of dissonance with themselves and the world around them. They may be hungry, exhausted, depressed, or ill. Such children need a place to rest, receive nourishment, and perhaps vent frustrations on a punching bag or cry in the arms of an accepting adult (Quint, 1994, p. 61).

The buffer zone may be a room staffed by a case manager, counselor, or resource teacher; or a staff member may meet the student in the cafeteria for breakfast or the media center for a transition period. Teachers can create transition time and space within the classroom as well, with individual activities and opportunities for consultation as students enter the classroom or begin the school day.

Teachers can use a variety of strategies to help a student become a member of the class by including newcomers' pictures on a class photo bulletin board, assigning a classroom responsibility geared to the student's interest, and pairing the student with a supportive peer (Christiansen, Christiansen, & Howard, 1997). Students benefit from explicit orientation and ongoing coaching in classroom routines and expectations as well as additional preparation for changes in the schedule. Establishment of designated work and storage space within the classroom is important for homeless students, who may have little personal space of their own. Secondary students may benefit from designated study carrels in the library.

RESOURCES

Christiansen, Christiansen, & Howard, 1997; Dryfoos, 1990; Eddowes & Butcher, 2000; Entwisle, 1993; Gonzalez, 1992; Henderson, 1997; Kling, Dunn, & Oakley, 1996; Mallory, 1995; Penuel & Davey, 2000; Quint, 1994.

● **STRATEGY 2.4:** EXPEDITE ASSESSMENTS OF STUDENT'S PHYSICAL, PSYCHOSOCIAL, AND ACADEMIC REQUIREMENTS. TEACHERS COLLABORATE WITH OTHER STAFF MEMBERS TO QUICKLY ASSESS AND IDENTIFY STUDENTS' SKILLS AND NEEDS FOR INSTRUCTIONAL AND SUPPORT SERVICES.

DISCUSSION

Comprehensive and speedy assessments help to determine the most appropriate placements and the range of programs and services needed for each homeless student (Anderson, Janger, & Panton, 1995). Expediting this process requires teamwork, shorter timelines, and flexibility (Hightower, Nathanson, & Wimberly, 1997).

The school team can assess a student's physical, psychosocial, and academic assets and needs. The nurse and community health services can evaluate the student's overall health, including nutrition, hygiene, immunizations, and any chronic or acute concerns. The school social worker or homeless education liaison may assess family needs for support services as well as student needs for clothing and personal care items. And the social worker, counselor, or psychologist may be involved in evaluating psychosocial issues regarding the student's development of coping strategies in response to homelessness. Sometimes a fellow student's family may decide to "adopt" a homeless student and her family, helping to assume responsibility for sibling and parent care.

Homeless students' life experiences may include trauma, violence, chronic discontinuity, or family disorganization; their responses can be highly varied, including anger, withdrawal, depression, or school phobia. As homeless students acclimate to the classroom, teachers' observations become a critical component of any evaluation.

Both classroom and resource teachers assess students' academic skills, interests, and prior school experiences. Curriculum-based assessments, interest inventories, and informal interviews contribute to the identification of meaningful instructional objectives as well as appropriate learning strategies (Idol, Neven, & Paolucci-Whitcomb, 1986; Tower, 1992). Referral for speedy, in-depth evaluations may be required to determine the student's eligibility for bilingual, gifted, special education, or other support programs (e.g., Title I or magnet programs). We should not overlook the possibility of giftedness or hidden disabilities; gaps in educational experiences may result in uneven academic skill profiles.

CLASSROOM EXAMPLES

Standard options for evaluation often need modification to provide timely information for placement decisions. The retrieval of evaluations—even partial ones—from previous schools may supply data that do not need to be gathered again. The child study committee can review existing information, determine the most important areas for assessment, and work together to complete assessments quickly (Walther-Thomas, Korinek, McLaughlin, & Williams, 1996).

Teachers use initial interviews as a quick, effective strategy to learn more about the student and to communicate their interest in understanding the student's assets and needs. New students complete an inventory of reading preferences (group, individual, oral, silent, and types of books) with the teacher, providing an opportunity for the teacher to gain useful information about the student's reading experiences and for the student to receive individualized support and orientation. The interview may include a tour of the classroom library to identify materials used previously. Through this process, students supply valuable information about their learning preferences, problem-solving abilities, and expectations about school.

Inquiries about previous learning can provide teachers with opportunities to recognize and validate students' previous accomplishments. Daily journal writing provides another avenue for students to describe their experiences, interests, and concerns. Teachers can construct curriculum-based assessments by drawing sample tasks from curriculum materials and activities; such tasks can probe students' current level of functioning.

RESOURCES
Anderson, Janger, & Panton, 1995; Hightower, Nathanson, & Wimberly, 1997; Idol, Nevin, & Paolluci-Whitcomb, 1986; Tower, 1992; Walther-Thomas, Korinek, McLaughlin, & Williams, 1996.

● **STRATEGY 2.5:** ADDRESS THE STUDENT'S BASIC PHYSICAL NEEDS. STAFF MEMBERS COORDINATE WITH ONE ANOTHER TO SUPPORT THE STUDENT'S BASIC NEEDS FOR FOOD, CLOTHING, REST, HYGIENE, SCHOOL SUPPLIES, AND ACTIVITY FEES.

DISCUSSION

A careful assessment of the student's full range of needs can determine needed supports and services (Anderson, Janger, & Panton, 1995). Sensitive teachers are often the first to recognize physical needs, including exhaustion, hunger, lack of clothing, and medical and hygiene concerns. These basic needs typically must be met before students can focus on learning and interacting with their peers. Teachers can anticipate student needs for school supplies, activity fees, and field-trip costs, which may be supported by volunteer organizations. Providing these resources in discreet ways avoids stigmatizing the student.

CLASSROOM EXAMPLES

Sensitive staff members and community volunteers can arrange creative approaches to supporting students' basic needs. School nurses, for example, can arrange for in-school dental and immunization clinics and accommodate students' needs for rest and for basic hygiene care (Black, 1994; Eddowes, 1992). An emergency fund supported by school festivals and other fund-raising activities can support costs of field trips, activity fees, and snacks (Quint, 1994). Community volunteers can organize extra clothing and school supply closets, complete with backpacks and assignment calendars.

Many homeless students have no study space available for completing homework (Vissing, 1996). Civic groups and booster clubs can purchase homework materials, complete with clipboards or lapboards and organizers to serve as portable desks.

RESOURCES

Anderson, Janger, & Panton, 1995; Black, 1994; Eddowes, 1992; Quint, 1994; Vissing, 1996.

● STRATEGY 2.6: FOSTER STUDENTS' PSYCHOSOCIAL WELL-BEING. TEACHERS DESIGN CLASSROOM ENVIRONMENTS TO PROVIDE SECURITY, SUPPORT, AND SENSITIVITY. THROUGH COLLABO-RATION WITH OTHER MEMBERS OF THE SCHOOL COMMUNITY, TEACHERS IDENTIFY ADDITIONAL RESOURCES TO MEET STUDENT NEEDS FOR SELF-EXPRESSION, COUNSELING, AND ENCOURAGEMENT.

DISCUSSION

Students' adjustment to a new classroom may require different types of support, depending on previous experiences, current living arrangements, and personal adaptability. Teachers can effectively support students' adjustment by understanding student behavior in light of their experiences.

For some students, the consistency of the classroom routine and the opportunity for personal space and belongings can make school a sanctuary from less pre-

dictable and protected settings. However, adjusting to structured expectations may be difficult for other homeless students, who may have learned to survive by fending for themselves or who have run away from hostile environments (Anooshian, 2000).

Teachers' observations of students' behavior and a willingness to listen may garner the best insights about the accommodations that will help homeless students become successful members of the class. Teachers may consult with specialists in domestic violence, counselors, school psychologists, and social workers to gain added information and support services for the student and family.

CLASSROOM EXAMPLES

Teachers use a combination of supports to help students understand the classroom routine and expectations. These supports include reviewing daily schedules, posting schedules and behavior expectations, providing personal copies of schedules and rules, and holding class meetings to review progress or plan activities. Providing coaching in appropriate behavior is preferable to depriving students of privileges, recess, or possessions as a consequence for inappropriate behavior (Black, 1994). Once students have adapted to the classroom routine, preparing them for any changes in the schedule or environment helps, too.

Homeless students usually live in shelters, cars, motel rooms, or share dwelling space with other families; they have little personal or quiet space for completing homework, reading, or playing. Designated classroom space for work and storage can be important for homeless students and they may become quite protective of it (Black, 1994). The school media center or library can provide quiet work space. And, just as with any student, music, art, or physical education may prove to be important avenues for these youngsters' self-expression and development.

If teachers are sensitive to the dramatic differences in homeless students' situations, they can be prepared to modify assignments that might require students to bring items from home, use reference materials for homework, or complete certain tasks at home (Vissing, 1996). School resources and time or community mentors may be needed to help homeless students accomplish such learning outcomes.

School counselors may provide instruction in conflict resolution, assertiveness training, or other skills that may be especially helpful to homeless students. Students who have experienced greater stress or trauma may need psychological support services for sexual abuse, school phobia, or depression (Anderson, Janger, & Panton, 1995). Situations involving domestic violence require additional precautions to protect the confidentiality of the student's location and the student's safety (Johnson, 1992).

RESOURCES

Anderson, Janger, & Panton, 1995; Anooshian, 2000; Black, 1994; Johnson, 1992; Vissing, 1996.

● STRATEGY 2.7: INDIVIDUALIZE INSTRUCTIONAL SUPPORTS AND SERVICES. INSTRUCTIONAL SUPPORTS AND SERVICES ARE BASED ON THE INDIVIDUAL STUDENT'S PROFILE OF ASSETS AND NEEDS. STUDENTS WHO ARE HOMELESS MAY REQUIRE SERVICES FROM GIFTED, TITLE I, BILINGUAL, VOCATIONAL, OR SPECIAL EDUCATION PROGRAMS.

DISCUSSION

The homeless student's individual profile, created in the initial assessment process, allows schools to identify necessary instructional supports. Gaps in schooling or broader experiences may produce uneven profiles of learning accomplishment, particularly for youngsters experiencing prolonged homelessness. Individual plans of instructional support (similar to those developed for special education) may be helpful.

Consider a full range of instructional services for these individual plans, including gifted, Title I, bilingual, vocational, alternative, and special education programs. Focusing on students' strengths as well as their academic deficits is a key factor in promoting resilience.

Including homeless students in the educational mainstream is an important means of promoting long-term success. Diverse classroom groupings and instructional differentiation within heterogeneous classrooms can help accommodate a wide range of student learning patterns and prior experiences (Beck, Kratzer, & Isken, 1997).

CLASSROOM EXAMPLES

Several kinds of learning environments may be particularly appropriate for homeless students. Increased individual attention is likely in classes with fewer students, with collaborative teachers (both general and special educators), and with groupings of varying size (individual, small, and large) (Gonzalez, 1992). Multi-age classes, intensive reading programs, and accelerated classes give students the opportunity to progress at varying rates—an important factor in accommodating differing experiences and learning profiles. No matter what the placement, dividing large projects into smaller chunks promotes a sense of accomplishment for students who are adjusting to changes, both in and out of school (Korinek, Walther-Thomas, & Laycock, 1992).

At the secondary level, a variety of effective approaches encourages students' participation, despite frequent disruptions or time constraints (Vissing, Schroepfer, & Bloise, 1994). Both magnet programs with varied emphases and alternative educational settings provide accommodating, engaging options. In Minnesota, Area Learning Centers offer flexible educational options; for example, courses that can be completed in shorter time periods or through independent study (Hightower, Nathanson, & Wimberly, 1997). Such options allow mobile secondary students to acquire course credit in less than one academic year or to continue work to support themselves. And in Madison, Wisconsin, staff members developed mini-courses that assist secondary students in acquiring credits toward graduation.

RESOURCES

Beck, Kratzer, & Isken, 1997; Gonzalez, 1992; Hightower, Nathanson, & Wimberly, 1997; Korinek, Walther-Thomas, & Laycock, 1992; Vissing, Schroepfer, & Bloise, 1994.

● STRATEGY 2.8: ENLIST MENTORS AND TUTORS FOR INCREASED INDIVIDUALIZED SUPPORT. STAFF MEMBERS, COMMUNITY VOLUNTEERS, AND OLDER STUDENTS CAN SERVE AS IMPORTANT MODELS FOR STUDENTS AND PROVIDE ADDITIONAL ACADEMIC SUPPORT, ENCOURAGEMENT, AND TALENT DEVELOPMENT.

DISCUSSION

Mentoring relationships with adults or older students are central to promoting resilience among homeless students. Through intensive, sustained attention, mentors nurture high expectations and talents, teach problem solving and consideration of alternative perspectives, and model competent behavior (Masten, 1994). The support of a mentor is key to building a homeless student's confidence in his ability to achieve goals and develop skills. Teachers may serve as mentors or they may recruit, orient, and coordinate with community members or older students to serve in this role (Quint, 1994). Assuring regular contact and ongoing coordination between teacher and mentor is an important means of enriching both schooling and support for homeless students. Mentors may focus on tutoring, enrichment activities, transition to work, and community involvement with students. Sustained relationships with competent, caring mentors allow youngsters to air their feelings, explore new interests, secure resources, and plan for the future (Henderson, 1997).

CLASSROOM EXAMPLES

Collaboration with corporate sponsors, universities, and community organizations can establish effective mentioning and tutoring options for homeless students. In Arizona, business and university personnel collaborate with teachers to find mentors who work with homeless students (Haas & Woods, 1997). Representatives from major corporations and university students provide in-class and community-based tutoring. Corporations provide opportunities for homeless students to "shadow" their mentors at work. Mentors help students recognize the links between school-based learning and subsequent work skills. Through sustained communication and commitment to this partnership, teachers and mentors have contributed significantly to homeless students' academic gains.

Students from William Penn College in Iowa serve as tutors to students who live in shelters (Hightower, Nathanson, & Wimberly, 1997). Although both young students and their college tutors rotate through the program, effective learning units and ongoing relationships have been built among school, shelter, and college personnel that sustain these creative instructional supports. In addition, teacher education programs such as those offered by Arizona State West, William Penn College, and University of South Carolina are preparing new teachers with the skills and sensitivity to effectively integrate homeless students into their classrooms (Popp, 2000; Swick, 2000).

Parent and other community organizations have also established volunteer programs that offer students individualized attention. Careful orientation of volunteers and ongoing interaction with classroom teachers maximize the results of these added supports. Teachers create a strong link with mentors and tutors by sharing relevant materials and information. Much of the information is in the form of current class work, e-mail and phone messages, and periodic conferences. In turn, mentors and tutors provide important insights into students' interests and concerns.

RESOURCES
Haas & Woods, 1997; Henderson, 1997; Hightower, Nathanson, & Wimberly, 1997; Masten, 1994; Popp, 2000; Quint, 1994; Swick, 2000.

● STRATEGY 2.9: FOSTER HIGH EXPECTATIONS WITHIN A SUPPORTIVE CLIMATE. TEACHERS DEMONSTRATE AND ENCOURAGE HIGH EXPECTATIONS FOR STUDENT LEARNING AND SUCCESS WITHIN A COOPERATIVE ENVIRONMENT.

DISCUSSION

High expectations by adults for students' educational participation and positive outcomes build youngsters' confidence and enthusiasm for learning (Henderson, 1997). Effective teachers communicate high expectations to homeless students through challenging content and supportive behavior.

Classroom management that promotes time on task continues to be one of the most important factors in successful learning. A review of 100 studies of learning showed increased learning time to be positively related to improved learning outcomes in 88 percent of the studies (Walberg, 1993). In fact, this link "is one of the most consistent findings in educational research" (Walberg, p. 1). Across several studies, Wang, Haertel, & Walberg (1994) identified additional factors that contribute to student learning outcomes, including focus on cognitive strategies, positive classroom environment, and family encouragement.

A study of urban elementary schools reveals that student perceptions of a cohesive school community were related to positive academic outcomes for students from high-poverty circumstances (Battisch, Solomon, Kim, Watson, & Schaps, 1995). School community was measured by students' judgments of support within classrooms and the larger school, as well as their sense of autonomy within the learning environment. Desirable academic outcomes included positive social and academic attitudes and academic performance.

Classroom Examples

Teachers can express high expectations for homeless students to learn and perform well without emphasizing competition with other students. Strategies for learning well include building on students' experiences and interests, including students in goal setting and monitoring, and identifying students' learning strategies while encouraging diverse approaches to problem solving (Ames, 1992). An emphasis on learning well is especially important for homeless students, whose schooling may have been interrupted frequently and who may lack confidence in their ability to learn.

Strategies designed for high-ability students may be integrated into the curriculum to the benefit of all students, particularly high-poverty students (Renzulli, Reis, Hebert, & Diaz, 1995). For instance, blocks of study time may be devoted to enrichment clusters organized around the interests of students and teachers, with the participation of community resource persons. These nongraded learning groups emphasize inductive and interdisciplinary approaches to learning and provide flexible, creative avenues for learners to demonstrate their knowledge and skills.

Other enrichment-focused strategies include thorough talent assessments, curriculum compacting, and specialized extensions (e.g., Odyssey of the Mind). Homes for the Homeless in New York City emphasizes accelerated and enriched learning experiences for homeless students whose schooling has been frequently disrupted (Nunez, 1994).

Resources
Ames, 1992; Battisch, Solomon, Kim, Watson, & Schaps, 1995; Henderson, 1997; Nunez, 1994; Renzulli, Reis, Hebert, & Diaz, 1995; Walberg, 1993; Wang, Haertel, & Walberg, 1994.

● **Strategy 2.10**: Foster Constructive Peer Relationships. Development of positive, meaningful peer interaction can be accomplished through cooperative learning activities, buddy systems, peer tutoring, shared classroom responsibilities, and modeling.

Discussion

Homeless students can be integrated more readily into heterogeneous classrooms that emphasize the valuable, diverse contributions of all members (Wang, Haertel, & Walberg, 1994). These settings are typically more desirable than variously segregated settings that may carry certain stigma and that also reduce access to the broader curriculum.

A welcoming environment and a sense of belonging are fundamental for students who have moved frequently, leaving behind friends, pets, and familiar surroundings. Classmates can—and many do quite naturally—assume the responsibility of orienting newcomers. Once homeless students have become acclimated to the classroom routine, they can assume this role with new students—a role that may give them particular satisfaction.

Multi-age instructional arrangements, whether fixed or occasional, provide opportunities for supportive peer interaction (with careful teacher instruction and monitoring). The combination of group goals and individual accountability is a central feature in cooperative learning groups that contribute to students' academic achievement (Slavin, 1991). Cooperative learning may also build student self-esteem, peer relations, motivation, and group work skills. Teachers naturally model and explain the process of sharing roles, responsibilities, and problem solving in their own cooperative relationships with other teachers, staff members, and volunteers (Gonzalez, 1992).

Classroom Examples

Several Texas programs employ a buddy system to help homeless students and other newcomers acclimate to the school environment (Johnson, 1992). This easily implemented strategy promotes prosocial behavior without stigmatizing newcomers.

Peer tutoring can furnish another interactive learning strategy that incorporates peer modeling, concept elaboration, skill practice, and supportive feedback (Walther-Thomas, Korinek, McLaughlin, & Williams, 1996). Teacher monitoring and feedback optimize the outcomes of peer tutoring.

Formal cooperative learning strategies provide specific guidelines for instruction in group contexts (Slavin, 1991). The frequent use of less formal collaborative learning arrangements gives students the opportunity to share ideas and resources and develop meaningful relationships. Ideally, teachers model many of the prosocial skills that students need through their respect for student diversity and their guidance in collaboratively solving a wide range of classroom issues. Class meetings can provide constructive resolution of group concerns and offer a chance to celebrate accomplishments (Bickart & Wolin, 1997).

RESOURCES
Bickart & Wolin, 1997; Gonzalez, 1992; Johnson, 1992; Slavin, 1991; Wang, Haertel, & Walberg, 1994; Walther-Thomas, Korinek, McLaughlin, & Williams, 1996.

● STRATEGY 2.11: ENGAGE STUDENTS ACTIVELY IN MEANINGFUL PROBLEM SOLVING. TEACHERS CREATE INCREASED OPPORTUNITIES TO INCORPORATE STUDENTS' INTERESTS, CONCERNS, AND EXPERIENCES INTO THE INSTRUCTIONAL PROCESS. STUDENTS ARE ACTIVELY ENGAGED IN IDENTIFYING RESOURCES AND SOLVING PROBLEMS.

DISCUSSION

An important feature of resilience is the ability to solve problems—an ability many homeless students and their families need as they address the challenges of poor employment and housing. Problem solving requires students to define issues, retrieve pertinent information, formulate potential solutions, analyze options, select and implement a solution, and evaluate outcomes. These skills, which can be acquired as an integral part of instruction, equip students to deal more effectively with academic, social, and personal tasks. This strategy shifts the focus from directed, rote learning to metacognitive processes that foster student ownership in learning.

Problem-based learning strategies engage students in active study of real-world issues. As students identify significant problems to study, they can examine their own experiences and communities for issues of concern. Studying real problems in depth and formulating solutions bolsters students' sense of responsibility, connectedness, and efficacy. Problem-based learning authentically capitalizes on the abilities of young people as they create new approaches to persistent problems and apply their enthusiasm to rally support for their plans.

Problem-based learning capitalizes on the natural diversity of student experiences and knowledge. One student who moved frequently (as her family searched for work) was quite knowledgeable about various areas of the United States. Her experiences with map reading and the public transit systems made her a key resource for the geography unit on urban areas in the United States.

Teachers and other staff members model problem-based learning strategies by discussing their own

approaches to solving real problems, both collaboratively and individually. Homeless students need to observe and practice these forms of decision making and resourcefulness in the safe environment of the classroom, as an alternative to the passive coping or survival-oriented strategies they may have learned in hostile circumstances (e.g., by being part of or witness to domestic violence). On the other hand, homeless students may have much to teach their classmates about problem solving, having "outmaneuvered, outlasted, outwitted, or outreached" myriad adversities (Henderson, 1997, p. 11).

CLASSROOM EXAMPLES

The members of Judith Norton's middle school civics class pursued their interest in governmental responses to homelessness by traveling to the Maryland state capitol. Their state representative sponsored a bill for homeless people. As the students learned about the realities of homelessness, they also learned valuable lessons about researching issues, developing bills, the effects of lobbying activities, and the satisfaction of taking political action.

In some schools, classrooms are transformed into a MicroSociety—complete with government, business, and service enterprises that reflect the structures and processes of the broader community. Students study traditional subjects in the morning and apply their skills in the afternoon by creating various work projects with the advice of community organizations and volunteers. Teachers using this strategy report improved attendance, academic performance, self-management, active learning, and creative problem solving (Coad & Wilson, 1996; Fedarko, 1992). Students wrestle with finding employment within the society, completing financial audits for their businesses, and conducting trials for classmates' violations of the law (Fedarko, 1992).

Teachers and students are using the resources of technology to implement problem-based learning strategies. Opportunities to access, analyze, and report information as well as to involve students in actual political, scientific, corporate, and professional projects on the Internet are expanding rapidly.

By employing technology effectively for investigation and communication, teachers help students develop skills in using a significant problem-solving tool. For homeless students and families without personal access, teachers, shelters, and local libraries can provide additional orientation to Internet access options. The SHELTRS (Support for

Homeless Edcucation: Linking Technology Resources to Shelters) Project in Texas creates connections among homeless students, tutors and Web-based resources (http://www.tenet.edu/shelters/index.html). The partnership among universities, community agencies, and businesses supports homeless students' access to the state curriculum as well as to the World Wide Web.

RESOURCES

Baltimore County, 1997; Bickart & Wolin, 1997; Coad & Wilson, 1996; Fedarko, 1992; Henderson, 1997.

● **STRATEGY 2.12:** PROMOTE AGE-APPROPRIATE SKILLS OF SELF-DETERMINATION. STUDENTS CAN ASSUME A MORE ACTIVE ROLE IN ASSESSING THEIR OWN SKILLS AND INTERESTS, SETTING LEARNING GOALS, AND MONITORING THEIR OWN PROGRESS.

DISCUSSION

Instructing students in strategies of self-determination includes specific attention to planning, self-advocacy, and decision-making skills. These strategies also incorporate the skills of self-awareness, self-regulation, and self-monitoring. The development of self-determination skills supports students' goal orientation and positive self-appraisal, two protective factors associated with resilience, independence, and life satisfaction (Reiff, Gerber, & Ginsberg, 1996; Werner & Smith, 1992).

Opportunities to develop self-determination skills can be included throughout the instructional day by means of students' active planning, decision making, self-appraisal, and self-monitoring (Bickart & Wolin, 1997). Collaborative instruction can occur across the curriculum and in a variety of settings (e.g., media center, physical education, specialized reading instruction), involving classroom teachers, guidance counselors, special educators, and resource personnel.

Self-determination skills are prerequisites for effective self-advocacy, which is especially relevant for students who need help in communicating their learning strengths, needs, preferences, and progress. Self-advocacy may be especially critical for homeless students who find themselves threatened with dangerous situations or need to communicate their academic status in each new school they

attend (Walther-Thomas, Korinek, McLaughlin, & Williams, 1996). Curricula exist specifically to help students with disabilities acquire these skills and to participate in the development of their own individualized educational programs (Martin & Marshall, 1995; Van Reusen, Bos, Schumaker, & Deshler, 1994).

When dealing with young children, many effective teachers describe their own planning and management strategies to their students and build student participation into those processes. The High/Scope early childhood curriculum incorporates a "plan-do-review" format that facilitates the participation of very young children in these goal-oriented and reflective processes (Hohmann & Weikart, 1995).

Luckner (1994) provided examples of simple inventories of students' responsibilities and values as well as daily goal-setting formats that are quite useful for elementary students. Several curricula for secondary students include their families in building appropriate levels of autonomy for decision making in both family and school arenas (Hoffman & Field, 1995; Serena & Lau-Smith, 1995). Teachers may need to adjust their expectations to individual students' circumstances, recognizing that some homeless students are overburdened with responsibility and may initially need considerable structure and encouragement for decision making.

CLASSROOM EXAMPLES

Strategies of self-determination—particularly planning, monitoring, and self-appraisal—are easily incorporated into research projects, work portfolios, and other familiar instructional approaches (e.g., writing workshops). Introduce each component in a large group, with individual student and teacher conferences and peer meetings to support implementation. Homeless students can actively participate in selecting and evaluating work for their own portfolios, with an emphasis on identifying their learning preferences and progress, thus laying the groundwork for effective communication with subsequent teachers. Portfolio review conferences with teachers, parents, and peers become opportunities for students to present their own appraisals and accomplishments.

Group projects provide another avenue for collaborative planning, decision making, and self-appraisal. With teacher facilitation, students can establish ground rules for participation, including role assignments, time lines, monitoring strategies, and reporting methods. These interactions require good communication skills as well as individual accountability to the work group.

RESOURCES

Bickart & Wolin, 1997; Hoffman & Field, 1995; Hohmann & Weikart, 1995; Luckner, 1994; Martin & Marshall, 1995; Reiff, Gerber, & Ginsberg, 1996; Serena & Lau-Smith, 1995; VanReusen, Bos, Schumaker, & Deshler, 1994; Walther-Thomas, Korinek, McLaughlin, & Williams, 1996; Werner & Smith, 1992.

● STRATEGY 2.13: CONNECT WITH EXTENDED AND FLEXIBLE LEARNING OPPORTUNITIES. TEACHERS COORDINATE WITH TUTORIAL AND ENRICHMENT PROGRAMS, PROVIDED BEFORE AND AFTER SCHOOL AS WELL AS DURING THE SUMMER.

DISCUSSION

Students whose schooling has been frequently interrupted profit from extended and intensified learning options. These options provide important protective factors, including meaningful learning experiences, talent development, constructive peer relationships, and mentors.

Heath and McLaughlin (1994) identified several authentic learning opportunities that various youth organizations (e.g., Boys and Girls Clubs, Scouts, athletic or arts groups) furnished in urban areas. Within these extended-day and extended-year activities, students are expected to function as resources for planning, preparing, practicing, and performing a wide range of activities, including study groups, neighborhood clean up, and fund raising. Here young people have a safe haven and a focus for their energies, which is especially important for students who live in shelters that may close in the afternoon.

Students whose living situations offer little freedom for exploration or expression can find important outlets in talent development and enrichment activities (Shane, 1996). Teachers who are aware of these community resources and activities can encourage students to participate and can then celebrate their accomplishments in these arenas.

Before-school or after-school programs in school, community, and shelter settings can offer tutoring and homework support for homeless students (Anderson, Janger, & Panton, 1995). When teachers communicate and coordinate with staff and volunteers in such programs, an effective extension of the classroom-based learning is cre-

ated. Together, teachers and community mentors can create a "tapestry of programs" that support students' active, high-interest learning (Freiberg, 1994).

CLASSROOM EXAMPLES

The Middle College High School, on the campus of Central Community College (Seattle), provides a flexible learning option for homeless secondary students. This effective program (75 percent of the graduates pursue post-secondary education) includes paid internships, interdisciplinary classes, mentors, and both high school and college credits (Hightower, Nathanson, & Wimberly, 1997).

Students who live in Residential Educational Training Centers (sponsored by Homes for the Homeless) attend the Brownstone School for after-school programs. This Learning Fast-Track program uses accelerated, rather than remedial, programs to help students bridge gaps in their learning. The program provides "high expectations, deadlines for clearly identified performance levels, and stimulating instructional materials" within the context of a low student-to-teacher ratio and individualization (Nunez, 1994, p. 75).

The programs and resources of community and school-based libraries are a useful source of learning enrichment and extension (Tower, 1992). Homework and tutoring sessions, as well as family literacy programs, are often available in these settings. Teachers use online bulletin boards or recorded homework hot lines to connect classroom activities with after-school tutors.

Summer programs can be used to extend students' learning experiences. The Brownsville Cultural Academy, a joint project of the public schools and a Native American cultural center, offers a two-month summer program for both homeless and nonhomeless students (Hightower, Nathanson, & Wimberly, 1997). Activities include high-interest academic, cultural, and recreational experiences. Computer and academic skill development is complemented by mural creations, Native American drumming, sailing, and horseback riding. Following these summer enrichment programs, academy participants are more active during the school year in both school and community extracurricular activities.

RESOURCES

Anderson, Janger, & Panton, 1995; Freiberg, 1994; Heath & McLaughlin, 1994; Hightower, Nathanson, & Wimberly, 1997; Nunez, 1994; Shane, 1996; Tower, 1992.

● STRATEGY 2.14: BUILD CONNECTIONS WITH FAMILIES AND SHELTER PROVIDERS. TEACHERS USE A VARIETY OF COMMUNICATION AND INVOLVEMENT STRATEGIES TO CREATE GOOD WORKING RELATIONSHIPS WITH FAMILIES AND SHELTER STAFF MEMBERS.

DISCUSSION

Both homeless families and shelter providers are usually interested in educational issues but are necessarily preoccupied with securing housing, employment, and basic resources (Yon & Sebastien-Kadie, 1994). Teachers and other school staff can initiate regular communication to encourage closer ties among families, shelters, and schools (Anderson, Janger, & Panton, 1995). Shelter staff can present information to the staff and school council about the realities of homelessness in the community; similarly, teachers can brief community boards on educational perspectives. A strong working relationship between school and shelter can support students' enrollment and encourage their ongoing successful participation. Shelter staff members can contact the school about new students and accompany the family to school for the first time.

Although homeless families are often hesitant about interacting with schools, teachers can welcome parents into the classroom and share orientation materials (schedules, classroom expectations, and current activities). The school counselor or homeless education liaison can provide a tour of the school and introduce other staff members, as well as review school resources.

Family-focused programs—including family literacy, life skills, or parenting classes—are important sources of support for families who have almost no safety net (Nunez, 1994). Many of these programs employ a two-generation approach to education in an effort to end the cycle of poverty and homelessness. Even Start, Head Start, and some adult or alternative education programs address the educational needs of both parents and children.

CLASSROOM ACTIVITIES

Before school starts each year, school staff and shelter providers can attend an open house in each other's settings. A tour of shelter facilities, together with discussions with residents and shelter staff, can help educators understand the realities of these students' lives. School tours help shelter providers and residents understand the realities of school life, including the expectations and the resources for students, as well as encourage communication.

Schools and shelters can exchange newsletters to maintain this awareness and to promote better coordination. Teachers can make weekly phone calls to give progress reports and invitations to family-oriented activities. Photos of students involved in classroom activities (with descriptions written by the students) are an effective strategy for sharing school experiences with family members. Conferences with families have been held at fast-food restaurants with play areas for children or other community settings with activities for youngsters to provide a more comfortable environment for some families (Walther-Thomas, Korinek, McLaughlin, & Williams, 1996).

Frequent contact between shelters and schools improves the recruitment and enrollment of homeless students. To encourage student enrollment, homeless education liaisons can travel to campgrounds or motels that transient families use (Johnson, 1992). Shelter-based tutoring programs can make use of community volunteers, college students, and teachers. Some shelter-based libraries and play areas have been equipped through donations from school and community groups (Klein & Foster, 1998).

In New Jersey, family literacy workshops include family-style meals, parent workshops, and student activities. Workshops for parents address such issues as substance abuse, discipline, and career planning. Students participate in study sessions with tutors (based on teacher input) and recreational activities with their peers (Hightower, Nathanson, & Wimberly, 1997).

RESOURCES
Anderson, Janger, & Panton, 1995; Klein & Foster, 1998; Hightower, Nathanson, & Wimberly, 1997; Johnson, 1992; Nunez, 1994; Yon & Sebastien-Kadie, 1994; Walther-Thomas, Korinek, McLaughlin, & Williams, 1996.

● STRATEGY 2.15: PREPARE FOR THE STUDENT'S DEPARTURE. TEACHERS COMMUNICATE WITH STUDENTS, FAMILIES, AND SHELTER PROVIDERS ABOUT STRATEGIES FOR EASING THE NEXT TRANSITION, INCLUDING AVAILABILITY OF WORK SAMPLES, ASSESSMENT INFORMATION, AND FOLLOW-UP COMMUNICATION.

DISCUSSION

Almost as soon as homeless students arrive, teachers need to prepare for the reality of their departure (Kling, Dunn & Oakley, 1996). From the time of enrollment, teachers and other staff members can communicate to families and shelter providers the importance of providing records and follow-up contact to subsequent schools. Students being evaluated for special education or receiving special services require particular care to avoid lags in services or unnecessary reevaluations (Korinek, Walther-Thomas, & Laycock, 1992).

Teachers can include students in preparing their records by involving them in work portfolios and assessing their academic progress. Emphasis on evaluating and saving student work communicates to both student and family the importance of the youngster's learning accomplishments. Students also need time and support to gather their possessions and to tell other students and staff goodbye. Methods for maintaining contact provide some connectedness, despite the general discontinuity of homeless students' schooling.

CLASSROOM EXAMPLES

Teachers can help students organize important information about their academic accomplishments to take to their next school. Student and teacher reviews of progress can center on the student's articulation of acquired skills, interests, strengths, and needs. Donated or discarded textbooks and workbooks can be given to students when they leave, complete with the school address, phone number, and perhaps the teacher's e-mail address to encourage continued contact.

A formal checkout procedure with the office staff, nurse, counselor, and teacher provides another opportunity to review student progress and needs with the family, as well as to communicate the school's commitment to send records and support the student's transition (Gonzalez, 1992). The school liaison can link the sending and receiving schools by faxing evaluations, progress reports, and other records. Whenever possible, teachers can exchange information about strategies that were particularly effective in supporting the student's adjustment and learning.

Classmates can encourage continued contact by giving the departing student a few stamped, self-addressed postcards and class photographs. Gonzalez (1992) suggested taking a photograph of the student and family during the final farewell and adding it to a bulletin board titled "Contributions to Our School's Greatness." Support during this transition establishes the school as a caring place and encourages homeless families and students to continue seeking educational opportunities.

RESOURCES
Gonzalez, 1992; Kling, Dunn, & Oakley, 1996; Korinek, Walther-Thomas, & Laycock, 1992.

BIBLIOGRAPHY

Ames, C. (1992). Classrooms: Goals, structures, and student motivation. *Journal of Educational Psychology,* 84(3), 261–271.

Anderson, L. M., Janger, M. I., & Panton, K. L. M. (1995). *An evaluation of state and local efforts to serve the educational needs of homeless children and youth.* Washington, DC: U.S. Department of Education.

Anooshian, L. J. (2000). Moving to educational success: Building positive relationships for homeless children. In J. H. Stronge & E. Reed-Victor (Eds.), *Educating homeless students: Promising practices* (pp. 79–98). Larchmont, NY: Eye on Education.

Baltimore County Public Schools. (1997, June 20). *Making a difference: Effective education of homeless students.* Workshop presented in Towson, MD.

Barton, M. L., & Zeanah, C. H. (1990). Stress in the preschool years. In L. E. Arnold (Ed.), *Childhood stress.* New York: John Wiley and Sons.

Bassuk, E., & Rosenberg, L. (1988). Why does family homelessness occur? *American Journal of Public Health, 78,* 783–788.

Bassuk, E. L., and Weinreb, L. (1994). The plight of homeless children. In J. Blacher (Ed.), *When there's no place like home: Options for children living apart from their natural families.* Baltimore: Brookes.

Battistich, V., Solomon, D., Kim, D., Watson, M., & Schaps, E. (1995). Schools as communities, poverty levels of student populations, and students' attitudes, motives, and performance: A multilevel analysis. *American Educational Research Journal, 32,* 627–658.

Beck, L. G., Kratzer, C. C., & Isken, J. A. (1997). Caring for transient students in one urban elementary school. *Journal for a Just and Caring Education, 3*(3), 343–369.

Bickart, T. S., & Wolin, S. (1997). Practicing resilience in the classroom. *Principal, 77*(2), 21–22, 24.

Black, S. (1994, February). At home in your schools. *The Executive Educator, 16*(2), 47–50.

Carnegie Council on Adolescent Development. (1992). *A matter of time: Risk and opportunity in the nonschool hours.* New York: Author.

Children's Defense Fund. (1995). *The state of America's children yearbook.* Washington, DC: Author.

Christiansen, J., Christiansen, J. L., & Howard, M. (1997). Using protective factors to enhance resilience and school success for at-risk students. *Intervention in School and Clinic, 33*(2), 86–89.

Coad, P., & Wilson, D. (1996, May). MicroSociety! *Alpha Delta Kappan.*

Doll, B., & Lyon, M. A. (1998). Risk and resilience: Implications for the delivery of educational and mental health services in the schools. *School Psychology Review, 27*(3), 348–363.

Dryfoos, J. (1990). *Adolescents at risk: Prevalence and prevention.* New York: Oxford University Press.

Eddowes, E. A. (1992). Children and homelessness: Early childhood and elementary education. In J. H. Stronge (Ed.), *Educating homeless children and adolescents: Evaluating policy and practice.* Newbury Park, CA: Sage Publications.

Eddowes, E. A., & Butcher, T. (2000). Meeting the developmental and educational needs of homeless infants and young children. In J. H. Stronge & E. Reed-Victor (Eds.), *Educating homeless students: Promising practices* (pp. 21–44). Larchmont, NY: Eye on Education.

Egeland, B., & Kreutzer, T. (1991). A longitudinal study of the effects of maternal stress and protective factors on the development of high-risk children. In E. M. Cummings, A. L. Greene, & K. H. Karraker (Eds.), *Life-span developmental psychology: Perspectives on stress and coping.* Hillsdale, NJ: Lawrence Erlbaum.

Entwisle, D. R. (1993). Schools and the adolescent. In S. S. Feldman & G. R. Elliot (Eds.), *At the Threshold: The developing adolescent.* Cambridge, MA: Harvard University Press.

Felsman, J. K. (1989). Risk and resilience in childhood: The lives of street children. In T. F. Dugan & R. Coles (Eds.), *The child in our times: Studies in the development of resilience.* New York: Brunner/Mazel.

Foscarinis, M., & McCarthy, S. (2000). Removing educational barriers for homeless students: Legal requirements and recommended practices. In J. H. Stronge & E. Reed-Victor (Eds.), *Educating homeless students: Promising practices* (pp. 135–164). Larchmont, NY: Eye on Education.

Freiberg, H. J. (1994). Understanding resilience: Implications for inner-city schools and their near and far communities. In M. Wang & E. Gordon (Eds.), *Educational resilience in inner-city America: Challenges and prospects.* Hillsdale, NJ: Lawrence Erlbaum.

Gibel, L. C. (1996). *Attitudes of children toward their homeless peers.* New York: Garland Publishing.

Gonzalez, M. L. (1992). Educational climate for the homeless: Cultivating the family and school relationship. In J. H. Stronge (Ed.), *Educating homeless children and adolescents: Evaluating policy and practice.* Newbury Park, CA: Sage Publications.

Haas, N. S., & Woods, C. J. (1997, October). *Building bridges from school to work through mentoring.* Paper presented at the National Association of State Coordinators of Education for Homeless Children and Youth, Columbus, OH.

Haberman, M. (1991). The pedagogy of poverty versus good teaching. *Phi Delta Kappan, 73*(4), 290–294.

Hagen, J. L. (1987). Gender and homelessness. *Social Work, 32,* 312–316.

Haggerty, R., Sherrod, L., Garmezy, N., & Rutter, M. (1994). *Stress, risk, and resilience in children and adolescents: Processes, mechanisms, and interventions.* Cambridge, MA: Cambridge University Press.

Hanson, M. J., & Carta, J. J. (1995). Addressing the challenges of families with multiple risks. *Exceptional Children, 62,* 201–212.

Heath, S. B., & McLaughlin, M. W. (1994). Learning for anything everyday. *Journal of Curriculum Studies, 26*(5), 417–489.

Helm, V. M. (1993). Legal rights to education of homeless children and youth. *Education and Urban Society, 25,* 323–339.

Henderson, N. (1997). Resilience in schools: Making it happen. *Principal, 77*(2), 10–12, 14, 16–17.

Hightower, A. M., Nathanson, S. P., & Wimberly, G. L., III. (1997). *Meeting the educational needs of homeless children and youth: A resource for schools and communities.* Washington, DC: U.S. Department of Education.

Hoffman, A., & Field, S. (1995). Promoting self-determination through effective curriculum development. *Intervention in School and Clinic, 30*(3), 134–141.

Hohmann, M., & Weikart, D. P. (1995). *Educating young children.* Ypsilanti, MI: High/Scope Press.

Idol, L., Nevin, A., & Paolucci-Whitcomb, P. (1986). *Models of curriculum-based assessment.* Rockville, MD: Aspen.

Jackson, S. (1989). *The education rights of homeless children.* Cambridge, MA: Center for Law and Education.

Jahiel, R. I. (Ed.). (1996). *Homelessness: A prevention-oriented approach.* Baltimore: Johns Hopkins University Press.

James, B., Lopez, P., Murdock, B., Rouse, J., & Walker, N. (1997). *Pieces of the puzzle: Awareness, understanding, and opportunity.* Austin, TX: Charles A. Dana Center.

Johnson, J. P. (1992). Educational support services for homeless children and youth. In J. H. Stronge (Ed.), *Educating homeless children and adolescents: Evaluating policy and practice.* Newbury Park, CA: Sage Publications.

Kaufman, N. (1984). Homeless: A comprehensive policy approach. *Urban and Social Change Review, 17*(1), 21–26.

Kimchi, J., & Schaffner, B. (1990). Childhood protective factors and stress risk. In L. E. Arnold (Ed.), *Childhood stress.* New York: John Wiley and Sons.

Klein, T., & Foster, M. (1998). Support and education programs for parents. In T. Harms, A. R. Ray, & P. Rolandelli (Eds.), *Preserving childhood for children in shelters* (pp. 99–109). Washington, D.C.: Child Welfare League of America Press.

Kling, N., Dunn, L., & Oakley, J. (1996, Winter). Homeless families in early childhood programs: What to expect and what to do. *Dimensions of Early Childhood,* 3–8.

Korinek, L., Walther-Thomas, C., & Laycock, V. K. (1992). Educating special needs homeless children and youth. In J. H. Stronge (Ed.), *Educating homeless children and adolescents: Evaluating policy and practice.* Newbury Park, CA: Sage Publications.

Liddle, H. A. (1994). Contextualizing resilience. In M. Wang & E. Gordon (Eds.), *Educational resilience in inner-city America: Challenges and prospects,* pp. 167–168. Hillsdale, NJ: Lawrence Erlbaum.

Linehan, M. (1992). Children who are homeless: Educational strategies for school personnel. *Phi Delta Kappan, 74,* 61–66.

Luckner, J. (1994). Developing independent and responsible behaviors in students who are deaf or hard of hearing. *Teaching Exceptional Children, 26*(2), 13–17.

Mallory, B. L. (1995). The role of social policy in life-cycle transitions. *Exceptional Children, 62,* 213–223.

Martin, J. E., & Marshall, L. H. (1995). ChoiceMaker: A comprehensive self-determination transition program. *Intervention in School and Clinic, 30*(3), 147–156.

Masten, A. S. (1994). Resilience in individual development: Successful adaptation despite risk and adversity. In M. Wang and E. Gordon (Eds.), *Educational resilience in inner-city America: Challenges and prospects.* Hillsdale, NJ: Lawrence Erlbaum.

McChesney, K. Y. (1993). Homeless families since 1980: Implications for education. *Education and Urban Society, 25,* 391–380.

National Alliance to End Homelessness. (1988). *Housing and homelessness: A report of the National Alliance to End Homelessness.* Washington, DC: Author.

National Center for Children in Poverty. (1997). One in four: America's youngest poor. *National Center for Children in Poverty News and Issues, 6*(2), 1.

National Coalition for the Homeless. (1997). *Homeless families with children: Fact sheet.* Washington, DC: Author.

Nunez, R. D. (1994). *Hopes, dreams, and promise: The future of homeless children in America.* New York: Homes for the Homeless, Inc.

Nunez, R. D. (1995). The new poverty in urban America: Family homelessness. *Journal of Children and Poverty 1*(1), 7–28.

Nunez, R. D. (1997). Common sense: Why jobs and training alone won't end welfare for homeless families. *Journal of Children in Poverty, 3*(1), 93–101.

Orozco v. Sobol, 703 F. Supp. 1113 (S.D. N.Y. 1989).

Oxley, D. (1994). Organizing for responsiveness: The heterogeneous school community. In M. Wang and E. Gordon (Eds.), *Educational resilience in inner-city America: Challenges and prospects.* Hillsdale, NJ: Lawrence Erlbaum.

Penuel, W. R. & Davey, T. L. (2000). Meeting the educational needs of homeless youth. In J. H. Stronge & E. Reed-Victor (Eds.), *Educating homeless students: Promising practices* (pp. 63–78). Larchmont, NY: Eye on Education.

Pianta, R. C. & Walsh, D. J. (1996). *High risk children in schools: Constructing sustaining relationships.* New York: Routledge.

Popp, P. A. (2000). Educating homeless students: Linking with colleges and universities. In J. H. Stronge & E. Reed-Victor (Eds.), *Educating homeless students: Promising practices* (pp. 247–265). Larchmont, NY: Eye on Education.

Powers, J. L., & Jacklitsch, B. (1993). Reaching the hard to reach: Educating homeless adolescents in urban settings. *Education and Urban Society, 25,* 394–409.

Powers, J. L., & Jaklitsch, B. (1992). Adolescence and homelessness: The unique challenge for secondary educators. In J. H. Stronge (Ed.), *Educating homeless children and adolescents: Evaluating policy and practice.* Newbury Park, CA: Sage Publications.

Stewart B. McKinney Homeless Assistance Act of 1987. P. L. 100-77 Codified at 42 U.S.C. 11301-11472 (1987, July 22).

Stewart B. McKinney Homeless Assistance Amendment Act of 1990. P. L. 101-645 (1990, (November 29).

Improving America's Schools Act of 1994. P. L. 103-382 (1994, September 28).

Project ACT. (1997). *Shelter art exhibition.* Cleveland, OH: Cleveland Public Schools.

Quint, S. (1994). *Schooling homeless children: A working model for America's public schools.* New York: Teachers College Press.

Rafferty, Y. (1995). The legal rights and educational problems of homeless children and youth. *Educational Evaluation and Policy Analysis, 17,* 39–61.

Rafferty, Y., & Rollins, N. (1989). *Learning in limbo: The educational deprivation of homeless children.* Long Island City, NY: Advocates for Children. (ERIC Document Reproduction Service No. ED 312 363).

Reed-Victor, E. (2000). Resilience and homeless students: Supportive adult roles. In J. H. Stronge & E. Reed-Victor (Eds.), *Educating homeless students: Promising practices* (pp. 99–114). Larchmont, NY: Eye on Education.

Reed-Victor, E. & Pelco, L. E. (1999). Helping homeless students build resilience: What the school community can do. *Journal for a Just and Caring Education, 5*(1), 51–71.

Reed-Victor, E., & Stronge, J. H. (1997). Building resilience: Constructive directions for homeless education. *Journal of Children and Poverty, 3,* 67–91.

Reiff, H. B., Gerber, P. J., & Ginsberg, R. (1996). What successful adults with learning disabilities can tell us about teaching children. *Teaching Exceptional Children, 29*(2), 10–16.

Renzulli, J. S., Reis, S. M., Hebert, T. P., & Diaz, E. I. (1995). The plight of high-ability students in urban schools. In M. C. Wang & M. C. Reynolds (Eds.) *Making a difference for students at risk: Trends and alternatives.* Thousand Oaks, CA: Corwin Press.

Schweinhart, L. J., & Weikart, D. P. (1989). Early childhood experience and its effects. In L. A. Bond & B. E. Compas (Eds.), *Primary prevention and promotion in the schools.* Newbury Park, CA: Sage Publications.

Serena, L. A., & Lau-Smith, J. L. (1995). Learning with a purpose: Self-determination skills for students who are at risk for school and community failure. *Intervention in School and Community, 30*(3), 142–146.

Shane, P. G. (1996). *What about America's homeless children?* Thousand Oaks, CA: Sage Publications.

Slavin, R. (1991). Synthesis of research on cooperative learning. *Educational Leadership, 48,* 71–82.

Stronge, J. H. (1992). Programs with promise: Educational service delivery to homeless children and youth. In J. H. Stronge (Ed.), *Educating homeless children and adolescents: Evaluating policy and practice.* Newbury Park, CA: Sage Publications.

Stronge, J. H. (1993a). Emerging service delivery models for educating homeless children and youth: Implications for policy and practice. *Educational Policy, 7,* 447–465.

Stronge, J. H. (1993b). From access to success: Public policy for educating urban homeless students. *Education and Urban Society, 25,* 340–360.

Stronge, J. H. (1995). Educating homeless students: How can we help? *Journal for a Just and Caring Education, 1,* 128–141.

Stronge, J. H. (1997). A long road ahead: A progress report on educating homeless children and youth in America. *Journal of Children and Poverty 3*(2), 13–32.

Stronge, J. H. (2000). Educating homeless children and youth: An introduction. In J. H. Stronge & E. Reed-Victor (Eds.), *Educating homeless students: Promising practices* (pp. 1–20). Larchmont, NY: Eye on Education.

Stronge, J. H., & Helm, V. M. (1991). Legal barriers to the education of homeless children and youth: Residency and guardian issues. *Journal of Law and Education, 20,* 201–218.

Swick, K. J. (2000). Building effective awareness programs for homeless students among staff, peers, and community members. In J. H. Stronge & E. Reed-Victor (Eds.), *Educating homeless students: Promising practices* (pp. 165–182). Larchmont, NY: Eye on Education.

Tower, C. C. (1992). The psychosocial context: Supporting education for homeless children and youth. In J. H. Stronge (Ed.), *Educating homeless children and adolescents: Evaluating policy and practice.* Newbury Park, CA: Sage Publications.

U. S. Department of Education. (1989, February). *Report to Congress: Education of homeless children and youth - State grants.* Washington, DC: Author.

Van Reusen, A. K., Bos, C. S., Schumaker, J. B. & Deshler, D. D. (1994). *The self-advocacy strategy for education and transition planning.* Lawrence, KS: Edge Enterprises.

Vissing, Y. M. (1996). *Out of sight, out of mind.* Lexington, KY: University Press of Kentucky.

Vissing, Y. M., Schroepfer, D., & Bloise, F. (1994). Homeless students, heroic students. *Phi Delta Kappan, 75,* 535–539.

Waddell, M. (n.d.). *Faces of homelessness: A study unit for grades K-12.* Redmond, OR: COCAAN.

Walberg, H. J. (1993). Productive use of time. In L. W. Anderson & H. J. Walberg (Eds.), *Timepiece: Extending and enhancing learning time.* Reston, VA: National Association of Secondary School Principals.

Walther-Thomas, C., Korinek, L., McLaughlin, V. L., & Williams, B. T. (1996). Improving educational opportunities for students with disabilities who are homeless. *Journal of Children and Poverty, 2*(2), 57–75.

Wang, M. C., & Gordon, E. (1994). *Educational resilience in inner-city America: Challenges and prospects.* Hillsdale, NJ: Lawrence Erlbaum.

Wang, M. C., Haertel, G. D., & Walberg, J. H. (1994). Educational resilience in inner cities. In M. C. Wang & E. Gordon (Eds.), *Educational resilience in inner-city America: Challenges and prospects.* Hillsdale, NJ: Lawrence Erlbaum.

Werner, E. E., & Smith, R. S. (1982). *Vulnerable but invincible: A longitudinal study of resilient children and youth.* New York: McGraw-Hill.

Werner, E. E., & Smith, R. S. (1992). *Overcoming the odds: High risk children from birth to adulthood.* Ithaca, NY: Cornell University.

Williams, B. T., & Korinek, L. (2000). Designing effective school programs for homeless students. In J. H. Stronge & E. Reed-Victor (Eds.), *Educating homeless students: Promising practices* (pp. 183–202). Larchmont, NY: Eye on Education.

Yon, M., & Sebastien-Kadie, M. (1994). Homeless parents and the education of their children. *School Community Journal, 4*(2), 67–77.

Zimmerman, M., & Arunkumar, R. (1994). Resilience research: Implications for schools and policy. *Social Policy Report of the Society for Research in Child Development, 8.*

3

DIVERSE TEACHING STRATEGIES FOR IMMIGRANT CHILDREN

JoAnn Crandall, Ann Jaramillo, Laurie Olsen, and Joy Kreeft Peyton[1]

This chapter addresses the challenges facing immigrant students as they make the transition to schooling in the United States, as well as the qualities of schools and instructional approaches that assist them most effectively. The older the students, the greater their difficulty in catching up with their peers and graduating from high school. Immigrant students can succeed in school if (1) they have access to knowledge that is presented in interesting, understandable ways, and (2) they are integrated into the school's social and academic life. In this chapter we describe instructional strategies intended to develop students' language and literacy skills and to make academic content challenging, interesting, and accessible. These strategies, by the way, represent excellent educational practice for all students.

Education is the fault line in America today; those who have it are doing well in the global economy, those who don't are not doing well. We cannot walk away from this fundamental fact. The American dream will succeed or fail in the 21st century in direct proportion to our commitment to educate every person in the United States of America.

—President Bill Clinton, remembering Franklin D. Roosevelt, 50th anniversary commemorative services, April 12, 1995

tion, which reached a record 25.8 million in 1997, roughly 10 percent of the population, the highest proportion since World War II (U.S. Bureau of the Census, 1997).

Public schools are at the heart of efforts to incorporate these immigrants into U.S. society, and the number of immigrant students grows rapidly. The diversity of these newcomers, the complexity of their needs, and the swiftness and magnitude of change require new programs, materials, and approaches. And these swift changes demand teachers who are knowledgeable, responsive, and prepared to work with students of diverse language, educational, and cultural backgrounds.

UNSTABLE LEARNING: THE EFFECTS OF IMMIGRATION ON EDUCATION

The United States is experiencing an unprecedented wave of immigration, with people from every continent joining an already diverse population. In 1997, roughly a million immigrants swelled the U.S. foreign-born popula-

THE IMMIGRANT POPULATION

Children who speak a language other than English, many of whom are immigrants, are the fastest-growing segment of the U.S. school-age population. Between 1986 and 1994, the number of students designated as limited-English proficient (LEP) increased by 43.8 percent to over 3 million (Donly et al., 1995; Macias & Kelly, 1996). Many of these

1. We are grateful to Les Greenblatt, Prince George's County Public Schools and staff member of Project WE TEACH; and Laura Woodlief, California Tomorrow, for their background research and other valuable contributions to this chapter.

students speak no English at all, and many have limited prior learning. These students are primarily in the western U.S., in urban areas, and in large school districts. California, Texas, and New York enroll the most LEP students, but schools throughout the United States are affected (Henderson, Abbott, & Strang, 1993). Forty-two percent of all public school teachers have at least one LEP student in their classes (Han & Baker, 1997).

This wave of immigration shows no signs of abating; in fact, most demographers predict an increase throughout the next decade. Furthermore, the situation is far from static. The number of immigrants in a school district, and the languages and cultures they represent, can vary dramatically from year to year. Figure 3.1 shows the definitions of the terms used in this chapter to describe immigrant student populations.

The majority of immigrant students enter school at the elementary level. Two-thirds are in grades K through 6, 18 percent are in middle school, and 14 percent are in grades 10 through12 (Fleischman & Hopstock, 1993). These youngsters represent more than 100 different language groups; the majority, almost three of every four students, speak Spanish (Fleischman & Hopstock, 1993). Increasingly, teachers are working with students who do not share their language, culture, or national background (see Figure 3.2).

CHALLENGES FACING IMMIGRANT STUDENTS

All immigrant students face the challenge of learning English well enough to participate fully in an English-speaking world. They also face the pressure of learning academic subjects *before* they are fully proficient in English. The U.S. Supreme Court—in *Lau v. Nichols* (1974) and the Civil Rights Act of 1964—addressed this problem, defining the school's obligation to take affirmative steps to overcome immigrant students' language barriers and provide access to education.

Specifically, immigrant children need to learn not only social English, but also the academic English required to participate in school successfully. They must learn to read in English; comprehend academic discourse; write coherently; and speak and produce English at cognitively complex, academic, abstract levels. And they need to do so *quickly*. Depending on the strength of students' language development in their native tongue, developing a mastery of academic English can take from four to seven years (Collier, 1989).

FIGURE 3.1
Definitions

The terms used in this chapter to describe the student populations represent distinct but overlapping categories.

English-language learners (ELLs) are students whose first language is not English and who are in the process of learning English. Not all English-language learners are classified as limited English proficient or are receiving special language or educational services.

Immigrant students, for the purposes of this chapter, include those students (including refugees, regardless of legal status) born outside the United States of parents who are not originally from the United States. It does not include those born and raised in non-English-speaking homes in the United States.

Limited English proficient (LEP) is an official designation originating with civil rights law, which defines rights of access for students in terms of national origin and language. The term stems from the 14th Amendment to the U.S. Constitution, the Equal Educational Opportunity Act of 1974, and the 1964 Civil Rights Act. Schools are required to take affirmative steps to identify students who are limited English proficient and provide services that will overcome their language barriers.

Newcomers are recent arrivals to the United States. Programs for newcomers vary in their definitions of who is a newcomer; some use the federal government's definition of three years or fewer in the United States, while others restrict newcomer status to one year or less (Short & Boyson, 1997).

While they are becoming able to participate fully in instruction presented in English, immigrant students need a comprehensive, comprehensible means of learning academic subjects. And they often need an accelerated curriculum to catch up with their English-speaking peers, whose progress is a moving target. Each year, native English speakers improve both in English and academic content knowledge. To catch up, immigrants have to make more than a year's progress each year.

From 4th grade on, when the school's academic and cognitive demands begin to increase rapidly, students with

FIGURE 3.2
LEP Students by Language Group

The sheer numbers of students who are LEP indicate our need to reach everybody's children. The numbers of students in the following language groups have been identified as limited English proficient.

Language Groups	Number of LEP Students	Percentage of LEP Students
Spanish	1,682,560	72.9
Vietnamese	90,922	3.9
Hmong	42,305	1.8
Cantonese	38,693	1.7
Korean	36,568	1.6
Laotian	29,838	1.3
Navajo	28,913	1.3
Tagalog	24,516	1.1
Russian	21,903	0.9
Creole (French)	21,850	0.9
Arabic	20,318	0.9
Portuguese	15,298	0.7
Japanese	13,913	0.6
Armenian	11,916	0.5
Chinese (unspecified)	11,540	0.5
Mandarin	11,020	0.5
Farsi	8,563	0.4
Hindi	7,905	0.3
Polish	6,747	0.3

Adapted from Fleischman and Hopstock (1993).

world; others, from urban, industrialized areas. Some flee wars and political repression, others join family members or seek work in the United States. All must adjust to a new culture and language, but the size of the gaps they must bridge, the resources they bring, and their success in making the transition differ enormously. Some immigrant students achieve at high levels, adapt quickly, and learn English well; others do not. Some are far more at risk of school failure than others. Understanding the factors that place students at risk helps educators recognize when extra support is necessary. The issues that particular groups of immigrant students face include the following (from Olsen & Chen, 1988):

• *Living in Transnational Families.* Many immigrants, especially those from Mexico and the Caribbean, maintain a binational life and sustain strong relationships on both sides of the U.S. border. For students, however, moving between countries can result in missed curriculum, loss of credits, and attendance problems, unless the school aligns its calendar with migration patterns, provides independent study options, offers partial credit, or provides other support.

• *Acculturating.* Immigrant students arrive in the United States with a variety of backgrounds. The shock of entering a new culture and making a place for oneself is a daunting task. Many young people must choose between cultures, which can create deep identity crises. The process of acculturation often involves painful decisions about what to save or sacrifice, what to adopt or reject (Aronowitz, 1984). Rifts can open within families as youth become "Americanized" and reject their family ways. Tension can erupt at school, too, as immigrant children seek to maintain key parts of their traditional or cultural identities. Few students find within their families or schools a strongly supported middle ground—where they can be bicultural and bilingual and not have to give up a part of themselves to become a part of the U.S. culture.

• *Arriving as an Adolescent.* Young children often have an easier time than older ones in making the transition to a new land. Approximately one-fifth of the English-language learners (ELLs) in U.S. schools arrive as adolescents (Minicucci & Olsen, 1991). Some go directly to work and never enroll in school (Cornelius & Rumba, 1995). Those who do enroll must leap from one school system and curriculum to another. Those with solid schooling in their native land have greater success in U.S. schools. Unfortunately, the number of immigrants arriving in secondary schools with little prior schooling and little or no

little or no academic and cognitive development in their first language do less and less well. Catching up, and maintaining gains, becomes increasingly difficult as the curriculum becomes more challenging.

PERSONAL AND SOCIAL CHALLENGES

Students labeled LEP are tremendously diverse, with differing national backgrounds, languages, cultures, schooling experiences, and reasons for immigration (First & Carrera, 1988). Some come from rural, isolated parts of the literacy in their home language is increasing (Fleischman & Hopstock 1993). For these students, accelerated basic literacy instruction is necessary, though few secondary schools are prepared to provide it.

• *Learning a New, Very Different System.* Immigrant students have an immediate need to learn how U.S. schools work. Bells ring, and people change rooms; lunch is served in cafeterias; students store materials in lockers. More profound are the differences in teaching approaches, relationships between students and teachers, and school structure and expectations. Students in the United States are expected to participate in discussions and voice opinions. Tests do not determine their whole future. Teachers are often not accorded respect and authority. Immigrant students need support and orientation that their parents usually cannot provide. Instead, parents rely on their children to explain the system of schooling and to translate materials provided only in English.

• *Recovering from Trauma.* Some students arrive from war-torn nations or refugee camps, scarred by the disruptions and trauma of war, trauma that may have dispersed their families (Rumbaut, 1994). They may have had little or no schooling; they may well have suffered hunger and disease. Nightmares and violent memories haunt them, and many suffer from post-traumatic stress syndrome (Ascher, 1984; Carlin, 1979), which is often largely undiagnosed and unrecognized.

• *Dealing with Isolation and Discrimination.* In recent years, anti-immigrant sentiment has swept the United States. Many immigrants find they have entered a racially divided society. Immigrant students often encounter unwelcoming, sometimes hostile or violent attitudes at school. Hate crimes and anti-immigrant incidents are on the rise. This unsafe atmosphere seriously hampers immigrant students' willingness to participate in school. Unfortunately, a common aspect of the immigrant experience is isolation and marginalization, the shame of being teased or ostracized for imperfect English and foreign ways. This isolation adds yet another barrier to acquiring English.

WHAT SCHOOLS CAN DO

Schools face a major challenge in responding to the needs of immigrant students, because most schools were designed (and most teachers prepared) for a more homogeneous reality. Studies have analyzed the characteristics of effective schools for immigrant and language-minority students (August & Hakuta, 1997; Berman et al., 1995; Carter & Chatfield, 1986; Garcia, 1988; Lucas, Henze, & Donato, 1990; Olsen & Mullen, 1990), and some schools boast innovative programs. But few schools have the capacity to deliver effective, comprehensive programs for immigrant students that support full participation in school, provide access to the entire curriculum and strong English-language development, *and* result in high achievement. Getting from where we are to where we need to be must begin with a vision of what a comprehensive program could include.

COMPREHENSIVE PROGRAMS

A comprehensive approach to schooling provides both a strong academic program and a support structure to facilitate full student participation (August & Hakuta, 1997; Crandall, 1994; Lucas, 1997; Olsen & Mullen, 1990). The academic program includes customized learning environments for students with varying levels of English fluency and academic achievement. Articulation and coordination within and between schools is also strong. The curriculum incorporates a focus on English-language and literacy development. A curriculum balanced between basic and higher-order skills incorporates students' native languages and cultures and offers opportunities for student-directed instruction (Garcia, 1988; Olsen & Mullen, 1990; Wong, Filmore, & Valadez, 1986). Teaching methodologies and curricula draw on students' home and community cultures (Moll, Amanti, Neff, & Gonzalez, 1992) to bridge the gap between home language and literacy experiences and those expected in school (Garcia, 1988; Heath, 1983).

A comprehensive program rests on a strong initial assessment process to ensure appropriate student placement and to inform classroom instruction. After assessment, teachers monitor student progress to enable students to move to new levels of curriculum as their fluency in English grows.

Full access to the curriculum is ensured through a combination of native-language instruction and sheltered-content instruction in English. Teachers are well prepared with strong training in the principles and practices of second-language acquisition (Crandall, 1994; Zeichner, 1992).

Finally, a comprehensive program provides extended time to allow students the extra support needed for the burden of learning English and academics simultaneously. Support services addressing war trauma, acculturation, orientation to a new culture and school system, and other challenges are either provided directly by the school or ensured through referral relationships with community agencies and organizations that can deliver such support bilingually and biculturally.

A supportive climate sets the tone for an educational program promoting high achievement for all students. Research shows that a supportive school climate that helps ELLs succeed includes the following components (August & Hakuta, 1997; Lucas, Henze, & Donato, 1990; Olsen & Mullen 1990; Zeichner, 1992):

- Valuing students' primary languages and cultures.
- Making high expectations concrete.
- Having school leaders who make the education of ELLs a high priority.
- Having school staff members committed to empowering ELLs through education.
- Enacting policies and programs that promote positive intergroup relations such as conflict resolution; community building; antiprejudice programs; and curriculum about scapegoating, racism, and exclusion.
- Building strong relationships to support parent and community involvement.
- Valuing diversity.

RESPONSIVE HABITS

Immigration provides a constantly varying stream of cultures, languages, and national experiences; therefore, effective schools have found they cannot simply institute a good program and leave it alone. Instead, they build habits and mechanisms for responding to the continually changing mix of cultures and languages. Responsive schools have the following characteristics (Olsen, & Jaramillo, 1999):

- They consciously and conscientiously build capacity to deliver an effective academic program by investing in sustained professional development in collaborative, inquiry-based, and individual formats. (See also Crandall, 1994; González & Darling-Hammond, 1997.)
- They internalize accountability for inclusion and access for immigrant students by creating data systems and processes that support ongoing analysis of data about immigrant student achievement, participation, and progress. These data become the basis for program improvement and new interventions.
- They recognize the importance of learning about immigrants' cultures, experiences, and needs, and they

build structures that support listening to and learning from immigrants.
- Their structures support optimal teaching and learning for immigrants, including time for teacher collaboration, reflection, data discussions, and inquiry.
- They create mechanisms that allow advocates to come together, shaping a voice in the school and district on behalf of immigrant students.

RESOURCES

Aronowitz, 1984; Ascher, 1984; August & Hakuta, 1997; Berman et al., 1995; Carlin, 1979; Carter & Chatfield, 1986; Collier, 1989; Cornelius and Rumba, 1995; Crandall, 1994; First and Carrera, 1986; Fleischman & Hopstock, 1993; Garcia, 1988; Gonzàlez & Darling-Hammond, 1997; Han & Baker, 1997; Heath, 1983; Henderson, Abbott & Strang, 1993; Lucas, 1997; Lucas, Henze, & Donato, 1990; Macías & Kelly, 1996; Minicucci & Olsen, 1991; Moll, Amanti, Neff, & Gonzalez, 1992; Olsen & Chen, 1988; Olsen & Jaramillo, 1999; Olsen & Mullen, 1990; Population Resource Center, 1996; Rumbaut, 1994; Short & Boyson, 1997; Wong, Filmore, & Valadez, 1986; Zeichner, 1992.

TEACHING AND LEARNING STRATEGIES FOR IMMIGRANT STUDENTS

While the number of immigrant students in U.S. schools continues to increase, the number of teachers from other countries and from non-English-language backgrounds is declining, as is the percentage of teachers who have special preparation for teaching ELLs. In 1997, Henke and colleagues found that 39 percent of public school teachers had ELLs in their classes; of these, only 28 percent had any training for working with these students.

Thus the more than 3 million ELLs in U.S. classrooms spend most of their day with teachers who have not been trained to work with them. Even in the basic area of instruction in ESL, in 1995 only 25 percent of Hispanic ELLs received any ESL instruction; of those who did not, 72 percent dropped out of school (National Center for Education Statistics, 1997a).

Unless both preservice and inservice teacher education programs change, this situation is likely to become worse, since the greatest population growth in public schools is expected to be among Hispanic, Asian and Pacific Islander, and Native American students. By 2005, the Hispanic public school population is expected to increase by 30 percent; Asian and Pacific Islander, 39 percent; and Native American, 6 percent. At the same time, the black population

AGAINST THE ODDS

SONJA LUTZ

With his high-top haircut and outdated clothes, Gabriel drew plenty of stares when he entered our school as a 9th grader. He lived with his father in a small apartment in the heart of what was once known as the "quarters" in Belle Glade, Florida. His father worked in the sugar cane fields; his mother remained in Haiti with his numerous brothers and sisters.

Records show that in middle school, Gabriel was tested and placed in a special education language arts class. Looking back, it isn't difficult to understand why he tested poorly. Though his spoken English was fair, his native language was Creole, and he had not been read to as a child in any language. He once said that he was one of more than 20 children. As a result, Gabriel had grown up without much home support. He was awkward, shy, and lacked social skills.

It wasn't long, however, before his special education teachers, realizing that Gabriel had been misplaced, transferred him to regular classes. Although he hadn't been cared for at home, he was a good thinker, and somewhere along the way, had developed terrific survival skills. His avid quest for learning and his constant questioning caused him to be regarded as a pest by some of his teachers.

By 9th grade, Gabriel found out that if he needed help, there were plenty of people in the community who could help him. The first person who contributed to his metamorphosis may have been his scoutmaster. The scoutmaster recognized that this young man wanted to *belong*. He found that Gabriel had an intense desire to succeed, so he not only gave him scouting responsibilities, but tried to give him help and encouragement with his schoolwork, especially in the area of science.

By 10th grade, with the scoutmaster's help, Gabriel designed a science fair project; because he had nowhere to set it up, it took up space in my garage. Twice a week, he would show up at my house to record the results of his experiment. Of course, he had no money to complete an elaborate science fair board to accompany his project, so we helped him. I can still picture his science board stretched out on our living room floor, and Gabriel carefully placing the letters in his title. His research and presentation won him first place in the biology division of the science fair and placed in the district. His achievements in scouting and his victory in the science fair were Gabriel's initial steps on his path to success.

By 11th grade, he had progressed to honors classes. In addition, he was involved in many extracurricular activities. He played drums in the marching band, made the wrestling team, and ran track. At about this time, his father returned to Haiti, and Gabriel was left to fend for himself. The scoutmaster helped with the legal work to have Gabriel declared a ward of the court and to help find him a suitable foster home. As a result, Gabriel found a room in a house with foster parents, but he still didn't find a home.

During the summer between his junior and senior years, he attended summer Boy Scout camp as a patrol leader. When he returned to school, he completed his community service project by painting the Kathryn Price Foundation's headquarters and was awarded the coveted honor of Eagle Scout. The community and its people were the closest thing to home that Gabriel had ever known.

By homecoming time in his senior year, Gabriel appeared and acted quite different from the odd-looking boy with the high-top haircut who had enrolled in 9th grade. With his short hair, wire-rimmed glasses, and semifashionable clothes, he was looked up to by his peers. In fact, he was elected Mr. Homecoming for the fall football celebration!

In the spring, he won first place for community service in the Pathfinder Awards Program sponsored by the *Palm Beach Post*. His ranking of seventh in a graduating class of 267 contributed to his receiving a full scholarship to college.

Gabriel's initial placement in special education classes stacked the deck against his later success. In fact, all the odds were against him—but he wasn't ashamed to ask for help, and he received it. His success is the result of his own initiative coupled with the support of caring teachers and members of the community. Perhaps his story can best be summed up by the final essay he wrote in my class. "I'm not a very good musician, and I didn't win many wrestling matches," he wrote. "I saw the soles of a lot of shoes when I ran track, but I tried and I know I'm a winner."

will increase by only 8 percent, while the white population is likely to decline by 3 percent (Annie E. Casey Foundation, 1997; cited in Maroney, 1998).

We found widespread agreement that teachers need to be adequately prepared to provide instruction that reflects an understanding of (1) second-language acquisition and development, (2) integration of language and content instruction, and (3) cross-cultural communication (Crandall, 1994). Some states (California and Florida, for example) have changed their certification requirements to reflect changing school demographics and address these areas of need. Even where certification requirements have not changed, districts and schools have undertaken various approaches to provide professional development in these three areas. Professional development includes programs of peer observation, mentoring and coaching, teacher inquiry and research groups, and college courses. For any of these techniques to be effective, however, they must be long-term, site-based, teacher-designed and teacher-directed; programs must be designed to improve student learning, and must allow adequate time for teacher inquiry and reflection (Crandall, 1998; Darling-Hammond, 1996; González & Darling-Hammond, 1997; National Commission on Teaching and America's Future, 1996).

One way to ensure long-term commitment is to establish partnerships between universities and schools that simultaneously address needed changes in teacher preparation and inservice professional development through a professional development school or center. In the professional development school, teacher educators, experienced and novice teachers, administrators, and other stakeholders in public education work together to provide a program of teacher education, much of which is taught on site by teams of experienced teachers and university faculty members.

Teacher candidates work alongside expert teachers, experiencing the reality of schools by spending more time in them than is now standard. In the process, teacher candidates provide schools with an additional, knowledgeable adult working in the classroom and help refresh potentially burnt-out teachers with their enthusiasm and new ideas. One result of this collaboration is that the gap between preservice and inservice teacher education and between theory and practice is partially bridged (Crandall, 1994, 1998; González & Darling-Hammond, 1997; Holmes Group, 1990).

In one such partnership, an ESL/bilingual teacher education program has provided a series of courses, workshops, and ongoing research and curriculum development that has helped to better prepare current teachers to work with their increasingly diverse student populations. In turn, these experienced teachers have helped both the teacher education program and current graduate students develop a far better understanding of the challenges and strengths these students represent (Crandall, 1994, 1998).

The following teaching and learning strategies are central to any program of professional development for teachers and other educators who seek to meet the needs of a multilingual, multicultural student population. Each strategy includes a rationale, followed by several classroom examples. References offer the opportunity for further exploration.

RESOURCES

Crandall, 1994, 1998; Darling-Hammond, 1996; González & Darling-Hammond, 1997; Henke, Choy, Chen, Geis, Alt, & Broughman, 1997; Holmes Group, 1990; Maroney, 1998; National Center for Education Statistics, 1997a; National Commission on Teaching and America's Future, 1996.

● STRATEGY 3.1: DEVELOP BASIC SKILLS FOR STUDENTS WITH LIMITED SCHOOLING. TEACHERS OF STUDENTS WITH LIMITED OR INTERRUPTED PRIOR SCHOOLING USE CAREFULLY PLANNED LESSON SEQUENCES TO HELP STUDENTS BECOME ACCUSTOMED TO SCHOOL AND LEARN BASIC ACADEMIC SKILLS. THESE SEQUENCES BUILD ON STUDENTS' PRIOR EXPERIENCES, AND TO THE EXTENT POSSIBLE, THEIR FIRST LANGUAGES.

DISCUSSION

Increasing numbers of ELLs come from countries where political or economic upheaval limited their opportunities for schooling. Significant gaps in their education result (Crandall, Bernache, & Prager, 1998). Others come from rural areas that lacked the opportunity or even the need for literacy or formal schooling (Hamayan, 1994).

Many students enter U.S. schools with limited prior education and literacy, as well as limited English proficiency. They face the double challenge of compensating for years of lost education as they try to learn English (Crandall, 1995; Crandall & Greenblatt, in press). Even if they do speak English, they may speak it in a way that is substantially different from that expected in school. Students who arrive in elementary grades face some diffi-

culty catching up to their peers, but the challenge facing secondary students is enormous, requiring many years of assistance by bilingual, ESL, and content-area teachers.

Like all newcomers to U.S. schools, these students need help in becoming accustomed to an educational environment that may differ greatly from what they left behind. Classrooms that encourage discussion, promote interaction with students of both genders, and allow some freedom for self-expression are likely to pose adjustment problems for any student used to classrooms with a dominant teacher who inflicts strict punishment and expects rote learning.

For students with limited experience with schooling, the adjustment is even more difficult. They need to learn a complex set of policies and procedures, such as how to follow schedules and what is expected of them when they come to class. These students may be challenged by requirements as basic as having to be seated for long periods of time, bringing books and materials, and raising their hands to ask or answer questions. Students with no prior education or literacy experiences need to develop basic literacy skills, such as discriminating among letters and numbers and understanding sound and symbol correspondences, as well as small motor skills. Children with two or three years of education may have developed some of these skills, but may have limited exposure to print and little experience with reading and writing and the myriad uses of literacy that are expected in schools. Their exposure to the basic academic skills of sequencing, measuring, classifying, and comparing may be limited, as well.

Students with little prior schooling need sequenced literacy and academic instruction to enable them to move through the stages of English language, literacy, and academic development until they can participate in regular courses. Ideally, they should first develop literacy and be introduced to the uses of reading and writing in their own language and then transfer these skills to English; doing so allows these new students to use their cognitive and oral-language resources as a basis for developing and understanding the uses of written language. If a classroom contains only a few students who speak the same language, or if appropriate materials or bilingual teachers are not available, then they may need to develop literacy in English first. Again, literacy in English takes more time and more steps than if literacy could be built on substantial oral-language development.

Literacy learners need different instruction from that of ELLs who have substantial education in their own language. Placing literacy learners and those with limited schooling in beginning ESL classes with no special attention to their literacy and cognitive needs is not sufficient, as many of their peers have first-language literacy and academic knowledge on which to build.

If limited numbers of these students prevent the formation of special first-language or ESL classes, then ESL and mainstream teachers need to explore ways to provide additional help. Peer tutoring, learning buddies, cooperative groups, or teacher aides can all help, as does the understanding that learning to be a student and developing basic literacy and academic skills takes time. Other students have acquired basic skills throughout their elementary education, an advantage that may have been denied to immigrant students.

Literacy instruction need not be thought of as sterile instruction in basic skills. While it is important to teach letter formation, basic sound and symbol relationships, and left-to-right reading and writing skills, it is possible to do so within a framework that validates students' prior experiences and uses them to develop more school-related knowledge and skills. A holistic approach to reading and writing, incorporating the teaching of basic skills where these become relevant, helps students see a role for reading and writing in their lives and makes literacy instruction both interesting and functional.

Time spent on drills and worksheets can cause boredom, especially among students who are new to formal schooling (Hamayan, 1994). Many ELLs come from cultures with strong traditions of story telling and oral history. Family histories, traditional stories, and rich personal experiences can provide a strong oral base on which to develop written language.

Linking students' life experiences to needed academic concepts and skills provides a sequence of instruction that can enable students to experience success, develop confidence, and make an easier transition to content-area classes. This takes time, however, and is likely to demand after-school or weekend tutoring, summer school, or additional years of high school, all of which are difficult for students who work to help provide family income. Strategies within classes can include the assistance of peer or cross-age tutors who share the students' first language or who have participated in higher-level ESL classes.

Educators need to distinguish between students with delayed (though normal) literacy development and students with learning disabilities. The difference can be hard to assess initially, especially when students are experiencing separation from family and country, dependence on extended family or friends, frequent movement from one home to another, memories of traumatic experiences, or isolation in their new community. Over time, however, if a student is not recognizing and understanding sound and symbol relationships or has difficulty remembering vocabulary or concepts from one day to the next, an assessment for special education services may be necessary.

CLASSROOM EXAMPLES

Ms. Thompson has taught only three years, but she is a masterful teacher of literacy learners. Her classes combine a predictable sequence of activities while fostering engagement and creativity. Her students keep journals, write stories about themselves and their families, and also focus on reading and writing conventions.

Ms. Thompson begins each class with a whole-class warm-up, in which she establishes that each student has the necessary materials and supplies and is ready to learn. She also uses this time to engage in conversation with each student, finding out what he did over the weekend or the previous evening (which usually involves substantial time working outside the home, thus leaving limited time for homework) or talking about school events. Ms. Thompson ends each class with journal writing and a writing workshop. She requires students to have a class notebook organized into categories that correspond to the various phases of the class (Tate, 1997).

The warm-up is often followed by the development of a language experience story, which the students dictate while Ms. Thompson records the words on the chalkboard (Allen & Allen, 1982; Dixon & Nessel, 1983; Taylor, 1993). The story may stem from something that students have talked about during the warm-up, a school event, a sequence of pictures, a short story or text that Ms. Thompson has read aloud, or something that happened in class. She draws out their experiences, writes vocabulary on the board, and makes mental notes of grammar or other items to work on later.

Ms. Thompson may use a semantic web or another graphic organizer to capture students' ideas and provide all students with access to the vocabulary that only some of them might know. She might ask students to work in pairs or small groups to fill out a storyboard identifying the setting, characters, and major events before trying to write a story together. Students build on that oral discussion as they dictate the story to Ms. Thompson. Together the students read what they have written and suggest changes. Ms.

Thompson also offers suggestions, providing a more appropriate word or tense, often seizing the opportunity for a mini-lesson on some aspect of English vocabulary or structure.

Students then copy the story into their notebooks; they may be asked to engage in additional writing, either at home or in the next class, perhaps adding an ending or describing a character. Ms. Thompson builds oral and written-language activities around these stories, focused on developing specific language skills. She might, for instance, give students a typed version of the story with key words omitted, listing them at the bottom for students to identify. Or she might develop vocabulary exercises such as word matching, fill-in-the-blank sentences, or synonyms and antonyms. She might focus on a specific aspect of spelling, perhaps encouraging students to find other words that exhibit the same spelling rule. She might also divide the story into sentences on strips and ask students to work in groups to put these sentences in an appropriate order. Eventually, she might ask them to try writing the story themselves, in their own words.

Students spend a great deal of time in this class writing. They write about themselves and their lives, their class, and their school. During writing time, they receive individual attention from Ms. Thompson or help one another to find appropriate vocabulary or verb forms. Their early writings may consist of collecting and labeling pictures and creating class bulletin boards or books. Or they might spend time illustrating a story they have heard in class and working in pairs to write captions.

Over time, their stories become longer and culminate in an "autophotography" (Moran-Ender & Ender, 1995), an autobiography using both photographs and words. Each student uses an inexpensive camera to take pictures of families, friends, pets, home, job, or anything they feel helps to identify who they are. They use these pictures to write a story about themselves, which is reproduced for both the learning resource center and Ms. Thompson's collection. Along with magazines and other reading materials, these books serve as readers that students may choose during periods of sustained silent reading or in developing ideas for their own writing.

Through their writing, students see the value of developing literacy and that serves to extend and reinforce literacy development. They come to understand that expressing oneself in writing is a process full of starts and stops; writing can be difficult and discouraging, but it can also be liberating. The students have the support of their teacher and each other in conferences and on review sheets. The review sheets begin simply by asking students to identify one thing they liked about their partner's story, and then asks questions that help writers extend their writing and suggestions for revision (Peyton, Jones, Vincent, & Greenblatt, 1994).

Students take turns using the computers, with priority given to those who are editing or in the final stages of publishing their work. Ms. Thompson finds that using computers encourages revisions and makes the task of writing less troublesome for students learning to read and write; it also reinforces alphabetization and supports reading and writing development. Students may illustrate their stories, produce a cover and title page, and even write a brief description of the author for the back cover. These activities build pride in students' newly acquired literacy.

Dialogue journals are central to Ms. Thompson's class. These written conversations between student and teacher offer private places where meaningful written dialogue can take place and students can receive immediate feedback on both their thoughts and their English (Peyton & Reed, 1990). In these journals, students are free to write about their concerns and their experiences, at whatever level they are able to or are comfortable with. Ms. Thompson responds to each journal, modeling appropriate English but never correcting the writing. Instead, she responds to thoughts, concerns, and questions, validating the importance of literacy in authentic communication. She provides something for students to read that is at their level of literacy and is interesting and important to them.

RESOURCES

Allen, 1982; Crandall, 1995; Crandall, Bernache, & Prager, 1998; Crandall & Greenblatt, in press; Dixon & Nessel, 1983; Hamayan, 1994; Moran-Ender & Ender, 1995; Peyton, Jones, Vincent, & Greenblatt, 1994; Peyton & Reed, 1990; Tate, 1997; Taylor, 1993.

● **STRATEGY 3.2: ORGANIZE INSTRUCTION AROUND THEMES. TEACHERS USE THEMATIC UNITS TO INTEGRATE ENGLISH LANGUAGE SKILLS WITH ACADEMIC CONCEPTS ACROSS THE CURRICULUM, ALLOWING STUDENTS TO BETTER SYNTHESIZE THE MATERIAL PRESENTED TO THEM.**

DISCUSSION

The importance of teaching reading and writing across the curriculum is now well established. When they help students perform experiments and write their findings in lab reports, science teachers are also writing and reading teachers. And mathematics teachers teach reading and writing when they ask students to read word problems and explain, in writing, how they solved them. Not surprisingly, recently established standards in the content areas now include communication standards involving writing as well as speaking, as students are unlikely to learn these skills in isolation, devoid of content.

The need to integrate reading and writing into content-area instruction is even greater when students are learning English. Students cannot be prepared for the academic language skills required for content-area classes without integrating these tasks, texts, and tests into their English-language instruction. ELLs benefit from a holistic approach that integrates language into content and content into language (Crandall, 1987; Curtain & Haas, 1995; Richard-Amato & Snow, 1992). Furthermore, students are unlikely to learn academic English unless they are provided with meaningful contexts and content in which to do so (Crandall & Tucker, 1990; Kessler & Hayes, 1989). Using thematic units to complement regular classroom instruction allows learners of English the opportunity to integrate their language skills in a variety of content areas. Studying relevant, meaningful topics increases motivation and enhances learning.

The use of thematic units may be schoolwide (e.g., in middle schools, organized into instructional teams), or the units may be developed by pairs of teachers (e.g., social studies and ESL) for use within a single classroom on any grade level that integrates language and content instruction. Teachers can choose (sometimes with student input) interesting topics or themes around which to build activities that tie in the content to be taught with corresponding language items from the areas of listening, speaking, reading, and writing (Enright & McCloskey, 1988).

As one teacher wrote in a reflective journal, "The approach that seems to be most successful is the approach that gets the most out of a lesson by stretching it across the curriculum." Thematic instruction helps students to see connections and relate what they are learning in one content area with that of another. Without thematic links, learning can seem fragmented and unrelated, especially for students who are new to U.S. classrooms.

The following steps are helpful in developing a thematic unit:

1. Identify a theme or topic.
2. Identify appropriate texts to use or adapt.
3. Identify needed language, especially new vocabulary.
4. Identify academic concept objectives.
5. Identify critical thinking and study skills objectives.
6. Develop activities that
   - Draw on students' experiences.
   - Are relevant to students' lives.
   - Are appropriate for a variety of learning styles.
   - Develop learning strategies (thinking and study skills).
   - Use a variety of grouping strategies.
   - Involve oral and written language.
7. Sequence activities.
8. If more than one teacher is involved, determine which teacher is responsible for each objective and activity.

In an ideal thematic unit, all ways of learning are addressed: bodily-kinesthetic, spatial, linguistic, musical, logical-mathematical, and interpersonal (Gardner, 1993). The ideal unit also uses Gardner's intrapersonal and natural intelligences to appeal to the learner.

CLASSROOM EXAMPLES

Mr. Garcia recognized that his students' interest in the Winter Olympic Games could provide a unifying theme for an ESL and social studies unit. He began by asking students what they knew about Japan, webbing their responses and organizing them into categories for further investigation by student groups (e.g., food, homes, sports, government, and families). Students presented their findings and used the information in a writing assignment that mirrored the functional writing test that the state required for high school graduation. In this assignment, students wrote a letter describing what they had learned about Japan to their cousin, who had just won a trip to Nagano to attend the Olympics.

During the two weeks of the Olympics, students added to their knowledge of Japan, filling the original web and keeping a tally of the medals that each country won. They also completed a daily chart of these medals and converted the information to line and bar graphs. They used these graphs and charts to help them learn English comparatives and superlatives, for example, better and best, more than and less than, worse and worst.

Mr. Garcia brought in the daily newspaper for students to use in determining when their favorite sports would be televised. They used that information and the results to report on the events as journalists, completing a

5-W Chart—Who, What, When, Where, and Why (Chamot & O'Malley, 1994) and summarizing the event. As a culminating activity, students worked in cooperative groups to prepare Olympic posters, taking roles such as poster designer and computer title creator. Social studies, mathematics, art, and English-language skills were all integrated into the project, and it was used as a means of preparing for their science fair projects in the spring.

Environmental and social issues provide particularly rich possibilities for thematic instruction. One high school used the rain forest as the focus of instruction for all students for eight weeks. A middle school team focused on endangered species for a similar period. After reading *Brother Eagle, Sister Sky* (Jeffers, 1991, Dial Books), in which a Native American laments humans' destruction of the environment, students worked in groups to investigate the status of specific animals, focusing on distribution, habitat, food, speed and mode of travel, interactions with humans, and causes of endangerment. The students used the five themes of geography—location, place, region, movement, and interaction with the environment—as the basis for their investigations.

The middle school students presented their research results in a poster session, similar to what would be required in a science fair. They used latitude and longitude to allow others to locate specific places where the animals live, illustrated and identified specific landforms in the animals' habitats, and explained why some animals are endangered. As a whole class, students brainstormed ways they might help reverse human destruction of the environment and move animals off the list of endangered species.

Even popcorn can unify concepts and language across the curriculum. Ms. Unger engaged her middle school students in a "Pop, Pop or Flop, Flop" unit that integrated mathematics, science, social studies, and language skills. To raise funds, students decided to sell popcorn. Ms. Unger suggested that they investigate which popcorn would provide the greatest return on investment and designed an experiment to compare various brands of popcorn. Students hypothesized that the most expensive popcorn would produce the fewest unpopped kernels. Each of her five classes tested one brand. They ran six trials for their brand, counting the number of kernels in a cup before popping and comparing that number with the number of unpopped kernels after popping, converting that to a percentage of popped corn, and then averaging the six trials. Each class contributed to a graph that enabled them to identify which popcorn produced the fewest unpopped kernels. To their surprise, the most expensive popcorn was not the best buy.

Other themes for secondary schools to use in integrating content and language instruction include immigration, nutrition, the solar system, the world family, themes from history, global issues, pollution, and peace.

RESOURCES

Chamot & O'Malley, 1994; Crandall, 1987; Crandall & Tucker, 1990; Curtain & Haas, 1995; Enright & McCloskey, 1988; Kessler & Hayes, 1989; Gardner, 1993; Jeffers, 1991; Richard-Amato & Snow, 1992.

● **STRATEGY 3.3: SHELTER INSTRUCTION IN CONTENT CLASSES. TEACHERS OF CONTENT AREAS THAT ARE TAUGHT IN ENGLISH "SHELTER" THEIR INSTRUCTION BY USING SEQUENCES OF TASKS INCORPORATING STRATEGIES DESIGNED TO ENSURE THAT ELLS COMPREHEND AND MASTER COGNITIVELY DEMANDING SUBJECT MATTER. THE TEACHERS SEEK NOT ONLY TO MAKE THE CONTENT COMPREHENSIBLE TO STUDENTS, BUT ALSO TO EXPAND THEIR STUDENTS' CAPABILITIES IN ENGLISH.**

DISCUSSION

Content classes designed for students who are acquiring English have been given several different names. The term "sheltered English" has been used frequently, as has Specially Designed Academic Instruction in English (SDAIE) in California. Whatever name is used, these classes serve an important function in a comprehensive program for students learning English.

Whenever possible, offering content classes in students' primary language is the most efficient, direct means of ensuring students equal access to difficult content, especially for those students for whom even a sheltered content class would be incomprehensible. When there are not enough students of a single primary language, or when students reach an intermediate level of fluency in English, creating sheltered content classes that are taught in English makes perfect sense. Many of the strategies described in the sections that follow work equally well in native-language content classrooms, in English-language development classrooms, and in sheltered content classrooms. In fact, students benefit even more when teachers use a consistent array of strategies across content areas.

Teachers of sheltered content classes need to master a repertoire of strategies to effectively teach a topic such as U.S. history, algebra, or biology in English to English learners who have been in the United States for less than two years. "Scaffolding" is the term used most frequently to refer to the tasks that teachers design to support their students as they encounter new concepts and complex language (Bruner, 1986). Just as the name implies, scaffolds should be used as long as students need them. As students become more capable and autonomous, use of the scaffolds decreases. For example, graphic organizers (charts that organize information) of various types can help students understand confusing content. Once it is clear that the students have gained control over the concepts, the graphic organizers may not be necessary.

While all students obviously profit from good instruction, what might be sufficient to enable a native English-speaking student to understand an idea may not provide a second-language learner with enough exposure or enough scaffolding to succeed. For example, a quick brainstorming session before starting a unit might be adequate for native English-speaking students in terms of assessing and activating prior knowledge. Second-language learners, on the other hand, usually need more investigation into what they know and do not know about the same topic. For these students, a brainstorming session might be followed by an anticipatory guide (see Strategy 3.6) and a journal entry on the topic. Each task approaches the topic from a slightly different perspective, giving students multiple opportunities to grapple with the ideas and language to be studied.

Thoughtful teachers in sheltered content classes spend substantial time thinking about what to teach. Approaching topics from different perspectives, using multiple tasks to ensure comprehension and mastery, and providing students with the tools to learn how to learn—all require the teacher to filter out unimportant or extraneous pieces of the curriculum and to get to the most essential, substantial concepts.

Teachers often feel uneasy at first about not "teaching the whole book." Once they have successfully taught a sheltered class, however, they become advocates for teaching with depth rather than breadth—for all students. Teachers carefully examine their curriculum with an eye toward what their students need to know most. They concentrate on foundation concepts in their particular subject matter and ensure that they teach ideas that are critical to their

students' success. The following strategies outline different types of scaffolding that can help teachers organize effective sheltered lessons. Designing an individual sheltered lesson involves a complex orchestration of many elements. Teachers might ask themselves the following questions as they plan:

• What will I do to assess and activate my students' prior knowledge? Can I relate course content to their personal lives?

• What are the big ideas, and how can I build my students' conceptual frameworks so they can comprehend and work with these big ideas?

• How will I incorporate explicit teaching of learning strategies into the lesson? How will these strategies promote my students' metacognitive development so that, over time, they will become increasingly independent learners?

• As I teach the lesson, how will I check for understanding and make sure the students are actively engaged? What kinds of pictures, graphics, and other contextual cues will help my students understand more?

• What kind of task can I give students at the end of the lesson to offer them a chance to attack the material in new or different ways?

• At the end of the lesson, how will we all assess the learning?

Classroom Examples

Mrs. Simons is a skilled teacher of sheltered content. Her primary responsibility is teaching literature to her advanced ESL students—the same literature that her students' native English-speaking peers are studying. After five or six years, she has become adept at incorporating a wide range of tasks into her sheltered language arts lessons. She is sensitive to the fact that students need extra instructional supports—scaffolds—as they study difficult content. She is also keenly aware that most of her students will be studying in mainstream classrooms the following year, sitting next to native English speakers and expected to compete. Thus, she is committed to making sure that her students not only learn the content of the literature class, but also are as prepared as possible for all of their classes.

This week, Mrs. Simons and her students in 8th grade sheltered language arts are finishing the novel *Dragonwings*, by Laurence Yep (Harper & Row, 1975), the story of a young Chinese boy's immigration to California at the turn of the century. Folders of student work related to the novel are on their desks. An examination of several folders shows the various kinds of scaffolds that Mrs. Simons has used to ensure that her students have understood the book. A reciprocal teaching chart and an active reading chart are stapled to the front of each students' folders.

Right now, the students are working in groups of four, using reciprocal teaching to read four pages of the last chapter: One student reads a paragraph and summarizes it, another asks for clarification, the third asks two questions, and the fourth makes a prediction (Jones, Palincsar, Ogle, & Carr, 1987; Palincsar & Brown, 1984; Palincsar, David, & Brown, 1989). After each paragraph, the students change roles.

The folders reveal that Mrs. Simons has used various tasks to assess and activate her students' prior knowledge throughout the reading of the book. There are two anticipatory guides (see Strategy 3.6)—one on Chinese immigration and one on earthquakes—with follow-up activities to show changes in students' ideas. Several journal topics relate the story to students' personal lives, for example, "Write about when you, or a member of your family, came to this country."

For several chapters of the book, the students have found important quotes, written them in a reading log, and responded to the quotes using the active reading chart. They have made several storyboards for other chapters, in which important events are summarized and related by using a graphic. All of these activities will lead to essays in which the students will write about whether the main character, Windrider, will fulfill his dream of becoming a dragon again. They must provide evidence from the story to support any claims. The folders show that the students already have experience with characterization through exercises in charting what Windrider says, what he does, what other characters say about him, and how the author describes him. Next to these direct quotes from the book, the students have written what this tells us about Windrider. It seems clear that, though the students' English is far from perfect, they are engaged in studying and mastering difficult content. They complain a little about "having to write an essay," but the complaints are tinged with pride.

RESOURCES

Bruner, 1986; Palincsar & Brown, 1984; Palincsar, David, & Brown, 1989; Jones, Palincsar, Ogle, & Carr, 1987.

● STRATEGY 3.4: USE INSTRUCTIONAL BEHAVIORS THAT PROMOTE EQUITY, COMPREHENSION, AND ACTIVE PARTICIPATION. TEACHERS OF SECOND-LANGUAGE LEARNERS UNDERSTAND THE SPECIAL ROLE THEY PLAY IN DELIVERING A STIMULATING AND COGNITIVELY DEMANDING, YET COMPREHENSIBLE, CURRICULUM. THEY CONSCIOUSLY TEACH IN A WAY THAT ACTIVELY ENGAGES ALL STUDENTS IN THE CONTENT AND PROVIDES RICH CUES TO MEANING THROUGH CONTEXT; THEY MAY USE A VARIETY OF STRATEGIES TO CHECK FOR UNDERSTANDING.

DISCUSSION

Teaching cognitively demanding subject matter to students learning in a second language requires tremendous skill. Teachers develop a wide repertoire of behaviors that assist student comprehension.

One effective strategy is to develop routines used in structuring the daily lesson and weekly plan. When students know the classroom routines, they are better able to tolerate ambiguities naturally encountered in learning a new language. If students know, for example, that the routine for the beginning of class every Monday, Wednesday, and Friday is journal writing, and they know the routine for checking the overhead to see the topic and the routine for passing out and collecting the journals, then they are able to concentrate on getting their thoughts on paper.

Increasing wait time (the time the teacher waits between asking a question and getting a response) gives second-language learners the extra time they sometimes need to construct a response in English. When teachers increase their wait time from five to seven seconds, they see student responses grow longer, a wider variety of students participating in discussions, and even an increase in student questioning.

In sheltered content and ESL classrooms, teachers need to be sensitive to the range of language proficiency levels. For students in the earlier stages of acquiring English, focusing on the meaning of their contributions rather than on grammatical accuracy lowers anxiety. When the teacher repeats, rephrases, and uses many examples throughout instruction, students understand more.

Teachers who call on all students in a systematic way know that this practice raises performance, especially of students who are considered low achievers. Attention to how students are seated in the classroom and in cooperative groups can also reap benefits (Johnson & Johnson, 1987; Johnson, Johnson, & Holubec, 1993; Kagan, 1994; Slavin, 1989-90, 1990; see Strategy 3.5). Teachers who promote equity in the classroom carefully plan cooperative groups and other activities so that "low status" students have equal opportunities to perform "high status" jobs.

Skillful teachers of sheltered content employ a variety of methods to check for comprehension. A simple "thumbs up, thumbs down" (indicating "Yes," "No," "I understand," or "I don't understand") gives the teacher immediate feedback. Using visuals, pictures, body language, snips of video, graphics, and models provides a rich, contextualized experience and greatly increases the possibility of student understanding.

Finally, the best teachers model *everything* for students, including procedures and processes. They show students, step-by-step, how to accomplish a task, including what each step looks and sounds like. They also teach and model how to ask for clarification if students don't understand. A teacher might even post possible clarification statements on the wall for students to see and use: "I need help with _____, please." "I don't understand this word (or sentence or paragraph)." "I am confused about _____."

Classroom Examples

Watching Mr. Jimenez and his students at work is a joy. As the students enter, the procedures for free voluntary reading are displayed on the overhead. The students get their books, sit down, and are reading when the bell rings. When the 15-minute reading period concludes, Mr. Jimenez moves to instruction. He is teaching the class how to use a compare and contrast chart. He speaks in a natural way and at an even pace, but his speech is sprinkled with such phrases as, "Let me say that another way" and "*Compare* means to show how things are the same" (and "how things are equal" and "how things are similar"). Mr. Jimenez not only uses extensive paraphrasing and rephrasing in his instruction, he also repeats key words and phrases that are crucial to understanding. Several times he repeats the phrase, "*Contrast* means to show how things are different."

Each student is assigned a number, which is written on a small card and placed in a box. Mr. Jimenez randomly draws numbers as a means of calling on students, but he also appears to target several who are not his top students. He consciously selects students who are struggling in class so that they have equal opportunities to respond. His ques-

tions are a mix of lower- and higher-order questions. Some center on ensuring that students are "with him" in the instruction, such as, "What does the word *contrast* mean?" Other questions ask students to think in new ways and to stretch their understanding of the topic: "What two characters in the story we're reading would make an interesting compare and contrast diagram? Why?" Or "When would this *not* be a good chart to use?"

Mr. Jimenez uses wait time to good effect. He understands the value of giving second-language learners extra time to construct an answer in their heads before responding. He tells everyone to think before answering, and he waits many seconds before calling on a student. He checks frequently for comprehension, asking students to respond nonverbally to such questions as, "*Contrast* means to show how things are different. Show me thumbs up if you say yes, thumbs down if you say no." Mr. Jimenez models explicitly how to fill out the first two parts of the compare and contrast chart. He says, for instance, "This is how I think about a comparison," or "This is not a comparison." And then he explains why. When the students move to work in preassigned pairs to complete the task, Mr. Jimenez refers to a poster on the wall that spells out the norms for working in pairs, asking several students to say what each pair should do and why.

References
Johnson & Johnson, 1987; Johnson, Johnson, & Holubec, 1993; Kagan, 1989; Slavin, 1989-90, 1990.

● Strategy 3.5: Use Cooperative Learning.
Teachers use cooperative learning strategies to encourage interaction and interethnic tolerance and acceptance among students of different ethnic groups. Cooperative learning enables students with different degrees of proficiency in English language and literacy, as well as academic knowledge and skills, to work together on tasks and projects and to contribute to each other's learning.

Discussion

All classrooms are heterogeneous in nature, with students having different backgrounds, expectations, strengths, and needs. But when students are from different countries and speak many different languages, the degree of heterogeneity increases dramatically. Students who have lived for years in African refugee camps join those whose entire lives have been spent in a large Asian city; rural Haitian or Jamaican children who have attended school sporadically join Russian or Chilean children with extensive education. In other instances, students whose families have fought one another sit next to each other, as do members of rival gangs, and students accustomed to wearing modest clothing in segregated classes are placed in mixed-gender classes, where some students wear shorts or other revealing clothes. Factor in differences in English-language proficiency, academic backgrounds and expectations, and socioeconomic status, and the mixture can be volatile. These differences, however, can also be the source of rich educational experiences, *if* students can be helped to work together and learn from each other.

Cooperative learning offers one means of having students learn from and help each other (Crandall, 1999). In cooperative activities, small groups of heterogeneous students work together to accomplish tasks and share rewards. When teachers structure these groups carefully, students from dramatically different backgrounds can maximize their strengths while learning from others. Each member of the group plays an important role. For example, a self-confident student who likes to talk in class may be given the role of reporting the group's accomplishments, while a quiet student who is a good reader might be responsible for leading the group through the assigned reading. Students with limited English proficiency may take on the roles of timekeeper or illustrator.

Cooperative learning promotes positive social interaction and communication, builds teamwork and a sense of community in the classroom, provides multiple opportunities for students to rehearse their contributions and receive feedback from peers before giving a presentation to the teacher or the whole class, and allows everyone to be both a teacher and a learner (Johnson & Johnson, 1987; Johnson, Johnson, & Holubec, 1993; Kagan, 1994; Slavin, 1990). Peer teaching helps students develop a deeper understanding of content and enables them to learn from others. As Tighe (1971, p. 23) states, "Real learning . . . is not a solitary task. One person cannot be expected to discover five different interpretations of a piece of literature. But five people can. This is where the real dialogue begins. Each student can examine his ideas in relationship to those of his peer group."

Cooperative learning has been found to do the following:

• Reduce anxiety by giving students time to practice and learn from each other in small groups.

• Increase motivation and promote authentic use of English as students communicate with each other to complete their tasks.

• Provide more opportunities for students to listen to and speak than is possible in teacher-centered classrooms.

• Allow students to receive support from and provide support to others in attempting to understand new concepts or differing points of view.

• Increase students' self-confidence and sense of self-worth as they view themselves as valuable members of their team.

• Offer opportunities for students to develop cross-cultural understanding, respect, and friendships (Crandall & Tucker 1990; Jacob, Rottenberg, Patrick, & Wheeler, 1996; Johnson, Johnson, & Holubec, 1993; Kagan, 1994; Slavin, 1990).

Sometimes teachers must assign students to groups on the basis of their strengths and needs; at other times, groups can be formed randomly. When groups do not work out, reassignment of some students may be necessary, and students who prefer to work individually may need time to adjust to group efforts. But cooperative learning can benefit all students: those who are academically successful, those who have more difficulty, those who are English-speaking, those who are just learning the language, those who are outgoing, and those who are less so. It addresses different learning styles while helping students become comfortable with new ones. And it can help students develop much-needed autonomy as learners.

Among the many cooperative activities available, some of the most effective for multiethnic and multilingual classes are think/pair/share, jigsaw, roundtable or round robin, and numbered heads together.

Classroom Examples

Mr. Li's biology class brings together 36 students from diverse backgrounds, many of whom are still enrolled in

ESL classes. Some of these students have substantial prior education; others have much less. Some of them clearly enjoy science; others do not. Mr. Li recognizes this diversity and organizes his course around thematic units that he hopes will motivate and interest students by focusing on issues relevant to youngsters' lives.

One unit centers on the rain forest and its potential destruction. Selecting a variety of readings that might interest different students, Mr. Li divides students into groups of four, each group responsible for teaching the rest of the class about their particular article. Each group reads and discusses the article and then answers a set of questions.

Mr. Li circulates among the groups to answer questions and stimulate discussion. When the students are comfortable explaining the article to the other members of their group, students return to the whole class to teach their peers. Mr. Li uses this jigsaw reading technique frequently, assigning shorter and less difficult articles and chapter sections to students with limited reading or English skills, and complex articles to those students prepared to read them. He finds that this approach helps students to think through and understand smaller portions of material. When students are responsible for reading an entire chapter, they may feel overwhelmed and either give up or resort to reading without understanding.

Sometimes Mr. Li checks to see how well students have taught each other by asking a group to answer questions about the article read by another group to build a sense of responsibility among students to make sure that they and their peers truly understand the material.

To introduce a new history chapter to her middle school students, Ms. Patterson asks them to write down what they know about that era and then to share it with a partner. After the two have shared, she asks them to join another pair of students, and together they combine what they know and develop a list of questions to be answered. This think/pair/share activity allows students to learn from each other in a nonthreatening way; it also establishes the beginnings of a set of objectives for the next unit. Ms. Patterson may use a K-W-L graphic organizer, in which students record what they know, what they want to learn, and then later, what they have learned in the unit.

Ms. Ramirez, who teaches a sheltered chemistry course to ELLs at various levels of proficiency, groups her students by language background and encourages them to help each other using their common primary language when necessary. Her class focuses on chemistry in the community, helping students to see the value of chemistry in dealing with community issues and problems. When students first arrive in class, they find a sign on the door warning them not to drink the water. They spend the next few weeks trying to find the source of the problem. As they learn the scientific method, they work in small groups to create bilingual posters illustrating their findings. Sometimes Ms. Ramirez has the help of a graduate student who is preparing to become an ESL teacher; at other times, she has a bilingual student aide. Even when she is alone, however, she finds that students help and learn from each other through their cooperative tasks.

Before a new unit, and again after the unit when students are preparing for the test, Ms. Ramirez uses a version of roundtable or round robin, assigning students to small groups and asking everyone to contribute to the overall task. For example, prior to a unit on petroleum, she asks students to identify as many sources of energy as possible. Each group passes a piece of paper and a pencil to its members until all ideas are exhausted. Then they share their ideas with the other groups while Ms. Ramirez writes a master list on the board.

Mr. Winter routinely assigns students in his ESL class to form teams for project work, bringing in topics and concepts from across the curriculum. Sometimes he places students who share a common language in the same group, so that they can use both languages in their projects. At other times, he requires all members of a group to use English to communicate. Students function as reader, recorder (writer), facilitator, timekeeper, materials organizer, reporter and speaker, or illustrator as they produce country reports, career posters, or science projects. After groups have been together for some time, he changes assignments to encourage a greater sense of community in the class and enable students to learn from a larger number of peers. Mr. Winter reports that cooperative group work has helped students from different ethnic groups recognize that they have things in common and can become friends.

RESOURCES

Crandall, 1999; Crandall & Tucker, 1990; Jacob, Rottenberg, Patrick, & Wheeler, 1996; Johnson & Johnson, 1987; Johnson, Johnson, & Holubec, 1993; Kagan, 1994; Slavin, 1990; Tighe, 1971.

● **STRATEGY 3.6**: ASSESS AND ACTIVATE STUDENTS' PRIOR KNOWLEDGE AND RELATE LESSON CONTENT TO THEIR PERSONAL LIVES AND EXPERIENCES. TEACHERS UNDERSTAND THE POWER OF ATTACHING NEW LEARNING TO PRIOR LEARNING, THEREFORE THEY SYSTEMATICALLY FIND OUT WHAT THEIR STUDENTS ALREADY KNOW. THOUGH STUDENTS DIFFER IN WHAT THEY BRING TO EACH NEW LEARNING SITUATION, ALL STUDENTS COME WITH LARGE STORES OF INFORMATION WAITING TO BE TAPPED AND DEVELOPED. STRATEGIC USE OF TASKS THAT ASSESS AND ACTIVATE STUDENTS' PRIOR KNOWLEDGE CAN GREATLY ENHANCE THE POSSIBILITY THAT STUDENTS WILL UNDERSTAND AND REMEMBER THE LESSON.

DISCUSSION

The work that teachers do with students at the beginning of a lesson can reap many benefits for everyone in the class. Tasks designed to assess and activate students' prior knowledge can serve many purposes. A well-designed task can show teachers immediately what their students know or don't know about a topic. Other tasks provide immediate links to the theme or topic by showing students that what they're studying connects directly to their own lives, thus establishing personal relevance and interest.

Teachers can ask themselves a series of questions before they decide which activity or task to use:

• What prior student knowledge do I want to try to activate that ties to the content most directly or powerfully?
• How can I show my students explicitly how the activity links to the theme or content?
• How can I show my students that they can use what they already know to understand something new?
• How can I best elicit my students' opinions, thoughts, or ideas about what they already know?
• What experiences can I provide for my students that will allow them to see and feel that what we are studying connects to their personal lives?

Most teachers have a repertoire of tasks for finding out what students already know. A journal activity allows students to write about personal topics that relate to something soon to be studied, for example: "Write about a time when you moved and had to leave something behind." As another example, brainstorming can be done in many ways, from a standard list format to more complicated semantic webbing. The K-W-L format (Chamot & O'Malley, 1994) provides a structured way for students to chart what they already know about a topic (K), what they want to know (W), and then, at the end of the lesson, what they learned (L).

Students who are second-language learners can profit from the use of not just one, but several, activities that allow them to uncover what they already know about a topic and see how it relates to their own lives, before they begin to study the lesson content.

CLASSROOM EXAMPLES

One valuable task designed to assess and activate prior knowledge is an anticipation and prediction guide, also known as an anticipatory guide (Chamot & O'Malley, 1994). Anticipatory guides are especially valuable tools for science teachers as they can reveal students' scientific misconceptions. Teachers can then structure their lesson so that students experience the scientific phenomena in a new way, giving them a chance to confront their misconceptions and restructure their thinking (Bruer, 1993).

In constructing an anticipatory guide, teachers select key concepts (or a key reading passage) and then create a short series of true or false statements encompassing the ideas they want the class to consider. The students respond to each statement individually, in pairs, or in groups. At this point, the teacher tells students that they don't need to know the correct answer—they should just make their best guess—but that they'll be responsible for knowing the correct answer by the end of the lesson.

Anticipatory guides are an effective addition to a language arts or literature class, before reading a story or studying a unit. Here the goal of the guide is to enable students to interact personally with the ideas or values expressed. In this version, there is no correct response, for students are dealing with individual feelings. For example, before studying a thematic unit on courage, students might be asked to respond with "yes" or "no" to the following statements or ideas they'll encounters in the readings:

• It is important to act brave even if you don't feel brave.
• Physical courage is more important than moral courage.

⚲ FIGURE 3.3
Anticipatory Guide: Action and Reaction

Assignment 1
Ask your students to read each of the following statements and to circle Agree or Disagree for each statement. The students need to save the paper for another assignment.

Agree   Disagree   1. When I hit the wall, the wall hits me back.

Agree   Disagree   2. The force that causes me to go forward when I walk is the ground pushing on me.

Agree   Disagree   3. When I drop a ball, both the ball and the earth move toward each other.

Agree   Disagree   4. The engine of a car generates the force that pushes the car forward.

Assignment 2
After studying Newton's Third Law of Motion, you can look back at your old beliefs. For each of the four statements, use examples to explain why your answer was either right or wrong.

Scoring Rubric
After completing Assignments 1 and 2, use this rubric to determine your score. Place your self-assessment in the first blank; your teacher will place the final assessment in the second blank.

10   Your original and final choices were clear. All of the final answers were correct. You explained your choices in a clear way, using examples where appropriate, saying why each statement was true or false.

8   You gave clear explanations, with examples, but your original choices were not clear. All final answers were correct.

6   Most of the final answers were correct and were explained using examples.

4   Most of the final answers were correct and explained in an understandable way, but without examples or with irrelevant examples.

2   Explanations were not clear. Many finals answers were incorrect.

0   The assignment was not complete.

Score _____ / _____

Source: (P. Quiggle, personal communication, May 1997, used with permission.)

• I have acted courageously at least once in my life.
• A person always knows what courage is when he or she sees it.
• A person can learn to have courage.

The teacher may ask students to periodically review their responses to the anticipatory guides as they progress through the unit, or to repeat the exercise at the end to see if their ideas have changed. In that case, students might be asked to supply evidence from the text that convinced them either to change their mind or to stick with their initial response.

Students in a physics class for second-language learners were given the anticipatory guide in Figure 3.3 prior to studying Newton's Third Law. The teacher systematically assesses his students' prior knowledge and possible misconceptions through the use of anticipatory guides. A key to understanding is in the "Later" activity at the end of the lesson, in which students are asked to examine their prior beliefs by redoing the anticipatory guide and explaining why their first answer was either right or wrong.

RESOURCES

Bruer, 1993; Chamot & O'Malley, 1994.

● STRATEGY 3.7: BUILD CONCEPTUAL FRAMEWORKS FOR NEW KNOWLEDGE. TEACHERS EMPLOY VARIOUS METHODS TO ENSURE THAT STUDENTS SEE HOW IDEAS OR CONCEPTS RELATE TO ONE ANOTHER OR HOW THEY FIT INTO THE LARGER PICTURE. SEEING THE RELATIONSHIP AMONG CONCEPTS HELPS STUDENTS GRASP THE MAJOR CONCEPTS AND IDEAS MORE QUICKLY AND EFFICIENTLY AND DEVELOP WELL-STRUCTURED MENTAL PICTURES RELATED TO THE CONTENT THEY ARE STUDYING.

DISCUSSION

For many students, especially those working in their second language, the content presented from lesson to lesson, unit to unit, or class to class often seems unconnected, unrelated, or even irrelevant. Students can sometimes repeat facts from U.S. history, earth science, or 7th grade language arts, but only rarely can they chart major historical trends and show how they are related, or explain how the study of the Earth's surface connects to the study of the moon and the solar system, or compare and contrast two characters in a novel.

Schemas are interpretive frames that allow us to make sense of information by relating it to previous experiences (Schank & Abelson, 1977). Providing students with graphic organizers such as a story map (Figure 3.4) that explicitly displays the different chunks of information to be studied helps alleviate the anxiety students naturally feel when they encounter new material in their second language.

Using a plot map (or story map; Figure 3.4) repeatedly while studying various short stories or novels provides a schema for the study of literature. All fiction is built by using characters, setting, and dialogue in a series of events or conflicts leading to some sort of resolution. The use of various graphic organizers showing the key ideas in a lesson or unit depicts what the teacher is teaching and what the students are responsible for learning. Graphic organizers can assist teachers in clarifying their teaching goals, especially in sheltered content classrooms, where depth rather than breadth of content provides the most linguistically rich experiences. Teachers can ask themselves, "What do I really want my students to learn here, and how can I display it to them graphically in a way that makes sense?" (See also Echevarría & Graves, 1998, pp. 313–333; and Short, 1991, for a discussion of graphic organizers with ELLs.)

CLASSROOM EXAMPLES

Before launching a semester's work on the biosphere, the science teacher displays a large concept map showing the connections among ideas and concepts to be studied, placed in a hierarchical fashion. She gives each student a map and shows an identical map on the overhead projector. Listed are ideas such as matter, living things, nonliving things, heat, energy, water, animals, and plants.

The teacher briefly explains what will be studied, in what order, how the ideas are related, and the importance of each. She pauses after each idea to give students time to draw something that will help them remember the concept. Later, she uses the same concept map to test the students, leaving parts blank. She refers to the map frequently throughout the semester. At the end, she asks students to construct their own concept maps that show their understanding of the biosphere.

The social studies class is about to study several civilizations from various perspectives. The students and the teacher construct a concept map of what they want to discover about each civilization or culture, and what they believe all cultures and peoples have in common. Their list of "big ideas" includes language, clothing, family structure, food, and religion. Through questioning and discussion with the teacher, the students decide to add "important values and beliefs" and "government" to the list. The list serves as a frame for the study of each civilization. Throughout the unit, the teacher uses various graphic organizers, such as Venn diagrams, to show how cultures are the same or different.

In a math classroom, after studying various geometric shapes, the teacher asks cooperative groups to create a con-

**FIGURE 3.4
Story Map**

TITLE

AUTHOR

SETTING

CHARACTERS

PROBLEM

EVENT 1

EVENT 2

EVENT 3

RESOLUTION

Source: (A. Jaramillo & K. Smith, 1995, used with permission.)

cept map showing the connections among a parallelogram, a quadrilateral, a rectangle, a rhombus, a square, a trapezoid, and a triangle. The teacher instructs the students to "put the biggest or most general mathematical idea at the top" and to "make sure you draw, not just write the name of, the shapes so you are sure that you put them where they belong." Animated discussions ensue as students clarify the connections, clear up misconceptions, and struggle to reach consensus on the map's structure.

RESOURCES

Echevarría & Graves, 1998; Schank & Abelson, 1977; Short, 1991.

● STRATEGY 3.8: TEACH LEARNING STRATEGIES. TEACHERS UNDERSTAND THAT ONE OF THE MAIN GOALS OF THE SHELTERED CONTENT CLASSROOM IS TO PROMOTE LEARNER AUTONOMY THROUGH EXPLICIT INSTRUCTION IN LEARNING STRATEGIES. STUDENTS LEARN HOW TO LEARN AND KNOW VARIOUS STRATEGIES THEY CAN USE THEMSELVES TO ACCELERATE THEIR ACQUISITION OF ENGLISH AND CONTENT KNOWLEDGE.

DISCUSSION

Research shows that instruction in learning strategies profits all students. Chamot and O'Malley's (1994) work with second-language learners reinforces the notion that students who learn to consciously monitor their own comprehension, and who have a storehouse of strategies to use when comprehension is a problem, fare better than students who stumble along, hoping that somehow they will eventually "get it."

Explicit instruction in how to learn empowers students in ways that almost no other instruction does. Second-language learners often feel anxious and powerless in their new culture, new school, and new language. Like other students who experience challenges at school, they may attribute their success on a task to luck and their failure to their own lack of abilities, or to forces outside their control (Borkowski, Johnston, & Reid, 1987). When students learn to use strategies, they begin to see the relationship between using strategies and success.

Effective instruction in the use of learning strategies contains several characteristics that can help ensure that

students eventually gain the skills and autonomy necessary for self-monitoring. Research has shown that teachers should identify the strategy, explain why it is being taught and its usefulness, demonstrate its use, give students abundant practice in applying it to real learning, and show students how to evaluate the effectiveness of using the strategy and what to do if it doesn't work (Duffy et al., 1986).

Skillful teachers of learning strategies value explicit instruction and teach in a way that reflects what they believe. A classroom that focuses on learning how to learn is full of language (from both teacher and students) such as

- This is how I think about this kind of problem.
- Before you read, you need to think about what you already know about the topic.
- Teresa, can you tell us what strategies you used to understand those two pages?
- I want you to write in your learning log what we learned yesterday, look at the picture up here, and predict how the lesson from yesterday is connected to the lesson today.
- I'm finished reading this section. Now I'm going to summarize. That's one thing that good readers do.

CLASSROOM EXAMPLES

Students in an intermediate ESL class have just finished reading a chapter of John Reynolds Gardiner's short novel *Stone Fox* (HarperTrophy, 1983). The teacher tells the class, "I'm going to model for you again today how to ask questions about a story. When I finish modeling, you and your partner are going to make some questions about this chapter. Take a minute and think, 'Why are we learning to make questions about stories?'" Hands pop up all over the classroom. The teacher calls on several students who answer, "To understand more," "A good reader makes questions," and "I get smart."

The teacher then says, "First I'm going to make one 'on the surface' question. Remember, that's a question that has an answer right in the story. You can point to the answer. Here's my 'on the surface' question: What kind of farm do Willie and Grandfather have?" The teacher tells the class to copy the question from the overhead onto their papers. She then asks them to give the answer and say why the question is an "on the surface" one. Together, the class then constructs two more similar questions.

Next the teacher says, "Now I want you to think about the other kind of questions we know how to make. We also make 'under the surface' questions. Remember, those are questions that you have to think hard about. Those are questions where you cannot point to the answer on the page. Who remembers what words 'under the surface' questions begin with?" Students respond with "why," "how," "should," or "could." As the lesson continues, the teacher models "under the surface" questions, including, "Why is Grandfather not speaking?" and "How should Willy help Grandfather?" The teacher asks the class to construct some questions with her, and then sets the pairs to work on making their own questions.

RESOURCES

Borkowski, Johnston, & Reid, 1987; Chamot & O'Malley, 1994; Duffy et al., 1986.

● STRATEGY 3.9: FOCUS ON READING IN ALL CLASSES. TEACHERS IN ALL CURRICULUM AREAS—WHETHER AN ESL CLASS, A SHELTERED CONTENT CLASS, OR A CONTENT CLASS TAUGHT IN THE STUDENTS' PRIMARY LANGUAGE—USE A VARIETY OF TASKS TO ENSURE THAT STUDENTS ARE ACTIVELY ENGAGED IN READING. TEACHERS EXPLICITLY TEACH WHAT GOOD READERS DO AND GIVE STUDENTS MULTIPLE OPPORTUNITIES TO INTERACT WITH BOTH TEACHER-SELECTED AND SELF-SELECTED TEXTS.

DISCUSSION

Academic and cognitive demands increase with every grade level. The need to concentrate on increasing every student's literacy becomes especially urgent for teachers of students who are struggling to close the achievement gap with their native English-speaking peers.

Collier (1989) has shown that some ELLs may need to gain as many as 14 months in reading comprehension for every year in school for several consecutive years to reach the 50th percentile on standardized achievement tests. Students who arrive in the United States with limited prior schooling and low literacy skills can take even longer—and require even more attention. With that challenge in mind, it is clear that the responsibility for teaching reading and writing can no longer be vested solely in the English or

ESL teacher. Teachers in all content areas need to know how to accelerate their students' literacy.

Several methods promise to increase the literacy of second-language students. Reciprocal teaching (Palincsar & Brown, 1984) can dramatically improve reading comprehension scores. When using reciprocal teaching, teachers explicitly instruct students in four distinct strategy areas: questioning, predicting, clarifying, and summarizing. The teacher models how to create questions about what is happening, how to hypothesize about what might happen next, how to ask for clarification and know what to do when you don't understand, and how to state the most important ideas in what was just read (Figure 3.5). Teachers and students can practice reciprocal teaching dialogues in a whole-class setting, and when students gain sufficient skill, they can then work in groups of four on selected portions of text.

When working in groups, students take turns with each of the four strategies. Reciprocal teaching makes it very clear to students what good readers do. Poor readers often believe that good reading consists of pronouncing all the words correctly (Crandall, 1981), or of being able to say the color of the main character's hair and eyes. When students understand the reading process thoroughly, they can begin to monitor their own comprehension and see the connection between application of the process and increased comprehension.

Teachers in all content areas can incorporate explicit instruction in reading strategies into their classrooms. A well-designed unit might include practice in the four skill areas of reciprocal teaching: On one day, students practice predicting by looking at pictures instead of text; in another session, they create questions based on reading the first paragraph of a text; they learn how to summarize by looking at a series of statements and deciding which are absolutely necessary for the summary and which can be omitted.

Teachers can also give students multiple opportunities to respond to text using various teacher-designed tasks: reading logs, in which students copy quotes from the text and then write their own response; first-response "writes," in which students read and then quickly write about what ideas came to them as they were reading; or graphic logs, in which students write quotes from the text and respond with a drawing or symbol that corresponds to the quote. The important idea is that teachers make sure that students are actively engaged with the text and that there is evidence of that engagement.

🏃 FIGURE 3.5
Reciprocal Teaching Strategies

Ask your students to use reciprocal teaching strategies to help everyone learn the curriculum.

Questioning
Create questions about what is happening or what you wonder about.

Make on-the-surface questions.
–What?
–When?
–Who?
–How?
–Where?

Make under-the-surface questions.
–Why?
–How?
–Would?
–Should?
–Could?

Clarifying
Be clear about what you don't understand or what is confusing to you. Use different methods to try to understand.
–Read ahead
–Read again
–Ask for help
–Look something up
–Ask a classmate or teacher for help: "What does _____ mean?" or "I don't understand _____. Can you please help me?"

Summarizing
Create a short version of the text. Use only the most important facts and ideas. Use your own words, but ask yourself these questions:
–What is most important here?
–What will I leave in the summary?
–What will I leave out of the summary?
–How can I say it in my own words?

Predicting
Think about what you already know from the text. Guess what is going to happen next or say what will come next. Use clues from the text to say why you make the prediction. For example, fill in these sentences:
–I think what's going to happen next is_____because_____.
–It says here_____, so my prediction is_____.
–I predict that_____. The evidence for my prediction is_____.

(Developed by teachers of the Salinas Union High School District, based on Palincsar & Brown, 1984; Palincsar, David, & Brown, 1989)

CLASSROOM EXAMPLES

Ms. Salinas, who teaches Spanish for native speakers, shares students with four other teachers: a science teacher, a social studies teacher, a math teacher, and a language arts teacher. All the teachers have been working throughout the semester to teach their students how to respond to written text. When they began, most of the students had no idea that they could interact with the text—that they could hold a conversation with the text and have their own important ideas about it as they were reading. They had no experience with assuming responsibility for

FIGURE 3.6
Active Reading Strategies

Use this chart with your students to remind them how to engage in active reading.

What does active reading mean?	Use these sentence starters to promote active reading.
Making predictions about what will happen next.	I predict that_____because _____. In the next chapter or section, I think_____.
Asking questions about what is happening in the story, or about the section or part of the text.	I wonder why_____. I wonder what it meant when_____. Why doesn't/didn't [the character]_____. How is [this concept or idea] related to_____?
Connecting what you are reading to your own life or to what you already know.	When I read about_____ it made me think about _____. Reading this reminded me of_____.
Giving opinions about what you are reading.	I felt_____when_____. I think [the character] should have_____. In my opinion,_____.
Reacting to events, figures, or what is happening in the story.	I was surprised when_____. I was disappointed when_____. I was confused when_____.
Creating a picture of what is happening in the story or text.	When I read about_____, I saw_____ in my mind.
Reading under the surface or thinking about what is happening but isn't being talked about.	This is what I think is really going on here_____. What this really means is_____.
Making connections to other books or stories you have read, movies you have seen, or ideas you have heard about.	When_____, it reminded me of_____ because_____.

(Used with permission from A. Thompson & A. Jaramillo, 1996)

creating personal meaning from the text. Most of them struggled simply to get through one or two pages of any reading; at the end, they had little understanding of what they had read.

The teachers in Ms. Salinas's school have been working on reciprocal teaching strategies in their different con-tent areas, and Ms. Salinas has just added elements of what the team calls "active reading strategies" (Figure 3.6). Ms. Salinas found that she had to teach her students the differ-ent ways to respond to text. The prompts on the right side of the active reading chart provided sufficient scaffolding for the students in the beginning.

The students are busy reading a short story and filling out a dialectical journal as they read. In the left column, they write quotes or ideas from the story that they find interesting or provocative. In the right column, they respond to the quote with a question, a speculation, a visualization, or some other response. The variety of responses shows that the students have internalized the notion that good readers are not passive, but rather active constructors of meaning as they work their way through a text. Students have written responses such as, "Why did the character do that? That doesn't seem like what he would do!" "This story reminds me of the story we read last week. The two characters are very similar." "In the next chapter, I predict that he will finally go visit his uncle because his uncle seems important to him." "This part is just like my life. I have felt just like that before."

RESOURCES
Collier, 1989; Crandall, 1981; Palincsar & Brown, 1984.

● **STRATEGY 3.10**: GIVE STUDENTS MULTIPLE OPPORTUNITIES TO READ SELF-SELECTED TEXTS. TEACHERS ACTIVELY SEEK WAYS FOR THEIR STUDENTS TO READ SELF-SELECTED BOOKS AND OTHER TEXTS SUCH AS MAGAZINES AND COMIC BOOKS. TEACHERS VIEW FREE VOLUNTARY READING OR SUSTAINED SILENT READING AS KEYS TO BUILDING STUDENT LITERACY, AND AS CRUCIAL IN DEVELOPING HABITS OF READING THAT EXTEND BEYOND THE CLASSROOM.

DISCUSSION

Getting students to read more of what they want to read is an often-overlooked strategy in teachers' attempts to raise reading scores and close the gap between second-language learners and native English speakers. Adding a voluntary reading program to the curriculum at any grade level provides what most second-language learners do not have at home or at school: access to books.

Many advantages accrue for students who begin to read on their own. A compilation of research (Krashen, 1993) on voluntary reading shows that students involved in free reading programs do as well as or better than students involved in more traditional skill-based reading

instruction. Second-language learners involved in free reading programs in school consistently outperformed those who received a more traditional language-teaching approach with a mixture of grammar and oral exercises. Free reading also has positive effects on vocabulary acquisition, spelling, and writing accuracy and style—thus the potential to dramatically increase the acquisition of English.

Frank Smith (1988) has written eloquently about the need to get students to feel that they are part of the "literacy club," that they are potential members of this powerful inside group who expect to be able to read and write competently. But access to books to read has been a problem for many poor and language-minority students. Spaces that abound with fiction and nonfiction books, magazines, newspapers, and comic books are often referred to as print-rich environments. Though it is understandable that many homes lack the economic resources to make such environments possible, many schools (especially secondary schools) have not made access to books a priority. Many teachers committed to getting books into their students' hands comb secondhand bookstores, their own bookshelves, and garage sales to build a classroom library of engaging books. Many teachers work together to ensure that a necessary portion of their school's discretionary money is allocated to the purchase of books for free reading programs, whether based in the school library or in individual classrooms.

Teachers who implement voluntary reading programs in their classrooms use a variety of methods to heighten interest in reading and ensure that reading happens regularly. Often they conduct research on what their students would like to read. They ask other teachers, see what kinds of books students check out on their own, and ask the students themselves. Teenage romances, horror books, Newbery Award winners, comic books, series—all qualify for inclusion if students want to read them (paperbacks work better than hardbacks). The idea is to get students to read *something*, so they will want to read more. High school teachers report that their ESL students even pick up a good children's book with no embarrassment if it is part of a classroom library that has many types of books from which to choose.

Most teachers set up some sort of system for voluntary reading. They want to make sure that the time for reading is extended and consistent. For example, reading may take place at the beginning of class every day for 15 minutes. Students are taught the process for selecting and checking out a book; they learn such strategies as perusing the back cover to see if it looks interesting. Teachers look for students who seem to be struggling to maintain focus and try to help them select a book more appropriate to their reading level or interest.

An open sharing of ideas and progress shows what others in the class are reading. As a means of sparking interest in a book, the teacher might conduct a talk on a selected book, giving a short description of the characters, plot, or setting. Recommended reading lists from fellow students can help to guide student selections. Teachers often incorporate some kind of accountability into the program, so that they are better able to chart individuals' progress. Progress may be assessed in the venue of a conference, in which teacher and student talk about what the student is reading, or it might involve asking students to keep a daily reading log, in which they indicate how many pages they have read and write short summaries. A reading folder might include a list of books read over the course of the year, reflections on progress in reading, and book reviews to be passed on to next year's class.

Classroom Examples

When 12-year-old Juan entered his 7th grade advanced ESL class, he wrote in his reading portfolio, "I don't like to read." Asked what kinds of books he liked, he wrote, "None." In response to a question about when he reads, he said, "I read only when I have to." He spent the first two weeks of free reading staring at the pages of books he picked up at random from the revolving bookshelf in his English classroom. Juan made no progress in reading a book and tended to pick up a different book every other day. He was easily distracted during reading time and often attempted to disturb students around him who were trying to read.

Ms. Alvarez, Juan's teacher, had experience with such students. She knew it might take him a while to settle into the routine of reading. She also knew that she would have to help him. After the second week, Ms. Alvarez took Juan aside during free reading time and said, "Juan, I see you've had some trouble finding a book you want to read. Let me help you find something today." Together, they perused a variety of books on the shelf. Ms. Alvarez selected three that she thought he might like, told him to sit down with them, look at the back covers, read the first page, and then decide on one. When he had done that, she said, "Now, for this book you need to read the first two

chapters. If, after that, you don't like it, we'll pick out another one together."

Over the next three weeks, Juan read the first two chapters of four different books. Finally, one day Ms. Alvarez noticed that Juan was a third of the way through a short novel by Gary Soto—way beyond Chapter 2. When she asked him later if he wanted to try a different book, he replied, "No. I kind of like this one." Over the course of the semester, Ms. Alvarez saw subtle shifts in Juan's behavior toward reading. He came in, sat down, and usually began the task of reading. Though he read slowly, the summaries in his reading logs showed that he understood most of what was going on. By the end of the semester, Juan had read two short novels (about 150 pages each) plus a short book on soccer stars. He wrote in his portfolio, "This is the first time in my life I ever read a whole book."

Resources
Krashen, 1993; Smith, 1988.

● **Strategy 3.11: Help Students Move Beyond the Text. As a culmination of a unit, lesson, or theme, teachers plan tasks that serve to move students back to the text or content to reexamine, reconnect, and rethink the major ideas or concepts. Students have the chance to gain deeper understanding of the content by representing the text in new and different ways.**

Discussion

The walls of many classrooms are filled with posters, drawings, and writings that students have created after studying a particular piece of literature, historical era or figure, scientific concept, or thematic unit incorporating several subject areas. The best examples of student work done at the end of a carefully planned sequence of tasks in the sheltered content classroom exhibit several characteristics. First, the task allows students to take ownership of the material and create meaning for themselves. A good end-of-study task builds on the strengths of different class members by giving them, over time, the chance to express themselves through an array of formats: poetically, dramatically, musically, or artistically.

A good "beyond-the-text" task forces students to go back to the text to clarify and question and to reread it with a different purpose in mind. In this way, such a task gives second-language learners the chance to refocus on the overall meaning of the text. Many excellent beyond-the-text tasks require students to transform one genre into another: a scientific text turned into a TV news item; a historical narrative turned into a live debate; a short story turned into an "open mind" task that displays, with graphics and phrases, the main conflicts a character is facing, from that character's point of view (Figure 3.7).

Teachers may find that a combination of individual and group responses to content works best. At times, the best approach may be for each student to create a poem or graphic of the content; other lessons may more naturally call for a group-constructed product. If the purpose of the task is to solidify a particular concept, then the teacher may ask groups to create a "team word web" showing their joint understanding of how the content fits together. In any case, if the task is a group task, the teacher needs to ensure that all members contribute equally to reach shared and joint accountability for the end product. For example, each student uses a different colored marker to write his part of a conversation or dialogue or is responsible for a different section of a storyboard. Constructing a rubric with students beforehand that specifies the features of a good text (e.g., story section or dialogue) and providing models from previous classes give students clear parameters for performance expectations (Walqui-VanLier, 1991).

CLASSROOM EXAMPLES

A quick tour of the sheltered content classrooms in one school hallway shows that the teachers ask their students to respond to texts with a variety of creative beyond-the-text tasks. In the social studies class, students have just finished studying the Renaissance. In groups, they are preparing to question classmates who will sit on the "hot seat" in front of the class. Students have volunteered to sit on the hot seat and assume the personae of da Vinci, Sir Thomas More, Cervantes, Machiavelli, and Shakespeare. The groups have been asked to design hard questions that will force the students in the hot seats to live in the shoes of the historical figure. Hot seat students have been asked to prepare themselves to answer the questions as a Renaissance person would respond, with appropriate viewpoints, attitudes, and ideas.

FIGURE 3.7
Open Mind Activity

Students can use this activity to help them understand what a character is thinking and feeling. They can "fill" the open mind with the following ideas:

–Pictures of what the character sees.
–Symbols to represent important concepts.
–Key words to show feelings or ideas.
–Questions the character wonders about.
–Statements of what the character says.

Explain how the symbols, images, drawings, or words in the open mind represent your ideas about the character.

_____

_____

_____

_____

One wall of the language arts classroom is covered with student-created journey maps for John Steinbeck's novel, *The Pearl* (Penguin, 1993). Each map shows "trigger events," or events chosen by the student as being most important. Displays of key learnings make clear what happened or what was learned as a result of the trigger events. Finally, each map contains detours or dead ends—events in the story that seem to have caused problems. Each paper uses a combination of words, phrases, symbols, colors, and pictures to explain what the student learned. The borders of each map are filled with symbols that demonstrate the students' understandings of *The Pearl*.

RESOURCES

Walqui-Vanlier, 1991.

● STRATEGY 3.12: MAXIMIZE AND RESTRUCTURE TIME TO MEET STUDENTS' NEEDS. TEACHERS TAKE FULL ADVANTAGE OF THE ALLOTTED TIME FOR EACH OF THEIR CLASSES. THEY THINK STRATEGICALLY ABOUT HOW TO STRUCTURE THEIR CLASSES SO THAT THE PERIOD IS USED MOST PROFITABLY. IN ADDITION, THEY WORK OUTSIDE OF THEIR OWN CLASSES WITH THE LARGER SCHOOL STAFF TO EXPLORE ALTERNATIVE WAYS OF SCHEDULING TO BETTER MEET STUDENT NEEDS.

DISCUSSION

Teachers often struggle with the traditional scheduling of the typical comprehensive secondary school. Students come and go every 50 minutes or so, based on a rigid, inflexible system of bells. Time for learning is sliced neatly into six or seven distinct subjects, each with its own slot. Teachers see a succession of groups of 25 to 35 students passing through each class—as many as 125 to 150 students each day.

Some schools are attempting to address the disconnectedness of this pervasive system by instituting such innovations as block scheduling, rotating schedules, career academies, and other strategies aimed at making education more cohesive and meaningful. Structural changes to the school day can play an important role by providing longer blocks of time (90 minutes or two hours) for teachers to instruct in the in-depth ways they so often covet (Olsen & Jaramillo, 2000).

Even a radical restructuring of time does not ensure that class time is well spent. Close examination of many secondary classrooms reveals wasted minutes, time ill spent on taking attendance, and a general lack of urgency about the preciousness of each moment. Newly arrived second-language learners often find themselves at odds with this kind of schooling, which is already less structured and formal than that of their homes. Thoughtful teachers (no matter what the schedule) seek ways to manage their classrooms so that every minute is used to maximum advantage.

Time-conscious teachers create clear classroom expectations about the use of time. They begin class as soon as the bell rings and do not stop until the last possible minute. They often begin class with the same procedure or routine, so that students always know what materials they need, where to look for instructions, and how long they have to complete each task. For example, a language arts teacher might routinely begin with a journal topic written on the overhead projector. Students know that they need to record the topic and date by the time the bell rings, and that they have 10 minutes to complete this first task. Math teachers might begin with a set of problems that reviews a previous concept. Free reading is another way to open the period with an academic focus. (See also Strategy 3.10.)

Routines for retrieving and storing materials, moving from one activity to another, and moving from pair to group to individual work help reduce wasted time. Students do not have to wonder how to accomplish the routine, and they know they are expected to complete it promptly. Explicit teacher modeling of tasks also reduces the amount of time students must spend getting started. When teachers invest instructional time showing "This is what it looks like" and "This is what it sounds like," students are more likely to get busy right away.

Careful attention to task assignments within cooperative groups helps all students work toward completion in a timely fashion. This means that each member of the group must have an important, carefully defined role to fill, reducing the possibility that one or more members will simply relax and let the others do all the work.

Another way of looking at time receives less attention and is often overlooked. Teachers need to anticipate ways of ensuring that students are actively engaged for as much of each period as possible. For instance, a whole class might have their books open to page 24; the teacher calls on individual students to read; and it appears that just about everyone is following along in the text. But how does the teacher really know that the act of following is not merely mechanical? Without evidence of engagement, many students may simply be pretending to pay attention, and are really thinking about the upcoming dance, the fight they had this morning with their brother, or the fact that they're hungry, and when will this class be over, anyway?

Evidence of active student engagement is the most powerful tool that teachers have to maximize their use of time. That evidence can take many forms. During instructional time, students are saying and doing many things, always with the idea that something specific can be pointed to as evidence of engagement. It can be as simple as, "Turn and tell your partner . . ." or as complex as "You have just taken notes on this minilecture (five minutes maximum). Now, in the right-hand column, write a few questions about what you have just heard."

Ensuring that students are actively engaged in any reading process can take the form of reciprocal teaching, responding to text through a reading log, or any method that forces students to periodically make public their understanding of what is being studied. Time-conscious teachers effectively manage not only the surface aspects of time use (such as routines and starting and ending at the bell) but also consider how they can determine student engagement.

CLASSROOM EXAMPLES

Mr. Malabonga, a mentor teacher, has spent his preparation period observing various teachers to find some good models for managing classrooms. Several new teachers are struggling with issues of classroom management, especially the wise use of time and expectations for how students use time. Mr. Malabonga plans to conduct joint observations of the good teachers with the new teachers, knowing that they can profit from seeing specific behaviors of good teachers.

On this day, Mr. Malabonga stops to visit Ms. Bart, a teacher widely respected by teachers and students alike. As he watches her teach, he jots down what he will highlight when he returns to do the joint observations with the new teachers:

• Procedures for individual, pair, and group work are clearly posted. She refers to the posters frequently to remind students of her expectations.
• Class begins at the bell. Students are in their seats, already working on the warm-up assignment, when the bell

rings. Ms. Bart spends this time explaining to a new student the expectations for beginning class, including where to keep his journal, how the journals are passed out, and how they are to be put away. She quietly monitors the progress of the class members as they work.
• When students move to a new kind of group project, she clearly directs them concerning where, how, and when to move. Each student in the group has a clearly defined role, and the group has a clearly defined time limit to complete the task.
• Ms. Bart uses a variety of methods to ensure that all students are actively engaged. She even uses such terms as, "I need to see that your brain is engaged." Part of the new group project requires that the group brainstorm a topic. As students brainstorm, each member is required to repeat what the other students say, and each is required to write it down.
• Ms. Bart and the students work until one minute before the bell rings.

RESOURCES
Olsen & Jaramillo, 2000.

● **STRATEGY 3.13:** BUILD A SENSE OF COMMUNITY IN THE CLASSROOM. TEACHERS ARE SENSITIVE TO THE MYRIAD CHALLENGES THAT FACE IMMIGRANT STUDENTS, NOT THE LEAST OF WHICH IS FITTING IN AND BEING AN ACCEPTED, INTEGRAL, VALUED MEMBER OF THE CLASSROOM COMMUNITY. TEACHERS VIEW THEIR CLASSROOMS AS PLACES WHERE STUDENTS LEARN AND PRACTICE VALUES OF UNDERSTANDING AND HONORING THE DIVERSE CULTURAL, LINGUISTIC, ETHNIC, AND RACIAL BACKGROUNDS OF INDIVIDUAL STUDENTS.

DISCUSSION

Many teachers today face classrooms that mirror the rapidly changing demographics of their states, communities, and school districts. Just a decade ago, a class might have included only one, or a small handful, of second-language or immigrant students; today, classrooms are filled with an unprecedented mixture of cultures, languages, national backgrounds, and ethnicities. Schoolwide efforts to address these pressing issues often center on more superficial aspects of building community—an assembly to honor Dr. Martin Luther King, a dance for Cinco de Mayo, or a parade for Chinese New Year. Teachers are left searching for ways in which they and their students can find meaningful common ground within the four walls of the classroom.

Careful teachers find ways of avoiding divisions, aware that classrooms can splinter along invisible fault lines. When a class is made up of students from many different primary language backgrounds, the teacher can ensure that work groups create interactions among students from different language groups. Even when a teacher must pair a proficient primary-language speaker with a less proficient one of the same language to provide peer assistance, the teacher sees that the pairing is not permanent, but merely a temporary arrangement.

Teachers also need to consider the range of language fluency in the classroom. Status often accrues to those who speak English more proficiently; structuring situations so that students of varying levels of proficiency must work together to complete a task can help break down barriers, especially if students less proficient in English can contribute a meaningful, valued portion of the task in their native language.

Several well-researched, well-documented approaches to cooperative learning (Johnson & Johnson, 1987; Kagan, 1994; Slavin, 1989-90, 1990) address some of the issues (see also Strategy 3.5). Each approach requires considerable skill and practice by the teacher to succeed. But teachers who invest the time notice improvements in intergroup relations as well as increased academic achievement (Crandall, 1999).

It is critical to distinguish between doing cooperative learning and simply putting students in groups to do some work. Although it is often called cooperative learning, group work is often a somewhat random collection of students completing some task together. In real cooperative groups, such as those Kagan describes, the teacher assigns students to groups; each group represents students with a range of abilities. True cooperative groups operate on the principle of positive interdependence: Each student has a role and is accountable to the rest of the group. The groups incorporate clear individual accountability and an emphasis on students' use of collaborative skills.

Some teachers have been trained in complex instruction (Cohen & Lotan, 1997), an approach to cooperative learning that goes directly to the heart of status in the classroom. Teachers make explicit the kinds of skills and abilities needed for groups to solve intrinsically interesting problems or to complete group products. Group norms govern expectations and behavior. For example, students who systematically engage in complex instruction projects know that "one will be good at all of the tasks involved; everyone will be good at some of them." Because the group tasks (e.g., an investigation focused on the theme of social stratification in medieval Japanese society) truly require the use of multiple abilities, not all of which relate to reading and writing, every student can contribute to the group product. Because of the way the tasks are structured, complex instruction units break down the hierarchies that exist in classrooms, which reflect the larger school and community.

Other teachers employ a variety of methods to build group inclusion and class cohesiveness. Many such activities make up the team-building portion of cooperative learning approaches. A common activity gives teams a problem to solve, but team members may not speak or use nonverbal cues. Team members receive an envelope with parts from different broken squares. Their group task is to reassemble the pieces into squares, following the above rules. Another interactive method of building teams is a variation of Kagan's numbered heads together activity (see also Strategy 3.5). Students count off in groups of four or five, so that every student has a number. The teacher poses a question to the class and asks groups to put their heads together to discuss their response. After allowing a minute or two for group discussion, the teacher repeats the question and calls out a number. The teacher then calls randomly on one group to answer, and the student with that number in the group answers.

Teachers who use methods of grouping and instruction to break down barriers find that their classrooms are significantly more equitable, lively, and happy for all students. Methods such as complex instruction, which directly address potential inequities and unequal status within the academic content, are powerful on multiple levels.

CLASSROOM EXAMPLES

Ms. Tan is dedicated to creating a classroom governed by mutual respect and understanding. The 32 students in her 7th grade social studies class represent a mix of cultures, languages, national backgrounds, ethnicities, and races. Seven students are black, five are Euro-American, two are newly arrived from Russia, ten are from Central America and Mexico, and seven are Southeast Asian—two from Thailand, one from the Philippines, and four from Vietnam.

Recently, racial tensions have been rising in the surrounding community and spilling over into the school. Ms. Tan notices that students are segregating themselves more by groups and sticking together more. Even though her classroom has been relatively calm, she has redoubled her efforts to promote inclusion and cooperation.

Today students are seated in their cooperative groups working on a jigsaw project. On the surface, there is no way to tell how they are grouped, though it is obviously not by ethnicity, language, or race. Some examples of group team-building projects are displayed on one wall—in one case, the groups have created a group identity and drawn a picture or symbol to match. The teams are reading short historical pieces related to different immigrant groups. Seated in topic-specific "expert" teams, the team members will soon return to their home teams with information on the immigrant experience they have read about—when it took place, why the person came, how the person felt on arriving, what conditions and attitudes greeted them here, and whether the immigration was voluntary or involuntary.

The work in home teams is productive and focused. Students are responsible for filling out a grid outlining what other team members are providing from their reading in the expert groups. Each team member will then choose an immigrant experience unlike their own or their family's. Their job will be to stand in the shoes of that person and write a diary-like account of that experience. Ms. Tan will spend considerable time making sure that students know and appreciate the differences between voluntary and involuntary immigration. She has planned several activities to help them process the hard feelings that are bound to come up as the unit proceeds, but she knows that avoiding the issues would be worse.

RESOURCES

Cohen & Lotan, 1997; Crandall, 1999; Johnson & Johnson, 1987; Kagan, 1994; Slavin, 1989, 1990.

● **STRATEGY 3.14: HELP STUDENTS DEVELOP PERSONAL SELF-ESTEEM AND LEADERSHIP SKILLS. TEACHERS USE STRATEGIES WITHIN AND OUTSIDE OF CLASS TO HELP STUDENTS DEVELOP SELF-CONFIDENCE, PRIDE IN THEIR HERITAGE, AND LEADERSHIP ABILITY.**

DISCUSSION

Bilingual and bicultural students are valuable resources. Unfortunately these students are often viewed in terms of what they *lack* (especially English-language proficiency), rather than what they contribute. The value of bilingualism in cognitive and economic terms is established in that it promotes cognitive flexibility and creativity, enabling bilinguals to view issues from multiple perspectives. In addition, bilinguals bring much-needed skills to an increasingly global economy (Hakuta, 1987; Tucker, 1990).

Not all schools recognize the value of knowing more than one language. Although schools may recognize the importance of foreign languages for English-speaking students, they often neglect the languages that immigrant students bring to school, relegating students' primary languages to the home or the community, rather than gradually adding English to that primary language.

This deficit model can have a profound impact on immigrant students, as well as on the teachers and administrators who work with them. Bilingual students may be overlooked when others are encouraged to run for student government, apply to honor societies, participate in advanced placement courses, or receive training as peer mediators. They may not receive equal consideration for college or career counseling. Their immigrant status may also limit their participation in government-funded work-study programs or college financial aid programs.

Marginalization often causes these students to internalize others' perceptions of them. Rather than taking pride in themselves and their backgrounds and recognizing the value of their bilingualism and biculturalism, they may doubt their self-worth or seek to prove it outside school. Some students must contribute to their family income, and the low-skilled jobs available to them may further diminish their sense of self-worth. Conflicting expectations of family, friends, and school can create incredible pressures.

Students need opportunities to identify and celebrate their strengths, not focus on their weaknesses. Fortunately, there are many ways to accomplish this. Perhaps the most important is to have high expectations of these youngsters and provide opportunities that allow them to live up to those expectations. For example, ELLs, or those who have recently exited from ESL or bilingual programs, may be ideal tutors for peers still enrolled in these courses. Older ELLs may be ideal tutors for younger children who are just learning to read. These tutors play an especially important role when they assist students at risk of failure in overcrowded elementary schools (Cook & Urzúa, 1993; Heath & Mangiola, 1991). Peer tutoring by older or more proficient students works nearly as well as teacher tutoring (Cohen, Kulik, & Kulik, 1982), and the benefits to the tutor are substantial. Teachers have long known that one of the best ways to learn something is to teach it. The act of tutoring increases students' confidence in themselves as learners, improves their academic skills, and increases the likelihood that they will stay in school. In addition, tutoring helps develop interpersonal and leadership skills. Cross-age tutoring programs have the additional benefit of encouraging young people to consider teaching as a career—a critically important possibility, since the declining percentage of Hispanic, Asian, and other minority teachers creates an absence of role models in schools.

Additional activities that celebrate students' languages and cultures are also important. International clubs and festivals, extracurricular activities involving sports or music in which students excel, and opportunities to learn each others' dances can help students develop pride in their heritage. When newly arrived immigrants help a school win the state soccer championship, everyone recognizes and celebrates their accomplishments. Similarly, the publication of student stories or poems in school journals or newsletters validates student efforts and offers a valuable outlet for self-expression. Simple banners or hall exhibits reflecting students' diverse backgrounds help establish a positive multicultural environment.

Teachers can provide opportunities for students to demonstrate special linguistic and cultural knowledge, such as asking students to teach a short lesson on their language or to relate a local proverb to one from their native country. Working cooperatively on class projects helps students recognize each others' strengths. Former students with successful careers may be invited to class to discuss their careers and the role that bilingualism may have played; current students can serve as experts in teacher development courses and workshops, helping teachers and administrators to understand their countries and cultural backgrounds. The important point is to emphasize students' strengths while addressing their linguistic and academic needs.

CLASSROOM EXAMPLES

Ms. Hernandez, a high school Spanish teacher, recognized that many of her Spanish-speaking students were having difficulties in regular Spanish classes, as their spoken language differed from the textbook variety, and formal instruction in their own language was limited. Rather than underscoring students' strengths, the classes were further eroding their self-confidence.

Ms. Hernandez decided to develop a sequence of Spanish courses for native speakers, building on their oral language and developing their formal (especially written) language skills to further their ability to use the language in academic and professional contexts. After taking this course sequence, students transitioned into advanced placement Spanish classes with mainstream students, where they were able to earn college credit. Ms. Hernandez also developed a cross-age tutoring program in which Spanish-speaking and English-speaking high school students tutored ELLs in a nearby elementary school. Some of the Spanish-speaking students found themselves helping the English-speaking high school students with their Spanish. After this experience, several students indicated an interest in becoming teachers.

Teachers at one high school developed a weekend cross-cultural leadership institute at an environmental education center, where students from many different backgrounds were encouraged to develop confidence, leadership, and cooperative skills. For many students, this was their first weekend away from home. One activity required students to help each other negotiate an obstacle course, which required teamwork, confidence, physical and mental agility, and determination. Other activities engaged students in creating a banner for the school, participating in a talent show, and working with a variety of arts and crafts. In addition, two student government leaders (formerly in ESL classes) led an evening session, providing a forum for students to articulate their concerns about the school and to act on them by developing resolutions, which were subsequently presented to the student government and the principal for action.

Through these activities, friendships developed among students who had previously viewed each other with suspicion. Several of the participants became volunteers, guides, and interpreters for parents and new students at the international student guidance office during registration week. In doing so, they gained community service credits required for graduation. Another source of community service credits grew out of a field trip to a local nursing home, where students found senior citizens eager to talk with younger people who spoke their languages. Several students began visiting seniors regularly.

Another teacher, Mr. Wu, initiated a writing workshop by asking students to list (1) things I like about myself, (2) things I can do well, and (3) things others like about me. Students expanded their lists to serve as a means of introducing themselves to the class. As a follow-up activity, students brought personal items to school, including photographs and other pictures explaining who they were. In small groups, they elaborated on why these things were important to them. They wrote captions for the photographs and pictures, in both English and their primary language, and combined them with other items in a collage that was later displayed in the classroom.

Ms. Johnson routinely uses cooperative learning to integrate diverse learners into her middle school social studies classes. She groups ELLs with English speakers who are sensitive to the needs of these students and assigns roles that allow them to demonstrate special skills, such as designing and illustrating group posters. In the same middle school, a science teacher and a graduate student serving an internship helped immigrant students develop science fair projects. One project, by a 7the grade Somali student, won first place in chemistry. This student, who had only recently arrived from a refugee camp, learned to use the computer to enter the findings for her project poster.

RESOURCES

Cohen, Kulik, & Kulik, 1982; Cook & Urzúa, 1993; Hakuta, 1987; Heath & Mangiola, 1991; Tucker, 1990.

● STRATEGY 3.15: FACILITATE STUDENTS' PARTICIPATION IN COLLEGE AND CAREER PLANNING. TEACHERS INTEGRATE INFORMATION ABOUT POSTSECONDARY EDUCATION AND CAREER POSSIBILITIES INTO THEIR CLASSES, HELPING STUDENTS TO BETTER UNDERSTAND THE RANGE OF OPPORTUNITIES AVAILABLE TO THEM AND TO TAKE THE STEPS NEEDED FOR ACCESS.

DISCUSSION

Immigrant students often dream of going to college, but even those who succeed academically may have little understanding of how to achieve that dream, or may even believe it is impossible for them. Their experiences in their home countries may have led them to think that college is available only to the wealthy or that options for women are restricted. They may be unaware of the variety of colleges available, the possibility of combining work with school, or sources of financial assistance. They may be expected to work to help support their families or even to increase the

number of hours they work after graduation. If they are the first in their family to consider college, they are quite likely to have a limited awareness of college requirements and the application process (Crandall & Greenblatt, 1999; Hutner, 1996; Hadlock, 1994).

It is easy to forget the difficulty of the college application process. Horn and Carroll (1997) found that only a few of the students considered at risk in their study completed all of the steps necessary for college participation: aspiring to a college degree, taking appropriate courses, passing entrance exams, completing an application, and enrolling in college. English-speaking students born in the United States find this process difficult to negotiate; it is even more difficult for ELLs who may not even be aware of the steps involved.

Teachers and guidance counselors often overlook students who are still receiving ESL instruction as possible candidates for college, confusing limited English proficiency with limited academic ability. In addition, teachers and administrators are seldom aware of the test requirements for immigrant students seeking higher education—these tests and policies governing entrance examinations vary widely (Bunch, 1995). Changing federal policies concerning immigration status further complicate the situation because these policies determine who is eligible for federal financial aid (federally funded scholarships).

Students need support structures to complete the application process and role models to help envision themselves as potential college students; they also need to have information presented in language they can understand. Role models can help students sort through the many types of colleges available: two-year or four-year, public or private, coeducational or single gender, large or small, and liberal arts, technical or trade. Students' choices are often limited to schools where friends or older siblings have enrolled or colleges in the immediate vicinity. Without visits to other colleges or opportunities to discuss options with peers or alumni, students are likely to rely on those institutions with which they're most familiar.

Support structures and modeling are also important in career planning. Students may not understand the economic value of postsecondary education or the fact that higher education correlates with higher earnings and more stable employment. Without opportunities to talk with or shadow potential role models, or to visit workplaces with diverse employees, they may focus on areas of work limited by their experiences. Most secondary schools have career planning facilities, often involving sophisticated job interest surveys or computer-assisted career planning programs; however, these instruments are not usually available in languages other than English, and the level of English may be beyond the proficiency of English learners. Even when appropriate materials are available, immigrant students may not be aware of them or know how to access them.

It is possible to address both college preparation and career planning through specific courses for immigrant students. In college preparation classes, focus on selecting colleges and filling out applications, developing a résumé and the student essay required in the application, preparing for the variety of tests that will be required (e.g., the Scholastic Aptitude Test (SAT), Test of English as a Foreign Language (TOEFL), or American College Testing Program (ACT)), and doing financial planning (identifying and accessing sources of financial assistance). In a career preparation class, the focus might be on identifying personal interests and strengths, analyzing potential jobs that use these strengths, reviewing required course work and ensuring that students' schedules are appropriate, identifying postsecondary education that might be needed, and helping identify potential postsecondary institutions.

It is not sufficient, however, to relegate career and college planning to separate courses. As one teacher put it, "We need *every* teacher to help with the college and career process." Teachers across the curriculum need to relate their course work to the world outside the classroom and help students to see the interrelationships between what is taught in class and further education and employment. Classroom activities can be augmented by guest speakers who can serve as role models and motivators and provide information on how they chose their own college or career. Inviting prominent bilingual community members communicates the importance of bilingualism and biculturalism as a job asset to all students, not just ELLs. Former students who attend local colleges or are home on vacation can also be invited to talk to classes or to dialogue with students through e-mail or letters, serving as valuable sources of encouragement and information.

CLASSROOM EXAMPLES

Mr. Elson (an ESL teacher) and Ms. Sing (a social studies teacher) are on the same middle school team, including both ELLs and native English speakers. They coordinate their instruction, sometimes including the math or science teachers. They routinely weave career and college information into their teaching.

For example, a unit on U.S. history dealing with slavery and the Civil War also included a visit to a former slave home (the site was an archaeological dig in the middle of an apartment complex). Students visited the dig, saw archaeologists at work, and interviewed college students at the site about their work. Though the middle schoolers may be too young to choose a career, they became aware of career possibilities and of the role that postsecondary education plays in these careers. Units emphasizing the importance of college and career planning are also developed for students to take with them when they are called back to their home countries for extended periods of time, which helps students maintain their English proficiency.

At the high school level, Ms. Vaznaugh teaches college and career planning in her intermediate ESL classes; she incorporates job interest surveys, college and career field trips, and test preparation. The latter is especially important, as students will have to demonstrate their proficiency in English for admission to college and successfully complete standardized tests.

Using a variety of test-preparation materials, students analyze individual items for test-taking strategies. Students also take simulated tests, analyze the results, and share their experiences with students who have taken the test. These activities help reduce students' anxiety about the tests and reinforce the importance of planning for the experience. As Ms. Vaznaugh says, "Kids know less about college than we think they do. They need direct information, guidance, and support."

Another teacher incorporates college applications into her English class, focusing on the personal essay in the application form. Yet another teacher, Ms. Haynes, includes an introduction to keyboarding and word processing, using résumé development and essay writing for college and career planning as the basis of instruction. These classes introduce students to the college and financial assistance available through the Internet or local software. Usually students work in pairs or small groups when using the Internet or the software programs, freeing Ms. Haynes to answer specific questions or to provide assistance to groups of students.

Special career and college visits are planned for ELLs and those who have recently exited the ESL program. During these visits, students can meet with other immigrant students to see what kinds of career paths they are pursuing. Some teachers pair career visits with planning as a means of meeting the school's community service requirement. Thus a visit to a nursing home or hospital not only makes students aware of the wide array of jobs available in the health and nursing care fields, but also provides potential sites at which students can perform community service required for graduation.

Much of what is introduced in these classes is reinforced through after-school programs or clubs such as the Honors Council, an extracurricular activity focused on college and career planning (Hadlock, 1994). When the council began, only high-achieving senior students (those with a 3.0 grade-point average or above) were included; over time, however, students with a 2.0 or above have been added, and a second council—for freshmen, sophomores, and juniors—has also been initiated (Hutner, 1996). The councils encourage an earlier focus on postsecondary planning and provide for the development of peer mentors; students in the upper-level council can earn community service credits by helping those in the lower council. A similar set of courses, one for juniors and another for seniors, has been added to the school's curriculum, though the after-school activities and the emphasis on postsecondary options in ESL and other courses continue.

RESOURCES

Bunch, 1995; Crandall & Greenblatt, 1999; Hadlock, 1994; Horn & Carroll, 1997; Hutner, 1996.

STUDENT PROFILES

HIGH-ACHIEVING STUDENT

When Marco was a boy, his father and older brothers moved to the United States, leaving Marco and his younger sisters to help their mother with the small family farm in rural Mexico. Though he was needed on the farm, Marco's mother demanded that he attend school as often as possible. When Marco was 15, the rest of the family was able to move to the United States. While Marco's parents completed only a few years of schooling, his mother was determined that her children would receive a good education. Marco often talked about his mother's dream that her children attend college.

Shortly after his arrival in the United States, Marco began working as a cook in his brother's restaurant. Though he worked 30 hours a week, Marco was able to maintain more than a 3.5 grade-point average. He wanted to attend college so that he could learn accounting or business management to help his brother manage the restau-

rant (and some day possibly have a business of his own), but neither he nor his family knew much about the college application process. Nor could they afford to help pay for college. In fact, they needed Marco's help just to keep the restaurant open.

Fortunately, during his junior year, one of Marco's teachers suggested that he participate in his school's Honors Council, where he received help in choosing a college and filling out the necessary forms for admission and financial aid. He learned that he was eligible for a state-guaranteed access grant for disadvantaged students with good grades, as well as a federal Pell Grant. He took a course to prepare him for both the SAT and the TOEFL and applied for and received both grants.

Unfortunately, Marco's scores on the SAT and TOEFL were lower than he had hoped; he feared that his dream of a college education would not come true. However, during one of the field trips he took with the council, Marco learned about the local community college, where he could earn an associate degree in accounting and perhaps be able to transfer to a four-year college. He also discovered that his grants would pay for all his expenses. Marco is now in his second year at the college—majoring in accounting and still working at his brother's restaurant. He plans eventually to transfer to a four-year college.

LITERACY STUDENT

Patricia was 14 when she left her mother in El Salvador to come to the United States to live with her father and stepmother. In El Salvador, Patricia lived in a rural area, where she had little opportunity or need to attend school. When she arrived in the United States, it was almost the end of the school year, and Patricia was placed in 8th grade, though she needed to learn English as well as the basic academic concepts that others in her grade had already learned.

When she moved to the high school, she was fortunate to be placed in a special literacy and basic skills course for ELLs, as well as in a beginning ESL class. Though she had to overcome many obstacles, her determination and the support of her teachers and family enabled her to make steady progress. In just a year, she achieved a 2.25 grade-point average; after another year of a special academic skills class, she was able to pass two of the four required state examinations as well as raise her grades substantially.

Much of Patricia's success was due to the highly structured, though flexible, approach of her literacy and basic skills teachers, who taught her the importance of attending class and being prepared to learn. They convinced her that she would succeed. In her class, she learned how to organize a notebook, work with other students, and ask for help when she needed it. Family problems (her father and stepmother separated, and her brother was injured on the job) have forced Patricia to work both at home and in a part-time job. Though these demands are taking their toll and Patricia's grades are falling, she is determined to finish school. Her ESL teacher has suggested that she enter the school's work-study program next year and finish the last two tests. If she does, she will be one of the proudest seniors when she graduates next year.

BIBLIOGRAPHY

Allen, R. V., & Allen, C. (1982). *Language experience activities* (2nd ed.). Boston: Houghton Mifflin.

Aronowitz, M. (1984). The social and emotional adjustment of immigrant children: A review of the literature. *International Migration Review, 18*(2), 237–257.

Ascher, C. (1984). The social and psychological adjustment of southeast Asian refugees. *Urban Review, 17*(2), 147–152.

August, D., & Hakuta, K. (1997). *Improving schooling for language minority children: A research agenda.* Washington, DC: National Academy Press.

Berman, P., McLaughlin, B., McLeod, B., Minicucci, C., Nelson, B., & Woodsworth, K. (1995). *School reform and student diversity: Case studies of exemplary practices for LEP students* (draft report). Berkeley, CA: National Center for Research on Cultural Diversity and Second Language Learning and BW Associates.

Borkowski, J. G., Johnston, M. B., & Reid, M. K. (1987). Metacognition, motivation, and the transfer of control processes. In S. J. Ceci (Ed.), *Handbook of cognitive, social, and neuropsychological aspects of learning disabilities.* Hillsdale, NJ: Lawrence Erlbaum Associates.

Bruer, J. T. (1993). The mind's journey from novice to expert: If we know the route, we can help students negotiate the way. *American Educator, 17*(2), 6–15, 38–46.

Bruner, J. (1986). *Actual minds, possible worlds.* Cambridge, MA: Harvard University Press.

Bunch, G. (1995). Five tests and five schools: Information for international students (and their teachers!) about entrance exams for higher education. In E. Holden (Ed.), *College-bound immigrants and international students: A manual for setting up a support network.* Baltimore, MD: Project WE TEACH, University of Maryland Baltimore County and Prince George's County (MD) Public Schools.

Carlin, J. E. (1979). The catastrophically uprooted child: Southeast Asian refugee children. *Basic handbook of child psychiatry (Vol. 1)* (pp. 290–300). New York: Basic Books.

Carter, T. P., & Chatfield, M. L. (1986). Effective bilingual schools: Implications for policy and practice. *American Journal of Education, 95*(1), 200–232.

Chamot, A., & O'Malley, J. M. (1994). *The CALLA handbook: Implementing the cognitive academic language learning approach.* New York: Addison-Wesley.

Cohen, E. A., & Lotan, R. A. (1997). *Working for equity in heterogeneous classrooms: Sociological theory in practice.* New York: Teachers College Press.

Cohen, P. A., Kulik, J. A., & Kulik, C. L. (1982). Educational outcomes of tutoring: A meta-analysis of findings. *American Educational Research Journal, 19*(2), 237–248.

Collier, V. P. (1989). How long: A synthesis of research on academic achievement in a second language. *TESOL Quarterly, 23*(3), 509–531.

Cook, B., & Urzua, C. (1993). *The Literacy Club: A cross-age tutoring/paired reading project.* Washington, DC: National Clearinghouse for Bilingual Education.

Cornelius, W. A., & Rumba, R. G. (Eds.). (1995). *California's immigrant children: Theory, research, and implications for educational policy.* San Diego: San Diego Center for U.S.-Mexican Studies, University of California.

Crandall, J. A. (1981). *A sociolinguistic analysis of the literacy demands of clerical workers.* Unpublished dissertation, Georgetown University, Washington, DC.

Crandall, J. A. (1987). *ESL through content-area instruction: Mathematics, science, social studies.* Washington, DC/Englewood Cliffs, NJ: Center for Applied Linguistics/Prentice Hall Regents.

Crandall, J. A. (1994). Strategic integration: Preparing language and content teachers for linguistically and culturally diverse classrooms. In J. E. Alatis (Ed.), *Strategic interaction and language acquisition: Theory, practice, and research.* Washington, DC: Georgetown University Press.

Crandall, J. A. (1995). Reinventing (America's) schools: The role of the applied linguist. In J. E. Alatis et al. (Eds.), *Linguistics and the education of language teachers: Ethnolinguistic, psycholinguistic, and sociolinguistic aspects.* Washington, DC: Georgetown University Press.

Crandall, J. A. (1998). Collaborate and cooperate: Preparing language and content teachers. *English Teaching Forum, 36*(1), 2–9.

Crandall, J. A. (1999). Cooperative language learning and affective factors. In J. Arnold (Ed.), *Affective factors in language learning* (pp. 226–245). Cambridge, England: Cambridge University Press.

Crandall, J. A., Bernache, C. & Prager, S. (1998, Autumn). New frontiers in educational policy and program development: The challenge of the underschooled immigrant secondary school student. *Educational Policy, 12*(6), 719–734.

Crandall, J. A., & Greenblatt, L. (1999). Teaching beyond the middle: Meeting the needs of underschooled and high-achieving immigrant students. In M. R. Basterra (Ed.), *Excellence and equity for language minority students: Critical issues and promising practices* (pp. 43–60). Washington, DC: The American University, Mid-Atlantic Equity Center.

Crandall, J. A., & Tucker, G. R. (1990). Content-based language instruction in second and foreign languages. In A. Sanivan (Ed.), *Language teaching methodology for the nineties.* Singapore: SEAMEO Regional Language Centre.

Curtain, H., & Haas, M. (1995). *Integrating foreign language and content instruction in grades K–8.* Washington, DC: ERIC Clearinghouse on Languages and Linguistics. [www.cal.org/ericcll/digest/int-for-K8.html]

Darling-Hammond, L. (1996). The quiet revolution: Rethinking teacher development. *Educational Leadership, 53,* 4–10.

Dixon, C. N., & Nessel, D. (1983). Language experience approach to reading (and writing). Hayward, CA: Aleman Press.

Donly, B., et al. (1995). *Summary of bilingual education state educational agency program survey of states' LEP persons and available educational services, 1993–1994.* Arlington, VA: Development Associates.

Duffy, J. L., Roehler, M., Meloth, M., Vavrus, L., Book, C., Putnam, J., & Wesselman, R. (1986). The relationship between explicit verbal explanation during reading skill instruction and student awareness and achievement: A study of reading teacher effects. *Reading Research Quarterly, 21*(2), 237–252.

Echevarría, J., & Graves, A. (1998). *Sheltered content instruction: Teaching English-language learners with diverse abilities.* Boston: Allyn and Bacon.

Enright, D. S., & McCloskey, M. L. (1988). *Integrating English: Developing English language and literacy in the multilingual classroom.* Reading, MA: Addison-Wesley.

Fathman, A. K., & Quinn, M. E. (1989). *Science for language learners.* Englewood Cliffs, NJ: Prentice Hall Regents.

First, J., & Carrera, J. W. (1988). *New voices: Immigrant students in the U.S. public schools.* Boston: National Coalition of Advocates for Students.

Fleischman, H. L., & Hopstock, P. J. (1993). *Descriptive study of services to limited English proficient students: Vol. 1. Summary of findings and conclusions.* Arlington, VA: Development Associates.

Garcia, E. (1988). *The education of linguistically and culturally diverse students: Effective instructional practices.* Washington, DC/Santa Cruz, CA: National Center for Research on Cultural Diversity and Second Language Learning/Center for Applied Linguistics.

Gardner, H. (1993). *Multiple intelligences: The theory in practice.* New York: Basic Books.

González, J. M., & Darling-Hammond, L. (1997). *New concepts for new challenges: Professional development for teachers of immigrant youth.* Washington, DC/McHenry, IL: Center for Applied Linguistics and Delta Systems.

Hadlock, C. (1994). College-bound immigrant and international students: A manual for setting up a support network. In J. A. Crandall & E. Holden (Eds.), *Raising college and career expectations and helping immigrant students to achieve them.* Baltimore, MD: Project WE TEACH, University of Maryland Baltimore County and Prince George's County (MD) Public Schools.

Hakuta, K. (1987). *Mirror of language: The debate on bilingualism.* New York: Basic Books.

Hamayan, E. (1994). Language development of low-literacy students. In F. Genesee (Ed.), *Educating second language children: The whole child, the whole curriculum, the whole community.* Cambridge, England: Cambridge University Press.

Han, M., & Baker, D. (1997). *A profile of policies and practices for limited English proficient students: Screening methods, program support, and teacher training: SASS 1993–1994 (NCES 97-472).* Washington, DC: National Center for Education Statistics.

Heath, S. B. (1983). *Ways with words: Language, life, and work in communities and classrooms.* Cambridge, England: Cambridge University Press.

Heath, S. B., & Mangiola, L. (1991). *Children of promise: Literate activity in linguistically and culturally diverse classrooms.* Washington, DC: National Education Association/American Educational Research Association.

Henderson, A., Abbott, C., & Strang, W. (1993). *Summary of the bilingual education State Educational Agency program survey of states' limited English proficient persons and available educational services, 1991–1992.* Arlington, VA: Development Associates. [ERIC Document Reproduction Service No. ED 369 292]

Henke, R. R., Choy, S. P., Chen, X., Geis, S., Alt, M. N., & Broughman, S. P. (1997). *America's teachers: Profile of a profession, 1993–94.* Washington, DC: U.S. Department of Education, National Center for Education Statistics.

Holmes Group. (1990). *Tomorrow's schools.* East Lansing, MI: Author.

Horn, L. J., & Carroll, C. D. (1997). *Confronting the odds: Students at risk and the pipeline to higher education.* Washington, DC: U.S. Department of Education, National Center for Education Statistics.

Hutner, J. G. (1996). Preparing freshman, sophomore, and junior immigrant and international students for entrance into college. In E. Holden (Ed.). *College bound immigrants and international students: A manual for setting up a support network.* Baltimore, MD: Project WE TEACH, University of Maryland Baltimore County and Prince George's County (MD) Public Schools.

Jacob, E., Rottenberg, L., Patrick, S., & Wheeler, E. (1996). Cooperative learning: Context and opportunities for acquiring academic English. *TESOL Quarterly, 30*(2), 253–280.

Jeffers, S. (1991). *Brother eagle, sister sky: A message from Chief Seattle.* New York: Dial Books.

Johnson, D. W., & Johnson, R. (1987). *Learning together and alone: Cooperative, competitive, and individualistic learning.* Englewood Cliffs, NJ: Prentice-Hall.

Johnson, D. W., Johnson, R. T., & Holubec, E. J. (1993). *Circles of learning* (4th ed.). Edina, MN: Interaction Book Company.

Jones, B. F., Palincsar, A. S., Ogle, D. S., & Carr, E. G. (1987). *Strategic teaching and learning: Cognitive instruction in the content areas.* Alexandria, VA: Association for Supervision and Curriculum Development.

Kagan, S. (1994). *Cooperative learning resources for teachers.* San Juan Capistrano, CA: Kagan Cooperative Learning.

Kessler, C., & Hayes, C. (1989). Foreword. In A. K. Fatham & M. E. Quinn (Eds.), *Science for language learners.* Englewood Cliffs, NJ: Prentice Hall Regents.

Krashen, S. (1993). *The power of reading: Insights from the research.* Englewood, CO: Libraries Unlimited.

Lucas, T. (1997). *Into, through, and beyond secondary school: Critical transitions for immigrant youths.* Washington, DC/McHenry, IL: Center for Applied Linguistics and Delta Systems.

Lucas, T., Henze, R., & Donato, R. (1990). Promoting the success of Latino language minority students: An exploratory study of six high schools. *Harvard Educational Review, 60*(3), 315–340.

Macías, R. F., & Kelly, C. (1996). *Summary report of the survey of the states' limited English proficient students and available educational programs and services, 1994–1995.* Washington, DC: National Clearinghouse for Bilingual Education.

Maroney, O. H. (1998). Who is teaching the children? More trained bilingual teachers are needed for excellent education. *IDRA Newsletter, 25*(1), 6–8.

Minicucci, C., & Olsen, L. (1991). An exploratory study of secondary LEP programs. In *Meeting the challenges of diversity: An evaluation of programs for pupils with limited proficiency in English (Vol. 5).* Berkeley, CA: BW Associates.

Moll, L. C., Amanti, C., Neff, D., & Gonzalez, N. (1992). Funds of knowledge for teaching: Using a qualitative approach to connect homes and classroom. *Theory into Practice, 31*(2), 132–141.

Moran-Ender, C., & Ender, M. G. (1995, March). A picture and a thousand words: Autophotography in the ESOL classroom and beyond. Presentation at the TESOL Annual Convention, Long Beach, CA.

National Center for Education Statistics. (1997a). *Findings from the condition of education 1997: The social context of education.* Washington, DC: U.S. Department of Education, Author.

National Commission on Teaching and America's Future. (1996). *What matters most: Teaching for America's future.* New York: Author.

Olsen, L., & Chen, M. (1988). *Crossing the schoolhouse border: Immigrant children in California schools.* San Francisco: California Tomorrow.

Olsen, L., & Jaramillo, A. (1999). *Turning the tides of exclusion: A guide for educators and advocates for immigrant students.* Oakland: CA: California Tomorrow.

Olsen, L., & Jaramillo, A. (2000). When time is on our side: Redesigning schools to meet the needs of immigrant students. In P. Gándara (Ed.), *The dimension of time and the challenge of school reform* (pp. 225–250). New York: State University of New York.

Olsen, L., & Mullen, N. (1990). *Embracing diversity: Teachers' voices from California schools.* San Francisco: California Tomorrow.

Palincsar, A. S., & Brown, A. L. (1984). Reciprocal teaching of comprehension-fostering and comprehension-monitoring activities. *Cognition and Instruction, 1*(2), 117–75.

Palincsar, A. S., David, Y., & Brown, A. L. (1989). *Using reciprocal teaching in the classroom: A guide for teachers.* Berkeley, CA: Campion Group.

Peyton, J. K., Jones, C., Vincent, A., & Greenblatt, L. (1994). Implementing writing workshops with ESOL students: Visions and realities. *TESOL Quarterly, 28*(3), 469–487.

Peyton, J. K., & Reed, L. (1990). *Dialogue journal writing with non-native English speakers: A handbook for teachers.* Alexandria, VA: TESOL.

Population Resource Center. (1996). *Immigration to the United States: 1996 update.* Washington, DC: Author.

Richard-Amato, P., & Snow, M. A. (1992). *The multicultural classroom: Readings for content-area teachers.* White Plains, NY: Longan.

Rumbaut, R. (1994). The crucible within: Ethnic identity, self-esteem and segmented assimilation among children of immigrants. *International Migration Review, 28*(4), 748–794.

Schank, R., & Abelson, R. (1977). *Scripts, plans, goals, and understanding.* Hillsdale, NJ: Erlbaum.

Short, D. J. (1991). *How to integrate language and content instruction: A training manual.* Washington, DC: Center for Applied Linguistics.

Short, D. J., & Boyson, B. (1997). *Secondary newcomer programs in the United States: 1996–97 directory.* Washington, DC: Center for Applied Linguistics.

Slavin, R. E. (December 1989/January 1990). Research on cooperative learning: Consensus and controversy. *Educational Leadership, 47,* 52–54.

Slavin, R. E. (1990). *Cooperative learning: Theory, research, and practice.* Englewood Cliffs, NJ: Prentice Hall.

Smith, F. (1988). *Joining the literacy club.* Portsmouth, NH: Heinemann.

Tate, O. (1997, May). Teaching literacy-level ESOL students. Presentation at Mid-Atlantic Equity Conference, College Park, MD.

Taylor, M. (1993). The language experience approach. In J. A. Crandall & J. K. Peyton (Eds.), *Approaches to adult ESL literacy instruction.* Washington, DC/McHenry, IL: Center for Applied Linguistics and Delta Systems.

Tighe, M. J. (1971). Creative dialogue: Teaching students to teach themselves. *New Directions in Teaching, 2*(4), 21–25.

Tucker, G. R. (1990). Cognitive and social correlates of additive bilinguality. In J. E. Alatis (Ed.), *Georgetown University Round Table on Languages and Linguistics 1990,* Washington, DC: Georgetown University Press.

U.S. Bureau of the Census. (1997; March 1997 Update). *The foreign born population,* (pp. 20–507; PPL-92). Available: http:///www.ensus/gov/population/www/socdemo/foreign.html]

Walqui-VanLier, A. (1991). *Sheltered instruction: Doing it right.* Unpublished manuscript.

Wong Fillmore, L., and Valadez, C. (1986). Teaching bilingual learners. In M. C. Wittrock (Ed.), *Handbook of research on teaching.* New York: Macmillan.

Yep, L. *Dragonwings.* Harper & Row, 1975.

Zeichner, K. (1992). *Educating teachers for cultural diversity.* East Lansing, MI: National Center for Research on Teacher Learning.

4

STRATEGIES FOR INCREASING ACHIEVEMENT IN CIVICS

MARY ELLEN BAFUMO AND BURTON COHEN

Knowledge will forever govern ignorance, and a people who mean to be their own Governors must arm themselves with the power knowledge gives.

—James Madison, 1788

Democracy attracts diversity. The appeal of freedom and opportunity the United States offers draws a steady stream of seekers from many lands and cultures; the pilgrimage continues today. The diversity that democracy attracts goes beyond that of different cultures. The visionary and the pragmatist, the poet and the illiterate, the revolutionary and the traditionalist—all have been drawn by the promise of U.S. democracy.

Democracy invites diversity because democracy is a great leveler. Everyone—the rich and the poor, the learned and the unschooled, the powerful and the powerless—is endowed with the same rights and responsibilities in a democracy. The very idea that a viable system of justice prevails, a concept most citizens of the United States take for granted, continues to make our democracy a beacon for those who suffer oppression in places around the globe.

In U.S. schools, however, the serious study of civics begins late in a student's education. The traditional one-semester U.S. government course in high school often marks the first focused study of democracy, along with the role of its citizens and their rights and responsibilities. Without sufficient prior knowledge, students reach high school lacking the context and preparation to find meaning in civics—a subject of paramount importance to a nation intended from the beginning to govern through the voice and power of its citizenry.

Just as unfortunate as the dearth of effective study is the number of students whose own or whose family's experience with the processes of law and government is negative. Motivating students who view organized government as a barrier to their rights, or as a necessary evil, is one of the most serious challenges facing civics education.

The connection between citizenry and democracy is an unbroken strand in U.S. history. Yet the study of civics and government is fragmented and inconsistent, despite national consensus about its importance and a historic affirmation of the school's responsibility in developing civic competence. A 1993 report on instructional practices from the U.S. Department of Education noted that civics was most often taught as part of the social studies curriculum in the primary grades, and that only 2.5 hours per week were devoted to social studies. In contrast, English and language arts were allotted 10.6 hours of instruction per week. At the middle school level, only 7 percent of the schools surveyed in 47 states offered separate courses in civics and government (NEAP, 1995). Twenty-one states mandated instruction in civics and government, but most prescribed the time-honored format—a one-semester offering in grade 12—which gives young U.S. citizens an inadequate preparation for understanding concepts vital to their performance as citizens.

The absence of a substantive background in civics was reflected in a 1994 survey of 238,000 college freshman administered by the University of California at Los Angeles

(UCLA) Higher Education Institute. The survey reported an all-time low of 16 percent of respondents who discussed politics frequently. And those who said they paid close attention to political affairs declined to the lowest recorded level in the survey's 29-year history.

Moreover, public opinion polls reflect a serious decline in our understanding of the democratic system of government. Low voter turnout for local, state, and national elections supports the notion that fewer citizens avail themselves of—or even *know* of—their rights and responsibilities. In 1801, Thomas Jefferson wrote, "The qualifications for self-government in a society are not innate. They are the result of habit and long training." (Coates, 1996) A disengaged citizenry is dangerous to the principles of democracy.

An effective education in civics and government must begin in the primary grades and continue through middle and high school. It must be characterized by relevance and coherence. Exemplary schools across the nation already engage in such practices. The maintenance and improvement of democracy requires that all schools be engaged in civic education at a high level.

ENHANCING STUDENTS' CIVICS ACHIEVEMENT

During the 1990s, several events focused attention on the need for early, consistent, high-quality civics education. The inclusion of citizenship in the Goals 2000 Educate America Act (1994) placed civics on a par with other national content-area priorities. The publication, also in 1994, of the National Standards for Civics and Government (hereafter called the Standards) created guidelines for competencies from kindergarten through grade 12. The NAEP Assessment in Civics (1998), and a growing national interest in character education, are fueling interest in citizenship and government issues in U.S. classrooms.

Beyond creating awareness, however, is the need to direct teaching toward student understanding and achievement. The Standards provide a guide for achievement by identifying the knowledge and skills that students require for proficiency in civics and government. The Standards recommend the following themes in age-appropriate contexts:

- What is government and what should it do? (K–12)
- What are the basic values and principles of U.S. democracy? (K–12)

- How does the government established by the U.S. Constitution embody the purposes, values, and principles of U.S. democracy? (K–12)
- What is the relationship of the United States to other nations and to world affairs? (K–12)
- What are the roles of the citizen in U.S. democracy? (K–12)
- What are civic life, politics, and government? (5–12)
- What are the foundations of the U.S. political system? (5–12)

The identification of clearly defined areas of study can assist teachers in creating opportunities for focused study as well as integrating the Standards into the entire curriculum.

THE STATE OF CIVICS INSTRUCTION

In schools across the United States, knowledge of citizenship and government is being developed through activities that focus on personal and civic responsibility, service projects, and affiliation with a variety of government agencies. Teachers are integrating these activities into the school's daily life. Such examples are still the exception rather than the rule, and national assessments demonstrate that greater effort is needed to incorporate civics instruction into the classroom in motivating ways that sustain and improve democracy.

The 1990 National Assessment of Education Progress (NAEP) Civics Report Card indicated cause for concern about the general scope and quality of civics education. Results showed that

- Achievement on the 1988 NAEP Civics Assessment by 17-year-olds in all populations studied showed significant decline.
- Only 6 percent of high school seniors demonstrated broad knowledge of political institutions and processes.
- Serious disparities in achievement were evident among subpopulations (males versus females, minorities versus whites).

On a positive note, the report demonstrated that student achievement in grades 4, 8, and 12 is related to the reported *amount* of instruction. This finding also held true in international studies (NEAP, 1995). Creating classroom time and opportunities for meaningful civics instruction during already tightly scheduled days is challenging, but can significantly influence achievement.

FIGURE 4.1
Summary of Standards for Curriculum and Instruction in Civics Curriculum

CURRICULUM

Traditional Emphasis

- Secondary to academic learning
- Knowledge and skills emerging from academic disciplines
- Study in high school
- Historical content

New Emphasis

- Central to academic learning
- Focus on integrating academic disciplines
- Awareness and study K–12
- Contemporary and historical content

INSTRUCTION

Traditional Emphasis

- Teacher-centered approach
- Text based
- Memorization
- Individual seat work
- Written testing
- Factual knowledge
- Classroom-based learning
- Passive learning

New Emphasis

- Student-centered approach
- Variety of resources and technology
- Understanding and application
- Collaborative learning
- Multiple testing formats
- Intellectual and participatory skills
- Community-based learning
- Active learning

ASSESSING STUDENT ACHIEVEMENT IN CIVICS

Assessment in civics and government must include varied ways of measuring the complex competencies required for proficiency. The Standards recommend that assessments measure mastery of content knowledge *and* the ability to apply it through intellectual and participatory skills. Intellectual skills include evaluating, explaining, describing, taking a position, and defending a position. Participatory skills range from monitoring a problem to negotiating, building consensus, persuading, compromising, and articulating interests.

The kinds of skills the Standards call for require curriculum and pedagogy that actively involve students in learning and provide opportunities for practice (see Figure 4.1). Multiple assessment formats that measure performance beyond test taking are essential. Portfolios can mea-sure both general knowledge and intellectual and participatory skills; they should contain audio, video, or CD-ROM presentations of student speeches, debates, simulations of mock trials or town meetings, or persuasive oral presentations on a civic issue. Research for position papers on a political issue, letters to editors and government agencies, or petitions can also assess such skills. Participation in design, implementation, and evaluation of service projects provides a nontraditional but effective basis for assessing the civic and governmental competencies students will need as informed citizens in a constitutional democracy.

CIVICS STRATEGIES THAT PROMOTE ACHIEVEMENT

The strategies that follow grow naturally out of research on brain-based teaching, character education, and domain-specific learning. They come alive in exemplary classrooms throughout the United States. Each promotes understanding through active learning and practice with civic and governmental competencies in a variety of contexts. These nine learning-by-doing strategies encourage achievement for all students by offering motivating, relevant learning experiences:

- Create a democratic classroom.
- Integrate civic virtues into the daily curriculum.
- Encourage school staff to exemplify civic virtues.
- Monitor relevant current events, political issues, and politicians.
- Use discussion forums, mock trials, and debates.
- Plan learning projects around civics issues.
- Plan and implement service projects with students.
- Create learning partnerships/internships with government and community agencies.
- Host speakers from government agencies and organizations.

● **STRATEGY 4.1: CREATE A DEMOCRATIC CLASSROOM. TEACHERS CREATE CLASSROOMS THAT PROVIDE STUDENTS WITH CHOICES AND LEADERSHIP OPPORTUNITIES.**

DISCUSSION

Students of all ages learn best in environments that mirror the concepts and values they are expected to learn. Participation and decision making are two critical skills for citizens in a democracy, and classrooms should provide ample opportunities to practice them. Students participate when they are encouraged to do so; they become decision makers by learning from their choices. When teachers create tightly structured schedules and routines and make every decision, they deny students opportunities to exercise choice, think critically about their classroom, and make decisions that affect them as individuals or as a group. Even the busiest schedules should allow ways for students to exercise choice. Voting on a book to read, identifying an activity for recess, determining the type of project in which to engage—all are ways to exercise choice and learn about balancing individual interests with the needs of the group.

Teachers can model democratic practices by encouraging students to express their ideas, listening respectfully, and guiding students to be tolerant of different opinions.

Teachers can also devise activities that give each student, at some point during the school year, an opportunity to exercise leadership. While some students eagerly accept this role, others need to be encouraged.

In a democratic classroom, community issues, national and local elections, and current events can be integrated into the curriculum. Such themes offer opportunities for expressing opinions, debate, service, research, and simulations, all of which provide a rich context for acquiring civic competence as well as content knowledge.

CLASSROOM EXAMPLES

The beginning of the school year is the time to establish a democratic climate. Teachers can encourage students to express their ideas about the ways they might best function successfully as a group. What guidelines will assist everyone in the class to interact positively? How can conflict be settled amicably? How will classroom responsibilities be handled fairly?

Students can identify and discuss the significant ideas that will guide classroom activities and behaviors for the year. The ideas should be positive and describe what *will* be done, not what won't: "We will share ideas and materials, and be kind, honest, and considerate with each other." The resulting guidelines can be posted prominently in the classroom and referred to when challenges arise.

Classroom meetings can be made a part of the weekly schedule; at these regular meetings, students discuss learning climate, issues of interest or conflict, and ways to meet individual needs. The meetings offer students a forum for listening to others, considering needs, offering opinions, and understanding that each student is responsible not only to herself, but to the entire group. These activities develop experience in thinking beyond oneself to the greater good.

Kristy Herrera's 5th grade students at Jackson-Keller Elementary School in San Antonio, Texas, held class meetings when the need emerged—and students determined the need for meetings more often than the teacher. Issues ranging from name calling to refusing to share the basketball during recess affected student interactions and the learning climate. Students established a few simple ground rules for class meetings: Be honest, let the speaker finish before commenting, search for fair solutions, and remember that everyone has feelings. Herrera reported amazing levels of sensitivity, solidarity, and reflection as students grappled with issues. During these meetings, students frequently made connections between topics of study and their own situation, referring to people or events that matched those in their classroom. Discipline referrals vanished and open discussion flourished in an environment where students knew that their needs would be addressed and that their voices counted.

As a class, students grew far more supportive and understanding of each other, which their teacher attributed to the openness of class meetings and the opportunities for students to come to understand what someone was thinking when they acted, instead of simply looking at the results of the act. Herrera's students learned about compromise, negotiation, and the good of the many by living those concepts during class meetings, not merely by reading about them.

RESOURCES
Bragaw 1991; Costa & Liebmann, 1997b; Morse, 1993.

● STRATEGY 4.2: INTEGRATE CIVIC VIRTUES INTO THE DAILY CURRICULUM. TEACHERS CREATIVELY INTEGRATE CHARACTER DEVELOPMENT INTO CLASSROOM LIFE, RATHER THAN AS AN ADD-ON PROGRAM.

DISCUSSION

The beginnings of public schooling in the United States were rooted in the acquisition of virtue far more than in academic mastery. Horace Mann, the father of the common school, spoke emphatically about the mission of public education. In 1837, he wrote that schools should " . . . teach virtue before knowledge, for although the latter should not be ignored, knowledge without virtue poses its own dangers. . . . " (Michaelson, 1970, p. 77) In our own century, the Holocaust and the horrors of Pol Pot's regime have taught us undeniably that knowledge without conscience leads to horrendous destruction.

Today's intense focus on academic achievement seems to narrow opportunities for teaching and learning about civic and personal virtue, which overlap extensively. Teachers pressed by mandates to teach content and skills are reluctant to add still another program. Yet the most effective programs that address virtues are *not* add-ons, but part of the school's daily curriculum and life.

History, community life, political issues, the sciences—just a few of the topics of study in schools—inherently contain ethical issues. The study of history illuminates a host of exemplary lives and events as well as those that are less exemplary. Environmental topics, immigration, and voting are samples of value-laden political issues. In the sciences, older students profit from examining the ethics of cloning, the integrity of the scientific process, and the legalization of drugs.

Lessons of civic virtue also abound in children's literature and the classics, many of which teachers already incorporate into classes from kindergarten through high school. Learning how to extract such issues from mandated topics of study, and then support them with literature and meaningful activities, is the key to integrating civic virtue into everyday classroom life. This approach fits with brain-based teaching and learning as it links themes and concepts for more efficient acquisition, storage, and retrieval of information.

CLASSROOM EXAMPLES

At Mantua Elementary School in Fairfax, Virginia, 6th graders study the early exploration of North America as a prelude to learning their state's history. In social studies, they read about the early navigators and settlements; in language arts, they augment their historical study by reading primary documents and accounts of voyages and settlements. These accounts abound with value-laden concepts: idealism, fortitude, and sacrifice—and their opposites, parochialism, laziness, and greed. Each attribute offers opportunities for discussion about how these qualities affected individuals and the settlement, and how these attributes manifest themselves in communities today.

In music, Mantua 6th graders learned songs of the early settlements and searched the songs for clues to lifestyles and values. In physical education, students learned about and played the games of Native Americans and early settlers, discussing the rules for the games, their purposes, and similarities to sports today. Rather than isolate issues of values in a separate "character education" program, teachers at Mantua Elementary School integrate them into content areas, making such study entirely relevant for both historical and contemporary topics.

At Prairie Star Elementary School in Leawood, Kansas, civic virtue begins as a visual phenomenon. In the school's media center, a colorful 60-foot mural depicts seven core virtues taken from *The Basic School: A Community for Learning*, a report from the late Ernest L. Boyer, president of The Carnegie Foundation for the Advancement of Teaching.

Prairie Star is a member of the Basic School Network, a reform initiative that promotes a commitment to character along with academic achievement. The mural sits at the very heart of the school; it is the first thing anyone sees when entering the media center. The concepts of honesty, respect, responsibility, compassion, self-discipline, perseverance, and giving are conveyed both in writing and in depictions of children engaged in activity. Gus Jacob, Prairie Star's principal, notes, "Having those virtues in front of us every single day is a powerful reminder for all of us—staff, students, parents, and visitors—of the things we believe in at Prairie Star."

The school's integrated teaching units connect these consensus virtues to all content areas and to daily classroom events so that the "language of the virtues" comes alive in the life of the school. Student vocabulary and writing are marked by references to responsibility, tolerance, patience, and perseverance. Making a schoolwide commitment to virtues that enhance a democratic community causes such issues to become part of Prairie Star's everyday life and language.

Making it easier for teachers to incorporate virtues into their classrooms is the work of the Developmental Studies Center (DSC) in Oakland, California. DSC develops literature units for Caldecott and Newbery award-winning books that emphasize consensus and civic virtues, promote character development, and teach literacy skills. Many teachers routinely choose such top-notch literature for their classrooms, and DSC materials show how teachers can use them to convey value-laden issues as well as to promote academic achievement. The units use an integrated format that includes the arts, other content areas, and an activity involving parents. Also available are videos and guidebooks that offer proven activities and strategies for class meetings, parent involvement, and noncompetitive events for students and families that support consensus virtues for a democratic society. These materials make it easy for teachers to infuse the values and virtues of a democracy into daily classroom life.

RESOURCES

Hamilton & Zeldin, 1989; Newmann, 1989; Vue-Benson & Shumer, 1995.

● STRATEGY 4.3: ENCOURAGE SCHOOL STAFF TO EXEMPLIFY CIVIC VIRTUES. ALL ADULTS IN A SCHOOL—TEACHERS, ADMINISTRATORS, CUSTODIANS, CAFETERIA STAFF, PARENTS, AND VISITORS—MODEL CIVIC VIRTUES AND ACTIVITIES.

DISCUSSION

Students from kindergarten through high school closely observe adult behavior and listen keenly to adult conversation. Frequently, students compare words and actions; they are quick to notice when adults around them are really "walking the talk" or just "talking the talk." Schools in which teachers collaborate, parents and visitors are welcome, students have a voice in issues that influence them, and everyone is respectful are places that model effective civil discourse.

In an era when students grapple with conflicting messages about personal responsibility and face an endless parade of fallen sports, entertainment, and political heroes, adults in schools have the critical responsibility of reflecting on their own behaviors and striving to serve as role models of civic virtue. More than ever, students need to be immersed in a culture that encourages personal and civic responsibility, surrounded by adults who model such values.

Exercising personal responsibility, respecting people and property, sharing resources, assisting those in need, and participating in the political process are civic virtues that mesh with the process of character development. Providing opportunities to discuss facets of civic virtue through the study of historic and contemporary exemplary lives and events offers an effective beginning for student learning in civics.

To assimilate the processes of worthy civil discourse and service, students especially need to be engaged in such activities themselves. Engagement in meaningful projects and endeavors that promote civic responsibility—in the classroom, community, state, and even the nation—is vital training for citizenship. Such activity provides firsthand experience with the intrinsic rewards that accrue from service; students can discover the motivation for establishing service as a way of life, rather than as a one-time requirement in school.

CLASSROOM EXAMPLES

Clinton Kelly Elementary School in Portland, Oregon, flourishes in a culture of poverty by focusing deeply on civic virtue. Under the leadership of Principal Mary Beth Van Cleave, the school has established a program (supported by state and federal funds) to provide extensive family support services on-site.

The program quickly outgrew its original space, and when a home across the street became vacant, both school and community launched an all-out effort to lease it to house a truly comprehensive program with ample space. School staff members, enthusiastic about the project, invested personal time to bring area families needed services while affording them the dignity of work.

The Kelly Community House serves families in need, who, in exchange for assistance, serve others. Ties to the Kelly School are strong; students are involved in a variety of ways. They feel a sense of pride and ownership in Kelly House because many use its services, and in return, give service through it.

When teachers planned a unit on plants and seeds, for example, they developed a service component for students around the theme. Students grew seedlings that they then planted in the Kelly House community garden. Each spring, service projects at the school invariably include tending the floral plots in front of Kelly House to make it an appealing place, volunteering to sort clothes for the community closet, keeping the house and grounds clean, and receiving instruction and working in the community garden. Families who use the Kelly House washing machine help with housecleaning. Schoolchildren who need a shower or a change of clothes know that they are welcome to take what they need, in exchange for service that contributes to the work of Kelly House.

Everyone becomes aware that service is a two-way street. Through their own experiences, students understand that being helped and being able to help others are two sides of the same coin.

Staff members at Benjamin Banneker School in Milford, Delaware, function as exemplars for students. At Banneker, teachers don't just talk about being friendly and welcoming; they model those qualities. Each morning as students enter the school, Banneker teachers, including Principal Kae Keister, welcome every child at the front door, by name. Students feel welcome and valued, and they have the opportunity to practice interpersonal skills each day as they respond to those who greet them and pass that greeting along to classmates.

In September 1997, civic activity and role modeling by adults crossed county lines in northern Virginia. As troubled schools in Washington, D.C., struggled to open in time for the new school year, they faced daunting odds; district crews, struggling to complete major repairs, could not be spared for regular cleanups. Staff and parents of Mantua Elementary in neighboring Fairfax County, Virginia, led by Principal Ellen Schoetzau, volunteered a Saturday to clean an assigned District of Columbia school. Wielding paintbrushes, brooms, and cleaning equipment, these adults helped make the school a welcoming place for children they would never see or work with, but who needed their assistance.

When students observe staff members at Willard Model School in Norfolk, Virginia, they clearly see adults who like one another and respect one another's expertise. Friendly smiles, hugs, laughter, cheerful inquiries, and concern abound as teachers traverse the hallways. Shared materials and ideas are reflected in grade-level meetings as staff members plan curricular projects.

Everyone at Willard serves children. One custodian directs the boys' choir after school. Each member of the custodial staff takes pride that the school remains consistently bright and clean every day. The message to students is clear: Every member of the Willard community is valued for their unique contributions.

When adults in a school work well together, they model community collaboration. When they serve one another, or engage in community service, they exemplify civic responsibility. The conscious decisions adults in schools make about their behavior have far-reaching impact on young people. What school staff members do and say, how they do and say it, and what they choose not to do or say—all convey clear messages. Adults who work with students must continually be mindful that their actions speak as loudly as their words; both actions and words should be aligned with the civic virtues that support our democratic system.

RESOURCES
Boyer, 1995; Goleman, 1995.

● **STRATEGY 4.4**: MONITOR RELEVANT CURRENT EVENTS, POLITICAL ISSUES, AND POLITICIANS. TEACHERS INCORPORATE CURRENT EVENTS, POLITICAL ISSUES, AND PERSONALITIES INTO THE CLASSROOM ON A DAILY BASIS.

DISCUSSION

Teachers in most schools are overwhelmed by the sheer volume of content and skill requirements for which they are accountable over the course of a year. Few are eager to add to the list, yet most are aware that they must attend to issues in the news as they affect their students' lives. Teachers also realize that in too many households, newspapers and magazines—the basic tools of literacy—are not available or valued. The school may be the only place where students are purposely made aware of the world around them. The school, in fact, may be the only place where students are engaged with positive ideas about their government, its benefits, and the responsibilities required of citizens.

Current events have traditionally been the responsibility of the social studies teacher. Usually, only such front-page events as presidential elections or the Olympic Games move social studies to center stage in the classroom. Yet vital *community* issues can be found in the local news nearly every day, and local issues are increasingly influenced by national and international events. Where do such events and personalities fit into a teacher's already crowded planbook?

Relevance is a key concept in brain-based learning, and local news and events are highly relevant, often on a personal level. When a new town ordinance declares that all bicycles must have a registration sticker, or the mayor imposes a curfew, students are directly affected. Creative, concerned teachers from kindergarten through high school have always found ways to connect relevant issues to classroom themes; such issues invariably contain vital content and concepts that support academics.

Real-world examples drive home the abstract concept of cause and effect. Hurricanes, tornadoes, and other natural disasters do not have to occur locally to have an impact on students. Those too young to understand the economic effects of catastrophes can consider ways of preparing themselves for the unexpected or offering assistance to victims. Similarly, a killing frost during a critical part of the growing season can wreak havoc overnight on Florida citrus farmers. But their misfortune translates later into skyrocketing prices for orange-juice drinkers.

The inclusion of current events helps us stretch our thinking beyond the usual learning boundaries. It is one thing to study weather patterns and learn that drought causes famine; it is quite another to come to understand how famine can result from war. Students need to begin to perceive the less obvious connections in the world around them, such as those between war and the resulting destruction of crops, livestock, and disputed lands.

Another important reason for monitoring current events is that local news often features community heroes whose selfless generosity of spirit contrasts sharply with most headline stories. In a culture bereft of genuine heroes, learning about those in one's own town—discussing their attributes and how their actions contributed to positive change—is an invaluable lesson in itself.

Studying political campaigns and the positions of the candidates not only creates an awareness of the political process, but allows elementary students to grasp the concepts of comparison and contrast. Older students begin to determine their own beliefs and where they fall within the political spectrum.

Analyzing the utterances of politicians is the first step in holding them accountable. Students need to learn how to make responsible decisions—based on facts as well as preferences—long before they are eligible to vote. Using student versions of weekly news magazines (*Time for Kids*, for instance) or taking advantage of classroom pricing for standard versions brings current events into the classroom and eases students into the habit of keeping abreast of current events.

CLASSROOM EXAMPLES

Across the United States, teachers at every grade level find a variety of ways to study the birth of democracy and the functions of state and local governments. Aligning this study with the tracking of current political and civic events can fit snugly with the need to fulfill district mandates.

Teachers generally use local, state, and national elections to highlight the study of past political events and show continuity and change in the political process. In monitoring local politics, students can become involved in researching issues and candidates, polling in the school and community, and watching local newscasts to gain information. Left to their own devices, few elementary-age students (or even many high schoolers) will do this without encouragement.

Many teachers invite local candidates to present their ideas in the classroom. Students of all ages thus have a firsthand opportunity to consider the issues, formulate thoughtful questions about them, and inquire about the candidate's motivation to run for elected office. Issues of altruism, patriotism, special interests, and talents come to the forefront in such discussions, offering students invaluable insights about the privileges and responsibilities of our democratic system.

As students define the issues inherent in elections, they will begin to discuss them, hear a variety of viewpoints about them, relate them to past issues, and connect them to future scenarios. By doing so, they begin the process of responsible decision making so essential to the maintenance of democracy.

Environmental topics—weather, pollution, recycling—are perennial issues of study in every school. Monitoring local, state, and national weather helps students to see the commonality of such issues nationwide, the interdependence of our choices with regard to the environment, and our connectedness to the natural world, no matter where we live. Many teachers are using the Internet to allow their classes to work collaboratively with others around the world—studying weather patterns, disasters, and environmental issues that have immediate or far-reaching effects on people everywhere. Affording students opportunities to observe and become engaged with events and people—whether in their neighborhood, city, state, nation, or beyond—provides a window to the world outside the school that helps youngsters acquire, understand, and practice skills that will make them contributing adults.

RESOURCES
National Education Goals Panel, 1992; Parker, 1989.

● **STRATEGY 4.5: USE DISCUSSION FORUMS, MOCK TRIALS, AND DEBATES. TEACHERS INCORPORATE FORMATS USED IN THE POLITICAL PROCESS FOR LEARNING ABOUT CIVIC ISSUES.**

DISCUSSION

The words "government" and "politics" may elicit indifference from students, but the political process is far

from dull. Yesterday and today, discussion, debate, and the trial process have always involved invective, overstatement, and outsized egos. The political process is colorful, controversial, and often larger than life. Students miss most of the intrigue when they limit their study to textbooks.

Encourage youngsters to look closely at political cartoons past and present, and at newspaper or TV coverage of debates, campaigns, and trials. A careful reading of the language of such events simultaneously evokes elegance, sensationalism, and crudity, providing a different (and far less stuffy) view of an intensely stimulating process that has the power to arouse partisan passions.

Engaging students in discussion forums, mock trials, and debates—and also experiencing such events firsthand or through media coverage—can turn learning into a truly active, exciting event requiring of participants a variety of skills and content knowledge.

CLASSROOM EXAMPLES

Many teachers use class meetings as a means of airing issues that affect the relationships in the room. This same format is particularly well suited to discussions of political issues, because it promotes tolerance of many viewpoints, reflective responses, and the useful practice of listening before speaking. Successful classroom meetings address issues highly relevant to students. In fact, establishing relevance is the key to using this format for more academically focused content.

Beyond classroom meetings, experienced classroom teachers use debate as an integral, challenging part of learning content through process. Debate requires a deep understanding of the issues at hand; it provides opportunities for persuasive oral presentations and requires students to articulate their point of view.

While middle and high school students may study the Scopes or Lindbergh trials and debate the pros and cons of these landmark cases, elementary teachers have introduced young children to the judicial process by putting characters from nursery rhymes and storybooks "on trial." Children gain a new perspective on familiar stories when they must think about Goldilocks as a housebreaker, or Jack the beanstalk climber as a common thief for stealing the Giant's possessions. Such activities encourage young children to ponder civic issues and behaviors and develop language skills, too.

Many students are willing to offer opinions or join in discussions, but only a very few students are eager to engage in public speaking. This forum plays a critical role in a democracy's political processes, however. Observing and critiquing local, state, and national candidates as they debate election issues gives students an opportunity to learn from politicians' styles of communication. Choosing important issues (e.g., nuclear power, toxic wastes, exploiting our national resources) and debating their pros and cons requires students to understand thoroughly the concepts inherent in each issue to persuade others to their way of thinking. Students can observe TV debates and critique them. Videotapes of student debates allow students to critique their own and others' performances.

RESOURCES
Caine & Caine, 1991; Costa & Liebmann, 1997a; Kiernan, 1990.

● STRATEGY 4.6: PLAN LEARNING PROJECTS AROUND CIVICS ISSUES. TEACHERS USE CIVIC ISSUES AND EVENTS AS A BASIS FOR DEVELOPING THEMES AND PROJECTS FOR STUDY.

DISCUSSION

Connecting learning to life experiences helps students acquire, store, and retrieve knowledge more effectively and efficiently. Planning themes of study and learning projects around important community issues gets students involved in learning that affects their lives directly.

Issues in every community have educational ramifications—community growth and development, for example. As farmlands, forests, wetlands, and quiet neighborhoods give way to shopping malls and housing developments, how should growth be regulated? How much area should be paved over? What happens to the wildlife displaced by urban and suburban sprawl? What are the ramifications of increased waste disposal for the local water supply? In becoming aware of such issues, students come to realize that the outcomes will directly affect their community's future.

Every community has values that define citizens' beliefs, attitudes, and behaviors. How do community laws and celebrations reflect those beliefs? Students can explore those aspects of their community and participate in them to the extent that is appropriate for them.

On a larger stage, what national issues affect all U.S. citizens? Environmental policies, health care, child care, minimum wage, and tax reform are civic issues well within the grasp of middle and high school students, especially

when teachers make such issues relevant through personal connections, so that students can relate them to their own lives. And all of these issues can come alive in any classroom—not just social studies, but science and math, too. Using newspapers and news magazines, which many students will read with more enthusiasm than a text, ensures early and frequent exposure to national, state, and local issues and provides the basis for lifelong interest in the political life of their community and nation.

CLASSROOM EXAMPLES

At Tiospa Zina Tribal School in Agency Village, South Dakota, five Dakotah values form the basis for community attitudes, beliefs, and regulations: *ohoda* (respect for self, earth, all living things), *okciya* (sharing, giving service), *tehinda* (tenderness and responsibility for children), *wicake* (truthfulness), and *waunsida* (empathy for all living things). Students at Tiospa Zina celebrated Earth Day by showing *ohoda* to Mother Earth. Armed with trash bags and gloves, all classes combed the areas approaching the school and its grounds to remove debris left after winter snows and spring winds.

The cleanup was followed by another form of *ohoda* to Mother Earth: exhibition dancing by students in full dress costume. Honoring community values through school activity and celebration is only one of the ways in which students can build awareness of the mores that define their region, state, or nation.

Schools nationwide used the 1996 presidential election not only to create awareness of the issues on which the candidates based their campaigns, but to learn about the polling process. Untold numbers of teachers created math lessons from school and community polling activities that involved students in understanding the purpose, mechanics, and uses of polling in the political process, while learning and using math skills appropriate to their grade levels.

Internet connections are allowing students to learn the effects of civic issues around the world. Teachers who use such technology report that students learn a powerful lesson when they examine issues in far-off communities; many are identical to those in the United States. Students learn rapidly that the world, for all its diversity and wonder, is indeed a small place, and that what is important in a distant culture quite often affects events close to home.

RESOURCES
Drake, 1993; Jacobs, 1997; Wade, 1997.

● STRATEGY 4.7: PLAN AND IMPLEMENT SERVICE PROJECTS WITH STUDENTS. TEACHERS INCLUDE SERVICE PROJECTS WITH UNITS OF STUDY TO GIVE STUDENTS EXPERIENCE IN REACHING AND THINKING BEYOND THEIR OWN NEEDS TO ASSIST OTHERS IN THE COMMUNITY.

DISCUSSION

The Puritans who settled Massachusetts Bay Colony shaped a plan for community governance even before landing in the New World. They made clear the communal responsibility to build a new settlement and provide for those who were unable to do so. That communal tradition existed on the North American continent long before the arrival of European settlers, of course, but the encoding of such civic responsibility has been part of U.S. democracy since its very beginnings, and was ever present in religious tenets long before that time.

Along the way, unfortunately, the focus of U.S. society changed, moving away from this commitment to the common good. Somehow the idea of service went out of vogue, lost amid the ever-increasing curricular demands on schools and the ever-shifting bandwagon approach to reform that seems to characterize U.S. education. The usual food drives at Thanksgiving and the dimes collected for various local charities persisted, as did other small-scale, scattered approaches to service, but no clear-cut, consistent emphasis on service existed in schools for some time.

In the 1990s, there was a resurgence of attention to service, however, as schools "rediscovered" best practices and the political climate focused on values. Today, schools across the United States engage in a variety of service projects, some of which have become institutionalized in the schools' culture. Observers of education agree that the best projects are developed by students and tied directly to classroom learning. Such projects offer students an opportunity to look beyond themselves and to experience the intrinsic rewards available only in giving service to others.

CLASSROOM EXAMPLES

At Jackson-Keller Elementary School in San Antonio, Texas, as part of a unit about being happy and healthy, kindergartners decided to make the Christmas season happier and healthier for those who might be unable to enjoy it. They worked diligently to create Christmas ornaments that they sold to classmates who purchased their handiwork enthusiastically, knowing that the proceeds would serve the community. Students purchased gifts that were placed under a community tree at the local shopping mall. Many were able to see the smiles and hear the cries of delight as children whose holidays would not have been quite so happy opened the gifts.

Throughout the project, teachers discussed the act of giving one's talents, time, and funds to others—and time was spent discussing the good feelings that such actions incur. The project's effects were profound. As a result, service projects became part of every thematic unit in kindergarten.

The Subaru Corporation awarded national recognition for a service project to Gina Rau's lower primary multi-age class at Irving Weber Elementary School in Iowa City, Iowa. In learning about their community, Rau's students discovered a homeless shelter near their school. How could people be homeless when there was housing in the community? they asked. How did they get that way? What was it like to be homeless?

Rau led students in exploring their questions. When they learned the answers, the class decided unanimously to do something for the homeless in Iowa City. They contacted the shelter and asked what would be helpful to the residents. Many everyday items were needed, the shelter director told the students: soap, shampoo, tissues, toothpaste, paper towels, and toys. Working in collaboration with other classes, Rau's students mobilized school families to donate items to the shelter. As Rau collected the donations, students put the items in baskets and wrote individual notes of encouragement to children at the shelter. The class members delivered the items themselves. Not only did these children have an opportunity to serve others, but they saw and understood firsthand how people become homeless and how homelessness can happen to anyone. Many wrote at length about that experience; clearly, they had developed a sense of empathy for the homeless as well as a greater appreciation of their own good fortune.

Many U.S. high schools now require a service project for graduation. Often these projects are large-scale endeavors that focus on environmental cleanups, petition gathering for community projects, or volunteer tutoring for children in elementary and middle schools. Most students enjoy seeing the results of their efforts, develop new awareness about their community, spark interest in a career path, and remain engaged with their project after its completion.

Resources

Lewis & Espeland, 1995; Wilson, 1994.

● **Strategy 4.8:** Create Learning Partnerships and Internships with Government and Community Agencies. Students become involved with community agencies for active learning experiences with a community focus.

Discussion

Learners of all ages learn best through active participation and hands-on experience. Reading about the work of government and community agencies leaves many students cold. Seeing the work firsthand, however, can generate interest and questions. And actually taking part in the work brings a whole new dimension to learning. Schools attuned to the benefits of active learning—such as motivation, investment, and continued learning—are going beyond the classroom to tap people, agencies, and projects in the community to provide experiential learning.

The traditional ceremonial field trip is being augmented or replaced by daylong placements in a variety of settings that match students' interests or classroom themes. In such cases, students studying an environmental issue may spend a day with those in the local environmental office to learn more about the issue and how it is being handled.

Students studying current events no longer need simply watch a TV news broadcast during school hours. Instead, they may spend a day at a television station shadowing journalists. Students interested in the origins of stories can learn about the wire services and their role in shaping the news.

During election campaigns, middle and high school students have served as volunteers at campaign headquarters, where they answer phones, distribute information, check polls, and participate in behind-the-scenes activity that often affords them time with the candidate and always offers a deeper understanding of the election process.

Increasing numbers of middle and high school students are spending a day in their local courthouse to learn about the roles of those involved in the justice system. As they observe proceedings, students learn the kinds of problems prevalent in their community and the consequences of certain actions; frequently they speak with a judge, prosecutor, or defense attorney. This real-life experience is far more compelling and lasting in its effects than any written description.

Classroom Examples

At the School of Environmental Studies in Apple Valley, Minnesota, the study of civics permeates the school's interdisciplinary curriculum, weaving through coverage of language and literature, social studies and environmental studies. High school juniors apply the skills and knowledge they acquired in an interdisciplinary study of the ecology of ponds (reading Thoreau and engaging in historical data gathering as well as simply studying pond ecology), working with the city engineer's office to monitor water quality in the community.

Students begin working at the pond site on the school's campus, and in groups of four or five are then assigned a community pond to study. They learn procedures for sampling water quality, analyzing their findings, and reporting them. Students learn how to blend process and content to produce authentic, verifiable results that meet standards of the engineer's office. Along the way, they are serving the community with information that eases the strain on the city budget.

Seniors at the School of Environmental Studies complete a final project intended to provide something of lasting benefit to their community. This civics-based exit project requires research on community needs and priorities. Students create proposals based on their research and contract with school officials and government agencies to define completion schedules and standards. Civic activity is an integral part of student responsibility and learning at this high school.

At Downtown Open Elementary School in Minneapolis, Minnesota, students in grades 3 through 5 focus on democratic government as part of a thematic unit. Downtown Open is located in an office building in the heart of Minneapolis, and students use the city as an extension of their classroom. During the study of government, students attended city council meetings and listened to debate in the council chambers. They addressed questions to council members during sessions that solicited community input. Young people observed the purpose and dynamics of the debate process and used their knowledge to stage their own debates in class.

In their study of citizens in a democracy, students at Downtown Open learned that "citizen" is defined as one who does the work of the people. As a result of their study, children learned to use class meetings to discuss school rules and solve issues that arise during the course of a day. Elections were held for class offices; these officers conduct class meetings. Students are working to change some school rules through the use of petitions—and they have learned that some other rules cannot be changed. Using such formats with elementary students creates a solid foundation for their participation in the democratic process as adults.

RESOURCES

Erickson, 1996; Seigel, 1993.

● STRATEGY 4.9: HOST SPEAKERS FROM GOVERNMENT AGENCIES AND COMMUNITY ORGANIZATIONS. GOVERNMENT AND COMMUNITY MEMBERS VISIT SCHOOLS TO ADDRESS THEIR WORK AND MODEL SERVICE TO SCHOOLS.

DISCUSSION

Just as government and community organizations are becoming extended classrooms for learning civics, members of these institutions are increasingly visiting classrooms to discuss their work with students. Teachers have always tapped the occasional parent with a community agency job or a government connection, but today the use of such community members is becoming an integral part of classroom learning. As a result of national attention being focused on education, government and community agencies seem to sense the wisdom of investing staff time in schools to add to their expertise and perspective.

In high schools, the school nurse as a speaker on health topics has been replaced by the local hospital director or coordinator of government health services. In addition to learning about health problems, students gain insight into the work of the agency, career options available, and qualifications involved in such work.

CLASSROOM EXAMPLES

Visits by authors of children's books (especially in the author's community) have long been standard fare in classrooms. Visits by local politicians were rare. Now politicians are learning that children benefit tremendously from adult involvement in education. A visit by an adult, especially an important or well-known adult, states clearly to students that education matters.

In Broadway, Virginia, Broadway High School hosted Oliver North, a controversial figure from the Reagan years, during his run for office in Virginia. The controversy surrounding North made him even more interesting to students and boosted attendance at his appearance. Students in the government class gained much more from being able to question North personally than from anything they could have read about him in the media.

At Danebo Elementary School in Eugene, Oregon, local architects visit the school and work with teachers to help children understand the ways in which function helps to shape building design and existing building designs shape the community.

At Public School #7 in New York City's Spanish Harlem, members of the city business community provide a variety of in-kind services and materials to the school, as well as funds to enhance students' learning opportunities. Members of the Juilliard School of Music donate their time and talents to bring the arts to students and present programs to a community that might otherwise miss such performances. While students and community members are exposed to the arts, they are also learning about the many professions of their New York neighbors, and about the ways in which people use their talents to serve their community.

RESOURCES

Bragaw, 1991; Costa & Liebmann, 1997c; Healy, 1990.

BIBLIOGRAPHY

Ackerman, S. (1992). *Discovering the brain*. Washington, DC: National Academy Press.

Armstrong, T. (1987). *In their own way*. Los Angeles: Jeremy P. Tarcher, Inc.

Association for Supervision and Curriculum Development. (1997a). *Topic pack: Brain-based learning*. Alexandria, VA: Author.

Association for Supervision and Curriculum Development. (1997b). *Topic pack: Integrated curriculum*. Alexandria, VA: Author.

Boyer, E. L. (1995). *The basic school: A community for learning*. San Francisco: Jossey-Bass, Inc.

Bragaw, D. H. (1989). In training to be a citizen: The elementary student and the public interest. *Social Science Record, 26*, 27–29.

Bragaw, D. H. (1991). Expanding social studies to encompass the public interest. *NASSP Bulletin, 75*(531), 25–31.

Caine, G., & Caine, R. N. (1991). *Making connections: Teaching and the human brain*. Alexandria, VA: Association for Supervision and Curriculum Development.

Caine, R. N., & Caine, G. (1997a). *Education on the edge of possibility*. Alexandria, VA: Association for Supervision and Curriculum Development.

Caine, R. N., & Caine, G. (1997b). *Unleashing the power of perceptual change: The potential of brain-based teaching*. Alexandria, VA: Association for Supervision and Curriculum Development.

Center for Civic Education. (1994). *National standards for civics and government*, Calabasas, CA: Author.

Coates, R. E., Sr. (1996). Thomas Jefferson on politics and government: Quotations from the writings of Thomas Jefferson. Available: JeffQuotes@eyter.freeservers.com

Costa, A. L., & Kallick, B. (Eds.). (1995). *Assessment in the learning organization: Shifting the paradigm*. Alexandria, VA: Association for Supervision and Curriculum Development.

Costa, A. L., & Liebmann, R. L. (Eds.). (1997a). *Envisioning process as content: Toward a renaissance curriculum*. Thousand Oaks, CA: Corwin Press.

Costa, A. L., & Liebmann, R. L. (Eds.). (1997b). *Supporting the spirit of learning: When process is content*. Thousand Oaks, CA: Corwin Press.

Costa, A. L., & Liebmann, R. L. (Eds.). (1997c). *The process-centered school: Sustaining a renaissance community*. Thousand Oaks, CA: Corwin Press.

Cutler, B. (1997). *Collaborating for integrated curriculum* [Audiotape]. Alexandria, VA: Association for Supervision and Curriculum Development.

Davis, J. (1997). *Mapping the mind: The secrets of the human brain and how it works*. Secaucus, NJ: Birch Lane Press.

Diamond, M. (1988). *Enriching heredity: The impact of the environment on the anatomy of the brain*. New York: Free Press.

Discovery Communications, Inc. (1994). *The brain within: Evolution and perception, memory and renewal, matter over mind* [Videotape Series]. Bethesda, MD: Discovery Enterprises Group.

Drake, S. M. (1993). *Planning integrated curriculum: The call to adventure*. Alexandria, VA: Association for Supervision and Curriculum Development.

Erickson, L. (1996). *Designing integrated curriculum that promotes higher-level thinking* [Audiotape]. Alexandria, VA: Association for Supervision and Curriculum Development.

Fitzpatrick, K., & Edwards, B. (1997). *A shared vision for student learning: Implications for designing an integrated curriculum*

[Audiotape]. Alexandria, VA: Association for Supervision and Curriculum Development.

Goleman, D. (1995). *Emotional intelligence: Why it can matter more than IQ*. New York: Bantam Books.

Greenfield, S. (1997). *The Human brain: A guided tour*. New York: Basic Books.

Greenspan, S. I. (1997). *The growth of the mind and the endangered origins of intelligence*. New York: Addison Wesley.

Hamilton, S. F., & Zeldin, R. S. (1989). Learning civics in the community. *Curriculum Inquiry, 17*(4), 407–420.

Hart, L. (1985). *Human brain, human learning*. New York: Longman.

Healy, J. M. (1990). *Endangered minds: Why our children don't think*. New York: Simon and Schuster.

Howard, P. J. (1997). *The owner's manual for the brain: Everyday applications from mind-brain research*. Tucson: Zephyr Press.

Jacobs, H.H. (1989). *Interdisciplinary curriculum: Design and implementation*. Alexandria, VA: Association for Supervision and Curriculum Development.

Jacobs, H. H. (1997). *Mapping the big picture: Integrating curriculum and assessment K–12*. Alexandria, VA: Association for Supervision and Curriculum Development.

Jensen, E. (1998). *Teaching with the brain in mind*. Alexandria, VA: Association for Supervision and Curriculum Development.

Kendall, J. S., & Marzano, R. J. (1997). *Content knowledge: A compendium of standards and benchmarks for K–12 education* (2nd ed.). Aurora, CO: McREL; Alexandria, VA: Association for Supervision and Curriculum Development.

Kiernan, H. (1990). Teaching civic identity and civic writing in the information age. *Social Education, 56*(1), 9–12. (ERIC Document Reproduction Service No. ED 348 340).

Kirby, K. (1989). *Community service and civic education: ERIC digest*. Bloomington, IN: ERIC Clearinghouse for Social Studies/Social Foundation Education.

Kotulak, R. (1996). *Inside the brain: Revolutionary discoveries of how the mind works*. Kansas City, MO: Andrews and McMeely.

Lewis, B. A., & Espeland, P. (1995). *The kid's guide to service projects*. Minneapolis, MN: Free Spirit Publishing, Inc.

Marzano, R. J., & Kendall, J. S. (1996). *A comprehensive guide to designing standards-based districts, schools, and classrooms*. Aurora, CO: McREL; Alexandria, VA: Association for Supervision and Curriculum Development.

Marzano, R. J., & Pickering, D. J. (1997). *Dimensions of learning teacher's manual*. Alexandria, VA: Association for Supervision and Curriculum Development; Aurora, CO: McREL.

Marzano, R. J., Pickering, D.J., & McTighe, J. (1993). *Assessing student outcomes: Performance assessment using the dimensions of learning model*. Alexandria, VA: Association for Supervision and Curriculum Development.

McBrien, L. J., & Brandt, R. S. (1997). *The language of learning: A guide to education terms*. Alexandria, VA: Association for Supervision and Curriculum Development.

Michaelson, Robert. (1970). *Piety in the public school*. New York: The Macmillan Co.

Morse, S. W. (1993). The practice of citizenship: Learn by doing. *Social Studies, 84*(4), 164–167.

National Assessment of Education Progress. (1995, March). *Issues concerning a national assessment of ethics: Executive summary*, Washington, DC: Author.

National Education Goals Panel. (1992). *Assessing citizenship: The goal 3 technical planning subgroup report on citizenship report*. (Report No. 92-06): Washington, DC: Author. (ERIC Document Reproduction Service No. ED 354 180).

Newmann, F. M. (1989). Reflective civic participation. *Social Education, 53*(6), 357–360, 366.

Novitt-Moreno, A. D. (1995). *How your brain works*. Emeryville, CA: Ziff-Davis Press.

Ornstein, R. (1991). *The evolution of consciousness: The origins of the way we think*. New York: Simon and Schuster.

Parker, W. C. (1989). Participatory citizenship: Civics in the strong sense. *Social Education, 53*(6), 353–354.

Pert, C. B. (1997). *Molecules of emotion: Why you feel the way you feel*. New York: Scribner.

Restak, R. (1991). *The brain has a mind of its own*. New York: Harmony Books.

Restak, R. (1993). *Receptors*. New York: Bantam.

Restak, R. (1995). *Brainscapes*. New York: Hyperion.

Schacter, D. L. (1996). *Searching for memory: The brain, the mind, and the past*. New York: Basic Books.

Seigel, S. (1993). Democratic education, student empowerment, and community service: Theory and practice. *Equity and Excellence in Education, 26*(2), 65–70.

Somer, E. (1995). *Food and mood: How the nutrients in food improve memory, energy levels, sleep patterns, weight management, and attitude*. New York: Henry Holt and Company.

Sylwester, R. (1995). *A celebration of neurons: An educator's guide to the brain*. Alexandria, VA: Association for Supervision and Curriculum Development.

Taylor, R. T. (1997). *Connecting the curriculum: Using an integrated interdisciplinary, thematic approach* [Audiotape]. Alexandria, VA: Association for Supervision and Curriculum Development.

Vue-Benson, R. C., & Shumer, R. D. (1995). *Civics, social studies, and service topic bibliography*. Minneapolis: National Service-Learning Cooperative Clearinghouse—University of Minnesota.

Wade, R. C. (1997). *Community service learning: A guide to including service in the public school curriculum*. Albany, NY: State University of New York Press.

Wilson, S. (1994). When students volunteer to feed the hungry: Some considerations for educators. *Social Studies, 85*(2), 88–90.

Wolfe, P., & Sorgren, M. (1990). *Mind, memory, and learning*. Fairfax, VA: MM & L.

Wurtman, J. (1986). *Managing your mind and mood through food*. New York: Harper & Row (Perennial Library).

5

STRATEGIES FOR INCREASING ACHIEVEMENT IN GEOGRAPHY

MARY E. HAAS

The teaching of geography, which I consider one of the great basic sciences, can help students discover for themselves the great complexity of the earth, its interlocking components and the manner in which it helps to determine human life.

—James A. Michener, 1991

The study of geography expands one's knowledge of and curiosity about the world. For many it leads to lives filled with travel, excitement, discovery—and sometimes danger! Realizing people's yearning for just such enrichment, in 1898 Alexander Graham Bell encouraged his son-in-law Gilbert Grosvenor to begin the process of turning a scientific journal into the popular magazine we now call *National Geographic*.

During the 21st century, our traditionally localized concerns will continue to grow in scope, increasingly affected by remote, far-flung events. Far more than our parents ever did, our children will have to learn to adapt to bewildering changes. Among such changes, the fact that common household items are manufactured with parts and materials from many other nations prompts migration and immigration, and often results in the loss of jobs close to home. Even those who do not move find themselves encountering a more diverse mixture of people, who see the world from a greater variety of perspectives, sometimes informative and sometimes quite threatening. Good old geography—a subject long taken for granted in our schools—has emerged as a dynamic and rapidly changing discipline essential to the lives of all citizens.

For decades, however, geography was a woefully neglected topic. There were a host of reasons for its neglect: the difficulty in breaking the topic into small, easily taught, easily tested parts; the desire of the United States to isolate itself from the political strife of other nations; an increased interest in attending to more interpersonal human relations (social sciences); the scarcity of geographic scholars in the universities to adequately prepare prospective teachers; and textbooks that turned geography into long lists of facts and map coordinates. Indeed, once students mastered the most elementary map skills, geography was no longer considered challenging and often became a course relegated to poorer students.

Today that perception has changed dramatically. Geography is considered an important topic for all students, beginning as early as kindergarten and continuing throughout the school years (see Figures 5.1 and 5.2). The content of geography is relatively well represented in the elementary and middle school curriculums and in various textbook series. However, the ways in which geography is integral to and integrated with the content of other social sciences, history, and the natural sciences is *not* clearly defined, in the minds of either teachers or textbook authors. At all grade levels, creative teachers who know the importance of geography and who approach its study enthusiastically can make better use of textbook resources and find in their local communities a ready-made laboratory. Moreover, computers now bring the resources of distant communities into every classroom, exponentially expanding available teaching resources.

FIGURE 5.1
Comparison Standards for Curriculum and Instruction in Geography

CURRICULUM

Traditional Emphasis

- Geography is part of the integrated social studies curriculum presented in a disorganized manner for grades K–8, with perhaps an elective course in high school.
- Local content is used in primary grades; national and world content is used in higher grades.
- Learn and use map and globe skills.

- Locate and describe places.
- Memorize facts and lists of resources.
- Emphasize regions, stressing economic importance to the United States.
- Perspective: Use or control physical environment for economic benefits.

New Emphasis

- Geography has a carefully identified role in the integrated social studies curriculum for grades K–12, with perhaps an elective course in high school.
- Local and world content is interspersed throughout all grades.
- Ask and answer geographic questions; acquire, describe, and analyze geographic information.
- Locate, describe, and analyze places.
- Stress geographic concepts and interpretations.
- Emphasize how people use geography to help solve life problems.
- Perspectives: Spatial relationships and ecological relationships affect how acts of people in the past, present, and future affect their lives and the policies of governments and businesses.

INSTRUCTION

Traditional Emphasis

- Textbook based
- Map reading skills; drill and practice work sheets

- Color maps
- Teacher or film delivers information
- Students absorb information

New Emphasis

- Multiple resources
- Active learning by asking geographic questions (where? why there?)
- Make, read, and interpret maps
- Seek relationships among places and factors
- Students perform research from multiple databases, chart and interpret data, solve problems, and apply findings from spatial and ecological perspectives

THE STATE OF THE ART

Results from the National Assessment of Educational Progress's (NAEP) 1994 assessment in geography provided information on what students knew and could do. At each of the grade levels tested (4, 8, and 12), about 70 percent of the students scored at or above the Basic level; 22 percent of the 4th graders, 28 percent of the 8th graders, and 27 percent of the 12th graders performed at the Proficient level, defined as "solid academic performance." Across the grades, students with scores in the higher percentiles were more able to work with a range of geographic tools, create maps based on tabular or narrative data, grasp processes and relationships, bring outside knowledge to bear on answering questions, and analyze data. Other major findings included the following:

- White and Asian students scored higher than black and Hispanic students.
- The higher the parent's level of education, the higher the student's performance.

FIGURE 5.2
National Geography Standards

The World in Spatial Terms
- Know and understand how to use maps and other geographic representations, tools, and technologies to acquire, process, and report information from a spatial perspective.
- Know and understand how to use mental maps to organize information about people, places, and environments in a spatial context.
- Know and understand how to analyze the spatial organization of people, places, and environments on the earth's surface.

Places and Regions
- Know and understand the physical and human characteristics of places.
- Know and understand that people create regions to interpret the earth's complexity.
- Know and understand how culture and experience influence people's perceptions of places and regions.

Physical Systems
- Know and understand the physical processes that shape the patterns of the earth's surface.
- Know and understand the characteristics and spatial distribution of ecosystems on the earth's surface.

Human Systems
- Know and understand the characteristics, distribution, and migration of human populations on the earth's surface.
- Know and understand the characteristics, distribution and complexity of the earth's cultural mosaics.
- Know and understand the patterns and networks of economic interdependence on the earth's surface.
- Know and understand the processes, patterns, and functions of human settlement.
- Know and understand how the forces of cooperation and conflict among people influence the division and control of the earth's surface.

Environment and Society
- Know and understand how human actions modify the physical environment.
- Know and understand how physical systems affect human systems.
- Know and understand the changes that occur in the meaning, use, distribution, and importance of resources.

The Uses of Geography
- Know and understand how to apply geography to interpret the past.
- Know and understand how to apply geography to interpret the present and plan for the future.

Source: Geography Education Standards Project. (1994). *Geography for life: What every young American should know and be able to do in geography.* Washington, D.C.: National Geographic Research & Exploration.

- Overall, male students performed better than female students at all three grade levels, though the differences were not consistent across content areas within geography. In one instance, females significantly outperformed males.
- Students attending nonpublic schools performed at higher levels than those in public schools.
- Some 68 percent of the 4th graders and 70 percent of the 8th graders reported that computers were never used for geography instruction. (This last finding raises questions concerning the opportunities provided to students to study geography. Computers provide much information for the study of geography and need to be available to and used by all students.)

ENHANCING STUDENT ACHIEVEMENT

The 1994 NAEP assessment attempted to identify ways in which students learn geography by asking both teachers and students about selected behaviors believed to be related to geographic achievement (see Figure 5.3).

⊰ FIGURE 5.3
Student Behaviors That Illustrate the Five Geographic Skills

Ask Geographic Questions
- Where is it? Why is it there? What is important about its location? How is its location related to other locations of people, places, and environments?
- Distinguish geographic from nongeographic questions.
- Plan ways to gather information
- Formulate geographic hypotheses and plan how to test them.

Acquire Geographic Information
- Locate, gather, and process information from a variety of maps, including primary, and secondary sources.
- Make and record observations of physical and human characteristics of places.
- Make and record field direct observations.
- Locate information in computer databases.

Organize Geographic Information
- Prepare maps to display data.
- Construct graphs, tables, and diagrams to display geographic information.
- Summarize data integrating various types of materials.
- Make models of physical and cultural landscapes.

Analyze Geographic Information
- Use maps to observe and interpret geographic relationships.
- Use tables and graphs to observe and interpret trends and relationships.
- Use text, photos, and documents to observe and interpret trends and relationships.
- Make inferences and draw conclusions.
- Interpret geographic information from many sources.

Answer Geographic Questions
- Prepare reports in oral and written formats that use maps and graphics.
- Acquire geographic information, draw conclusions, and make generalizations.
- Apply generalizations to solve problems and make decisions.
- Assess validity of generalizations and revise if needed.
- Apply theories from geography to help explain events and places.

Adapted from Geography Education Standards Project. (1994). *Geography for life: What every young American should know and be able to do in geography.* Washington, D.C.: National Geographic Research & Exploration.

Reporting the responses by age and average test score allows us to infer some guidelines for what have been effective teaching strategies and curriculum. Helpful strategies included the following:

- Doing geography projects.
- Using audiovisual materials such as films, videos, and filmstrips.
- Discussing studies at home.
- Studying geography regularly as part of the K–12 social studies curriculum.

Schools and teachers can translate these findings into assignments and instructional procedures beginning in kindergarten and continuing at each grade level until graduation. Teachers across all disciplines can promote the study of geography by

- Using maps and information presented in graphic formats to illustrate practical applications of spatial and graphic skills.
- Encouraging the use of maps, pictures, and graphs in student reports, projects, and presentations, and requiring students to explain the graphics.
- Incorporating examination of local issues and related problems identified in texts or trade books used in class.
- Using and providing additional trade books devoted to cultural and physical geography when investigating geographic questions, issues, and problems.

• Encouraging students to seek out additional sources of information in research books or electronic resources and to share books with friends and parents.

• Using field research to investigate everyday encounters and uses of geography locally when studying current events.

• Inviting parents and others who use geographic data in their work to assist classes or individual students.

• Promoting curiosity and adventure through recreational reading and films related to travel and biographies.

• Providing access to the world and information about it through computer and Internet sources.

ASSESSING ACHIEVEMENT

Recent years have brought frequent reports that U.S. children do not know geography because they fail to correctly locate places on a blank map of the world. Knowing correct location is important to the study of geography, but it is not the only measure of geographic knowledge.

The same reports indicated that children had considerable knowledge about geographic problems related to environmental issues, pollution, and conservation. Past test questions tended to ask for recall of randomly selected, isolated facts and locations. Such tests unfairly selected specific content from textbooks. More recent tests ask students to use geographic skills and read answers from charts and maps and to interpret the information presented by adding short-answer questions to standardized, national tests.

The NAEP assessment reported that most students at each grade level could read maps and graphics to attain information or recognize correct answers illustrated in graphic formats. At each grade level, however, far fewer students were able to use the information to explain relationships or form conclusions. Perhaps this is because they do not encounter the tasks required for performing this more complex mental processing during instruction, or perhaps insufficient time was given to providing opportunities to investigate and consider the reasons for and relationships between answers.

We have long known the importance of grounding instruction in important concepts rather than in isolated facts. If teachers' questions and standardized tests are restricted to isolated facts, however, students will concentrate their learning on these same facts. Why? Because they believe these will be tested instead of the more important relationships between information and an understanding of larger ideas. Therefore, it is vitally important that objectives

related to geographic standards be used in both planning instruction and assessing learning. Students must know, too, that the teacher will assess *all* aspects of study.

Teachers can and should assess student learning through many types of tasks and questions. Locating places on outline maps should continue to be one measure of geographic knowledge, but children should also be asked to describe how they would tell people where a site is located. Giving students new information in graphic and chart form and asking them to read and organize the information provides quick assessments of mastery of important geographic skills. Keeping careful records of personal observations during field trips or exercises and organizing that information upon returning to class measure both understanding of content and the actual use of geographic skills.

Authentic assessment tasks and projects requiring various amounts of time to complete are especially important; they illustrate the use of geography in real-life situations. Such tasks include construction of maps and models of landscapes, group or individual research projects, presentations illustrated with graphics, problem-solving or decision-making tasks, and simulations. Each such task illustrates how citizens and people in many jobs use geography-related knowledge, skills, and perceptions. All provide opportunities to identify and examine the conflicting values citizens and geographers experience in their investigations and when making policy.

Teachers can provide students with a clearly defined set of expectations for the various tasks required to successfully complete authentic assessment projects, along with rubrics describing the evaluation scale. Rubrics should include such criteria as defining the problem, locating appropriate and accurate information, organizing information, illustrating with maps and charts, providing geographic interpretations of information, making appropriate conclusions or recommendations, and making presentations clearly. Teachers can share each rubric with students prior to the assessment.

Final assessments of progress need to reflect what is taught throughout the course, and thus it is important for teachers to set their final assessment goals before beginning the course. The complete list of rubrics can then be used throughout the entire course, and teachers can emphasize improving outcomes through the use of ongoing assessments. They can do this by using assessments to measure progress toward completion of individual lesson objectives and projects, applying appropriate rubrics to the grading of shorter projects, and using rubrics during closure of individual lessons. Teachers can also ask students to use rubrics to evaluate their own work and that of their classmates.

Geography Strategies That Promote Achievement

To raise achievement in geography, teachers and curriculum planners can include a systematic selection of content to be learned; this selection can be based on the essentials of geography defined by the national standards, with emphasis on the procedures for studying and interpreting geographic questions. Instructional strategies that involve students in actively *doing* geography and that require analytic and critical thinking when making decisions are more effective in promoting higher achievement and greater depth of understanding. Teachers at all grade levels can use the strategies in the remainder of this chapter to help them make developmentally appropriate decisions related to geographic instruction, write curriculum at each grade level, and determine the K–12 scope and sequence.

Students of all ages can be involved in making maps, models, personal observations, graphs, and doing fieldwork. As skills in reading and cognition increase, so should the frequency of using narrative information, documents, and project presentations.

All grade levels can include geographic content and examples that focus on local problems as well as national and world examples. Local studies bring to life the complex abstractions in textbooks. Local resources also help to provide examples of the use of geography's spatial and environmental perspectives in medicine, engineering, social sciences, architecture, art, and the construction trades.

All grade levels can use multiple data-processing skills. In-depth learning of geography requires young people to ask, and also answer, geographic questions, and to acquire, organize, and analyze geographic information (Joint Committee on Geographic Education, 1984). Throughout the grades, new and more complex skills can be taught whenever they are needed to address geographic content and perspectives. Experts recommend avoiding the teaching of skills in isolation from the content that requires use of a given skill. When initially teaching a skill, consider using systematic instruction to perform the skill, followed by practice until the skill is accurately performed. Throughout the curriculum, consider planning activities that reinforce the proper use of the skill, to ensure its continued mastery. For example, as students learn to use simple statistics such as averages, percentages, and

ratios in mathematics and to access databases in computer instruction, they should also learn to use these skills in processing and interpreting geographic information and problems.

The lesson and activity ideas that follow illustrate specific strategies to use when teaching geography in grades K–12. These strategies illustrate how to teach various topics, but they are most powerful and successful in increasing learning when they are combined thoughtfully with appropriate content and teaching materials.

● **Strategy 5.1: Develop a Mental Map of the World. Teachers help each child create a personal mental map of the world to develop spatial knowledge of the earth.**

Discussion

Early in life, people begin to develop a mental map that helps them locate places and items they deem important. The development of these mental maps begins in the crib with the immediate environment; it expands every day as the child encounters more and more of the world.

Expanding youngsters' mental maps to include places they infrequently or never encounter personally is an important school task, fundamental to the building of spatial relations. Through formal education, students' mental maps expand to encompass the world; they help students form patterns and store information about the world.

When geographers examine questions and problems, the key variable is location. Simply recognizing a name does not mean that students can locate a place or understand its importance. This higher level of understanding occurs only when students incorporate the place into their mental map.

Teachers at all grade levels and in all subjects can make generous use of maps and verbal descriptions of locations that include where the location is in relation to other important locations that students might already know. Atlases, with their many types of maps, are certainly a key resource for locating places, but people's own mental maps are an equally important resource in daily life.

Beginning with 1st grade, systematic programs to learn map and globe skills are available for students from major map makers. These programs introduce all of the most frequently used map skills; when time is provided, they can be mastered by the end of grade 6. More advanced skills (for example, those used in the trades and professions) are more appropriately taught at the secondary level. At all grades, initial systematic instruction and practice should be followed with frequent usage of a wide variety of maps. By the time students enter school, they are ready to begin expanding their mental maps to embrace locations of places that are ever farther from personal daily encounters and to develop a mental map of the entire world.

Teachers have many opportunities to use information from maps to answer questions and make decisions in science and mathematics or to deal with economic, social, and political problems requiring legal consideration or conflicts between people and nations encountered in the middle school and high school curriculums. In every subject, map-making and map-using strategies provide answers to a wide range of questions.

The visual impressions that maps present make them powerful teaching resources. Working and playing with three-dimensional models helps the brain to make abstract images come alive. Similarly, three-dimensional models help many students to understand more difficult concepts related to maps, such as elevations or projections. So also does comparing a map with pictures and aerial photographs of a region.

Relative location (location in relationship to other places), or a person's perception of a location, may prove to be of far greater practical importance than the dryly specific location that latitude and longitude provide. Relative location tells us where a place is in relation to the physical and cultural features important to us. Key questions are Where is it? Why is it there? Have changes over time resulted in changes in its importance?

Individual globes, atlases, and laminated place-mat-size maps allow students a close look at places and invite outlining and underlining with water-based pens or crayons. Three-dimensional maps and models of landscapes help students understand elevation; they are especially helpful to children with limited vision or those living in regions with little variation in elevation. Thin strips of paper and yarn or string can be used to measure distances and emphasize lines of latitude and longitude.

CLASSROOM EXAMPLES

Beginning in kindergarten, students can take walking field trips and then make maps, or they can use maps to record information gathered on the trip. Ask students to describe what they saw, decide which features are impor-

tant to include on the map, and determine where on the page to locate each item.

Students can begin to improve the locations and scales of their maps by folding the paper in half and then quarters and recording their observations in the correct quadrants of the paper. In making maps of classrooms, school grounds, neighborhoods, and field-trip destinations, students decide what to include and what symbols represent various sites. This helps them understand the role of maps and appreciate the information that maps provide.

Important skills needed to read, gather information from, or interpret locations on globes and maps include directions, scale, symbols, legend/key, and grid systems. Drill-and-practice activities, as well as verbal, card, and board games, provide opportunities to master map and globe skills.

Reports and projects allow students to use their knowledge of maps to gather, organize, and display information. Entire reports depicting a variety of facts and relationships about places can be written using only the atlas as a reference. Assignments requiring middle and high school students to describe and explain a place by using information found on political, physical, and topical maps reinforce the importance of using a variety of maps and provide a stimulating challenge. The Internet also provides access to a multitude of maps and atlases; it also provides U.S. Census data for communities, states, and the nation, as well as similar types of information for many large cities and nations.

The local availability of goods and services affects the job market and the quality of life in a community. Mapping the locations of business and community services on local and county maps using addresses from the telephone book reveals patterns of the availability of essential public and private services. Armed with such information, students can actively develop plans or policies for promoting changes in their community or region.

The more advanced skill of reading and interpreting contour lines requires mastery of numbers and estimation. Contour lines (often encountered for the first time on weather maps) are an important tool for showing elevations and ocean depths on topographic maps. Using contour lines and other symbols on weather maps, students can make (and quickly check) predictions concerning changes in the weather. If their predictions prove to be wrong, students can investigate the next day's maps and explain why. They can also predict and follow the paths of storms using their map-reading skills.

Teachers at all grade levels can reinforce map skills by, for instance, using pins or marks on inexpensive paper maps to locate cities and nations that have been discussed in current events or literature. Students can plot the route for field trips and write out directions for the driver, or given the written directions, they can plot the bus route on a map and follow it during the trip.

Spatial relations are based on the recognition of patterns in the shapes of regions such as states, nations, and continents. Recognizing these shapes helps in learning place names. Mnemonics can help teach students to locate a variety of political regions. Encourage students to describe the shapes or associate them with familiar objects: "Which continent has a shape similar to an ice cream cone?" Outline the shape of a region and encourage students to tell you what they think the shape resembles. Other patterns may be found in the regularity of, concentrations of, and absence of cultural and physical features on the map. Geographers describe these patterns and seek to explain the causes and relationships among them.

It is easier to recognize and see patterns on a single map. When information cannot be placed on only one map, placing several maps one atop the other and holding them up to the light helps many students to distinguish common or partially shared locations.

RESOURCES

Gutierrez & Sanchez, 1993; Geography Education Standards Project, 1994; Salter & Riggs-Salter, 1988; Stimpson, 1991; Sunal & Haas, 1993.

● **STRATEGY 5.2: INCREASE PRACTICAL AWARENESS OF GEOGRAPHY. TEACHERS HELP STUDENTS BECOME AWARE OF THE IMPORTANCE OF GEOGRAPHY BY IDENTIFYING THE ROLE GEOGRAPHY PLAYS IN PEOPLE'S DAILY LIVES.**

DISCUSSION

Learning the practical implications of a subject helps to motivate many students. Geography affects *everyone's* everyday life; for some professions, knowing and understanding geography is a requirement.

Although people may seldom have occasion to look at a map, everyone (including very young children) uses geography every single day in simply moving about and locating things and places. Driving a car and taking public transportation may require a person to read a city map to get to a job interview or work, or to find the home of an acquaintance.

Perhaps the most frequently encountered map is the TV weather map. Students (and teachers, too!) celebrate when inclement weather shuts down the schools. But most children—and probably most adults, too—seldom stop to think that it is the shape of the land and its elevation that direct air currents that bring storms to one area and not another. Geography contributes to weather patterns, which in turn help determine the foods we may eat or the natural disasters or diseases that can threaten our safety. Geography is the stuff of our everyday lives!

Physical features affect the settlement patterns and transportation resources that isolate some locations and bring others together. The presence or absence of resources limit the number and types of occupations available within a geographic region. Many occupations, such as civil engineering, landscaping, and truck driving require an understanding of geography. Students may want to vacation at sites famous for their unique geography, such as the Grand Canyon or the Pacific Coast.

CLASSROOM EXAMPLES

Schools can display maps of the building near the front door to help guide new students, parents, and visitors. (Maps that students make are much better than commercially prepared maps.) Yearly changes in faculty make it necessary to display new maps each year.

Students can use maps of their own community and state to measure the distance to familiar places when beginning to study the skill of measuring distances. Students can take surveys to learn how frequently adults use maps and which types of maps they use most often. Studies of historically important military engagements can illustrate vividly the crucial nature of terrain, weather, and movement of troops and supplies.

Knowing the location of a place helps us know what temperatures to expect and what activities and tourist attractions might be available there. When studying regions of the United States, for example, teachers can ask students to pack a suitcase with clothing suitable for a week's vacation in a given area. Use a state's tourist information page on the World Wide Web to check average monthly temperatures and the availability of activities.

Studying the weather involves students in predicting weather patterns that can then be checked for accuracy. Following major storms can involve students in explaining how the storm will affect people's activities, as well as studying the responses of individuals and governments to the natural disasters by listening to news broadcasts and reading accounts on the Web from local newspapers.

Students can survey their own community, identifying needed or wanted services and recommending which services to increase and where to locate them. Maps can be used to illustrate their recommendations and to help explain why they selected particular services and locations. Interviews with the mayor, city planner, or members of planning commissions can illustrate the practical use of geography locally. The departments of natural resources, transportation, or tourism can provide evidence of geographic problems that must be solved related to automobiles, outdoor recreational activities, and jobs. Members of the business community can explain what they look for when they seek to locate sites for new stores, offices, or plants, and how geography becomes a key tool to target advertising campaigns or seek trade with other nations.

Geographical factors affect the costs of such everyday goods and services as food, housing, and insurance. Youngsters can investigate the reasons for regional differences in prices. Students can decide if the cost differences are justified, if people in the region are paying unfairly high costs, and if governments or collectives of people might possibly act to reduce prices.

Can community service projects assist in reducing the price of food for the schools, the elderly, or poor people in a neighborhood? Is land available for a gardening project? If so, what are the best plants to grow? Do the people in this group like to eat them or know how to prepare them? Are the growing season and the water supply sufficient? All these questions require an understanding of geography and the ability to locate answers.

RESOURCES

Association of American Geographers, 1999; Geography Education Standards Project, 1994.

● STRATEGY 5.3: DESCRIBE PLACES AND REGIONS. TEACHERS ENCOURAGE STUDENTS TO IDENTIFY BOTH COMMON AND UNIQUE CHARACTERISTICS OF VARIOUS LOCATIONS TO ANALYZE AND APPRECIATE THE PHYSICAL AND CULTURAL VARIATIONS ON THE SURFACE OF THE EARTH.

DISCUSSION

Earth is unique among the planets in our Solar System. Geographers study the surface of the earth and

seek to describe, explain, and understand it. The study of geography is filled with adventure, danger, and beauty. Understanding all that is happening at any one time is impossible. Therefore, geographers divide the earth into various regions in the hope of understanding each region's characteristics and its interdependence with every other region. Each region has many common characteristics and few differences internally, but is significantly different from other regions.

CLASSROOM EXAMPLES

Virtually all schools—and even individual elementary classrooms—contain regions. Students can make maps of their own school building, identifying and describing regions, and giving each one a name that describes its characteristics, (for example, quiet place, conversation pit, activity center, administration).

Older students will find it more appropriate (and more challenging) to examine the economic and administrative regions of cities, states, and nations. Migration to the United States has been dominated at various times by people from different regions of the world; students can identify the origins of these migratory groups, investigating the reasons for their migration and the regions in the United States where they settled.

Building models of places can help young people to understand their characteristics and the relationships among them. Young children may build models of their immediate neighborhoods using data they personally gather on walks with their classmates. Computer programs such as the *Neighborhood Map Machine* and *Community Construction Kit* from Tom Snyder Productions provide patterns for models of various buildings that can be printed, colored, and folded into three-dimensional models, even by young students. Half-pint milk cartons can be decorated with construction paper to form buildings. Historical models of cities, castles, and plantations require students to include cultural features, people, and elements of the physical environment and to locate each feature on the model. Such projects can integrate art instruction by adding appropriate decorative features and mathematics by building the models to scale.

Locating different types of businesses can help students better understand their community. With the help of a phone book, students can pinpoint all the locations of particular types of businesses—pizza restaurants, shoe stores, furniture stores, grocery stores—and locate them on a city map. After they have identified the common characteristics of these business sites, students can attempt to predict sites where new businesses might locate.

A study of other nations is also the study of the characteristics of a political region. Students can make posters, murals, or collages that illustrate their chosen nations. Rubrics for evaluation can include the use of symbols, graphics, pictures, and illustrations showing the major physical characteristics of the nation, cultural traditions, and landmarks. Advanced students can be asked to produce graphs illustrating the characteristics of various populations.

Students can listen to popular or folk songs that describe cities, states, and nations, picking out those factors the songwriter considered important and discussing why they are important and how they differ from their own local area. Translations of national anthems and pledges to nations can be analyzed in much the same way.

RESOURCES

Association of American Geographers, 1997, 1999; Haas, 1988; Hoge & Allen, 1991; National Council for the Social Studies, 1994; Geography Education Standards Project, 1994.

● **STRATEGY 5.4:** EXAMINE HOW PHYSICAL PROCESSES SHAPE THE EARTH. TEACHERS ENCOURAGE THE EXAMINATION OF THE PHYSICAL SYSTEMS TO EXPLAIN HOW THE FORCES OF NATURE BOTH CREATE AND DESTROY LAND AND LANDFORMS.

DISCUSSION

If there were no people, our planet would still be in constant flux; the atmosphere, lithosphere, hydrosphere, and biosphere interact constantly to create and change it. Because each system has its own set of internal interactions and processes, which tend toward equilibrium, we can observe predictable trends. These processes, working together, maintain our physical environment. Earth's patterns of vegetation, weather, and landforms change as a result of these dynamic physical processes. Over time, disruptions bring dramatic alterations—slowly, but inexorably.

Key questions to ask when leading an investigation of geography and physical systems include the following:

- What physical features are located in the region?
- What natural forces have created and changed the landscape?
- Which physical forces seem to be dominating the landscape at this time?
- What is the probability of a large disruption in the physical landscape occurring in the near future?
- What types of changes will this bring in the appearance of the landscape?

CLASSROOM EXAMPLES

Make a bulletin board locating pictures of national monuments or national parks around the periphery of a larger U.S. map. Students can describe what they see in the pictures and compare pictures of similar landforms, discussing similarities and differences. Students can also be encouraged to decide what they like about the pictures and if they would like to visit or live in such places. (Students might be required to make forced choices by being asked to select only five of, say, ten locations.) Attach strings to the pictures and ask students to locate the scene on the map by attaching the string from the picture to the correct location on the map.

Landforms are best studied by examining them in relation to one another: river, delta, flood plain, canyon. When studying rivers, for example, use both aerial and ground-level photos. Follow the course of one river with a series of pictures or a video. If possible, follow the course of a local stream on a field trip. Locate major rivers on a world map and trace their courses. In small groups, research some of the rivers using the World Wide Web and learn of any large floods or unusual disasters. Classify landforms by the forces that create them, and discuss the forces that might change them. Learn the particular resources associated with a landform, such as water, precious metals, or coal.

Throughout the school year, follow current events related to changes in the natural environment. Plot these events on a world map, using appropriate symbols to designate the cause or event. Examine the map periodically to discern any emerging patterns. Read books and stories about these types of events to better understand their cost in lives, money, and human emotions. Examine photos of scenes before and after a natural disaster. Describe the pictures in words, locate the places on the map, and research explanations for the causes.

Examine a local ecosystem. Learn its characteristics and locate it on a map. (Older students can use a topographic map.) Research how the ecosystem has changed over time and what is happening to it today. Interview local people who can tell you how the ecosystem has changed during their lifetime. Survey people in the region to see how they feel about the ecosystem and its future. If there are major changes to this ecosystem, predict what will happen to the lands that border on the system in the next five to ten years.

RESOURCES

Association of American Geographers, 1997, 1999; LeVasseur, 1996–97; McKeown-Ice, 1994; Geography Education Standards Project, 1994; Peters, 1994.

● **STRATEGY 5.5: EXAMINE THE PATTERNS OF HUMAN SYSTEMS FOUND ON THE PLANET. ENCOURAGE STUDENTS TO IDENTIFY WHERE PEOPLE LIVE AND WHY THEY HAVE CHOSEN TO LIVE IN PARTICULAR REGIONS OVER TIME.**

DISCUSSION

Human systems include continual changes in settlement patterns, the movement of resources, and struggles and conflicts to control the earth's surface. People have found ways to inhabit all regions of the world, even those that some might consider too hostile to permit survival.

Changes in a region's physical conditions often force people to move constantly in search of food and grazing lands. Sometimes people have decided not to return to their old habitat, but to settle in new locations. The need for safety has prompted people to live close together, enclose their settlements, and seek out locations protected from invaders. The need for new resources or trade has spurred people to find or create pathways over which they could move quickly to trade or communicate with others.

Today there are few unpopulated places on our planet. By employing varying technologies, we have populated areas that have a meager capacity to support life. Even very young children enjoy learning about areas of the world that are quite different from their own region—and also about those that are quite similar to their own. Children also enjoy communicating with each other and learning directly from other children.

Learning about people's different lifestyles and needs is more than idle curiosity. The period known as the "Age of Discovery" was prompted by a search for commerce and for food and spices to preserve food and make it taste better. The search today is for new forms of wealth; we even use photographs taken from space to help locate natural resources and sources of underground water. Just as in past centuries, conflicts arise over ownership of the land and sea. Such struggles spawn conflicts that span borders and lead to wars between and within nations, requiring international treaties.

CLASSROOM EXAMPLES

Given sets of pictures, young students can search for signs that people have inhabited or now inhabit an area. They look for signs that many people, or only a few, inhabit an area. They identify evidence of how the inhabitants might earn a living. Young children can study the differences between rural, urban, and suburban communities, communicating by letter or e-mail with children living in other types of communities to learn the kinds of stores and recreational facilities available. Students can read a multitude of books about other cities and regions of the United States and their inhabitants. They will learn that many U.S. citizens come from a staggering variety of nations and that some of their own neighbors may celebrate ethnic holidays or festivals very different from their own.

Students will begin to realize that they have the power to learn the many reasons why people and goods move from place to place. Students can plot the origins and movement of their own families on maps. They can examine the involvement of their families in international trade by studying the origins of the food they eat and where their toys and clothing are made. They can record these findings on world maps, drawing lines from around the world to their own city. They can ask local businesses to tell where they purchase their raw materials and where they send their finished goods. Older students can be asked to determine which nations of the world share important common interests with the United States. Historical maps of trading patterns can help students understand the facts behind past decisions by world leaders that resulted in treaties and wars.

Where people live is a reflection of many different factors. Students can research why people selected particular sites for cities or factories. They can look for common elements in the sites of those cities that have grown to be very large. Students can investigate where rapidly growing cities are located and compare the sites with the sites of cities founded one or two centuries ago.

Using U.S. Census data, older students can identify places where the population is growing and where it is decreasing. They can identify places where they might have good opportunities to work at a given occupation. They can examine the truth of claims that jobs are leaving the Unites States for particular nations.

Occupations in other locales and times have varied greatly. Students can compare their own lives with those of people in other nations by learning about the predominant occupations of men and women. Students might research such questions as, "How is the life of a rural woman in the developing world different from the life of a woman living on a farm in the United States?" What differences exist? What is the role of technology in contributing to these differences? Why might women in another region of the world prefer their lives to those of women in the United States? Would U.S. men and women be willing to trade their workday for the workday of someone living in another nation?

RESOURCES

Association of American Geographers, 1997, 1999; LeVasseur, 1996–97; Geography Education Standards Project,1994.

● **STRATEGY 5.6: UNDERSTAND RELATIONSHIPS BETWEEN THE ENVIRONMENT AND SOCIETY. ASK STUDENTS TO EXPLAIN RELATIONSHIPS BETWEEN THE WAYS PEOPLE VIEW THE ENVIRONMENT AND ACT TOWARD VARIOUS ENVIRONMENTS IN TODAY'S WORLD, AND MAKE PROJECTIONS OF HOW THE DECISIONS WE MAKE TODAY WILL AFFECT OUR HABITAT IN THE FUTURE.**

DISCUSSION

Every region of our planet provides varying resources of food, fuel, water, and energy; there are natural limits on the capacity of any given region to support life. Human beings have for centuries willfully altered their habitats, but it now seems obvious that the changes have not always been desirable ones. Nor, we see, do people in similar habitats make the same choices concerning their habitat.

It is impossible to change a part of the environment without destroying some degree of natural balance. Today we find ourselves in conflict, for instance, over the most appropriate use of land. Is preservation of the natural habi-

tat more important than the creation of jobs? The result of such decisions may be new inhabitants who will need additional services and places to live, which of course places greater demands on the habitat. On the other hand, people may choose to leave the region, creating a depressed economic situation, and in some cases, complete abandonment of the locale.

Questions to ask in examining human influence in a region include the following:

- What changes have people made to the landscape?
- What are the perceived advantages and disadvantages of a region?
- What natural forces are at work?
- How do people view local resources?
- Are people's views toward the site changing human distributions and relationships or changing the physical conditions of the site?

Resources helpful in teaching about the environment and society include current and historical maps, pictures, newspapers, books, documents, and diary entries. Studying geography problems at multiple scales from an early age is essential. Geography helps students understand the relationships within physical and human systems and their mutual interdependence. Maps for primary-age children should be of local sites, but youngsters know, too, that they live on the planet Earth, and they should begin to study the entire planet through the use of globes and maps showing worldwide distribution of natural and cultural phenomena.

CLASSROOM EXAMPLES

Ask small groups of students to examine photos of the landscape and classify them into those that show signs of changes made by people and those in which the changes appear to be brought about by nature. Ask the groups to share one or more photos and describe the kinds of changes people make and the kinds of changes nature can make. Then ask the groups to divide the photos into good and bad changes and discuss their reasons for doing so. Any photos on which the groups cannot agree may be sorted into a third pile, and then discussed with the entire class. Students will see that even friends can disagree on any given event or issue.

Present students with a problem that they are allowed to discuss, but must solve for themselves. Here's the problem: Make plans to move to another state, and decide which state and where in that state to settle. The students will have to locate the chosen place on the map and describe its location, relating the advantages and disadvantages of living in this location year-round. Older students can describe the types of occupations they might find available to them and their families.

Students can interview family members to learn why their ancestors came to the United States and settled where they did. Where else did their families live before they moved to their current location? The class can make a map of this information; each student can draw his family's answers on a paper map with a colored pencil. Students might create a promotional announcement for their community, encouraging people or a business to move to their community. Or they may decide to write an announcement *dis*couraging people and businesses from moving to their area!

Given pictures of scenes from a community, students can identify how people have used available resources from their natural habitat to provide for their needs. When studying history, students can determine how people's buildings and occupations used available resources. Students can also locate buildings in their own community that they believe were built using only locally available resources.

Follow a controversy concerning the use of a given piece of land. Identify the issues related to the controversy and the views of various groups. Ask speakers to visit the class to explain opposing views. Discuss both their presentations and the merits of their ideas. Also consider how they react to other people's viewpoints—with respect or ridicule. Do they disagree with the facts? Do they have facts to support their views? If so, how accurate are those facts? (If speakers are not available, consider asking the entire class to research the views of various groups and to hold a debate. Or students can write letters expressing their views.)

Study the types of ecosystems that attract local birds and small animals. With the help of parents and the permission of appropriate authorities, build a site on or near the school grounds that will attract birds and animals. Observe the changes that take place there throughout the school year. If building a complete environment is not possible, learn what individual families do in their homes to provide an inviting habitat.

Read books that describe the lives of people who live in particular regions of the world—the rainforest or grasslands, for example. Identify ways in which people have changed the habitat and how those changes are viewed. Is

anything left of the original habitat? Has the land use created controversy? Who makes decisions about what happens there now and in the future? What will be the costs of such changes? These costs can be calculated in dollars and cents by students with the necessary mathematical skills or described in terms of the types of buildings that will be built and the types of vegetation or landforms that will be removed or modified. Identify which people will benefit by the changes and what others will have to give up. Are the benefits long term or short term?

RESOURCES

Association of American Geographers, 1997,1999; McKeown-Ice, 1994; National Council for the Social Studies, 1994; Geography Education Standards Project, 1994; Peters, 1994.

BIBLIOGRAPHY

Allen, R. R., & Hoge, J. D. (1990). Literature study for geographic literacy, grades 3–6. *Social Studies and the Young Learner, 3*(2), 42–44.

Association of American Geographers. (1997). *Argus print materials.* Washington, DC: Author.

Association of American Geographers. (1999). *Argus Interactive CD* [CD-ROM]. Washington, DC: Author.

Backler, A., & Stoltman, J. (1986). The nature of geographic literacy. *ERIC Digest* No. 35.

Bednarz, R. S., & Tetersen, J. (1994). The reform movement in geographic education: A view from the summit. *Journal of Geography, 93*(1), 61–64.

Cole, D. B., & Ormrod, J. E. (1995). Effectiveness of teaching pedagogical content knowledge through summer geography institutes. *Journal of Geography, 94*(3), 427–433.

Downs, R. M. (1994). The need for research in geography education: It would be nice to have some data. *Journal of Geography, 93*(1), 57–60.

Dulli, R. E. (1994). Improving geography learning in the schools: Efforts by the National Geographic Society. *Journal of Geography, 93*(1), 55–56.

Galvez-Hjornevik, C. (1991). Reaffirmations of a permanent liberal. In *James A. Michener on the social studies: His writings in publications of national council for the social studies from 1938 to 1987.* Bulletin 85. Washington, DC: National Council for the Social Studies. 113–18.

Geographic Education National Implementation Project. (1996). *Spaces and places: A geography manual for teachers.* Distributed by the National Council for Geographic Education, Indiana, PA: Author.

Geography Education Standards Project. (1994). *Geography for life: What every young American should know and be able to do in geography.* Washington, D.C.: National Geographic Research & Exploration.

Gutierrez, E. D., & Sanchez, Y. (1993). Hilltop geography for young children: Creating an outdoor learning laboratory. *Journal of Geography, 92*(4), 176–179.

Haas, M. E. (1988). What is the name of the mystery nation? *Social Studies and the Young Learner, 1*(2), 19–20.

Haas, M. E. (1989). Teaching geography in the elementary school. *ERIC Digest* EDO-SO-89-6.

Hickey, M. G., & Bein, F. L. (1996). Students' learning difficulties in geography and teachers' interventions: Teaching cases for K–12 classrooms. *Journal of Geography, 95*(3), 118–124.

Hoge, J. D., & Allen, R. R. (1991). Teaching about our world community: Guidelines and resources. *Social Studies and the Young Learner, 3*(4), 19–22.

Joint Committee on Geographic Education of the National Council for the Geographic Education and Association of American Geographers. (1984). *Guidelines for geographic education: Elementary and secondary schools*. Washington, DC: Association of American Geographers. (ERIC Document Reproduction Service No. ED 252 453).

LeVasseur, M. L. (1996–97). Is it geography? *Update, 33*(2), 6.

McKeown-Ice, R. (1994). Environmental education: A geographical perspective. *Journal of Geography, 93*(1), 40–42.

Morrill, R. W. (1993, June). One perspective on geography, part two. *Perspective, 21*, 3–5.

Muir, S., & Cheek, H. N. (1991). Assessing spatial development: Implications for map skill instruction. *Social Education, 55*(5), 316–319.

Murphy, C. E. (1991). Using the five themes of geography to explore a school site. *Journal of Geography, 90*(1), 38–40.

National Council for Geographic Education (n.d.). *How to help children become geographically literate*. Indiana, PA: Author.

National Council for the Social Studies. (1992). *A vision of powerful teaching and learning in the social studies: Building social understanding and civic efficacy*. Washington, DC: Author.

National Council for the Social Studies. (1994). *Expectations of excellence: Curriculum standards for social studies*. Bulletin 89. Washington, DC: Author.

Nellis, M. D. (1994). Technology in geographic education: Reflections and future directions. *Journal of Geography, 93*(1), 36–39.

Persky, H. R., Reese, C. M., O'Sullivan, C. Y., Moore, J., & Shakrani, S. (1994). *Geography report card: National assessment of educational progress*. Washington, DC: U. S. Department of Education.

Peters, R. (1994). Nurturing an environmental and social ethic. *Childhood Education, 70*(1), 72–73.

Salter, C. L., & Riggs-Salter, C. (1988). Five themes in geography and the primary-grade learner. *Social Studies and the Young Learner, 1*(2), 10–13.

Self, C. M., & Golledge, R. G. (1994). Sex-related differences in spatial ability: What every geography educator should know. *Journal of Geography, 93*(5), 234–243.

Stimpson, P. G. (1991). Is it a long way to Tipperary? Suggestions for improving students' locational knowledge. *Journal of Geography, 90*(2), 78–82.

Sunal, C. S., & Haas, M. E. (1993). *Social studies and the elementary/middle school student*. Fort Worth, TX: Harcourt Brace Jovanovich College Press.

6

Strategies for Increasing Achievement in History

Virginia E. Causey and Beverly J. Armento

How exciting it is to uncover the voices and lives of our ancestors by becoming detectives solving historical mysteries, making sense of the events and issues of the past, and struggling with alternative interpretations of critical points in history. The study of history in our schools should also be exciting, stimulating, engaging, and provocative. Yet critics charge that our schools are turning out a generation of history illiterates, and students and their parents often condemn history teaching as boring, repetitious, and anything but stimulating and engaging. Clearly schools and teachers must move in new directions if they are to facilitate a deeper historical understanding among all young people.

History belongs in the school programs of all students, regardless of their academic standing and preparation, of their curricular track, or of their plans for the future. It is vital for all citizens in a democracy, because it provides the only avenue we have to reach an understanding of ourselves and our society, in relation to the human condition over time, and of how some things change and some things continue.

—Bradley Commission on History in the Schools, 1988

1988 NAEP tests noted that instructional activities in history classes emphasize reading and memorizing textbook materials, writing short answers to questions, and taking tests or quizzes. Similarly, in recent studies, students report that the most common class activities are listening to discussions and lectures, reading textbooks, completing worksheets, and taking tests. Teachers tend to select teacher-centered instructional options to exercise more control over student behavior, not because those approaches lead to a deeper understanding of and engagement with history.

The 1988 and 1994 results of the NAEP tests confirmed the criticism of students' knowledge of history. The latest NAEP tests indicated that students in 4th, 8th, and 12th grades demonstrate a very limited grasp of U.S. history. Even more discouraging, a wide disparity in performance exists between white students and black and Hispanic students, and between socioeconomic groups. Somewhat more favorable news is that the gender gap has shrunk slightly since 1988.

The ways teachers present history to students have not changed significantly for decades; undoubtedly, this is a big factor in continuing poor student performance. The

History teachers have tended to focus on the political aspects of history, emphasizing dates, heroes, and wars. The part often omitted is the more interesting and complex social history, the story of people's lives. As a result, women, people of color, and poor people who have traditionally had little access to the political process are excluded. History textbooks and curriculums also reflect this mainstream approach, contributing to students' general lack of interest. Females and ethnic minorities often look in vain for authentic depictions of themselves in curricular materials; when they do appear, it is usually as a sidebar or an addendum. The resulting message is that they and their contributions to history are of secondary importance. To ignore the controversial aspects and play to the middle takes away all the drama of history—and some of the teacher's best oppor-

SMILEY MEMORIAL LIBRARY
411 Central Methodist Square
Fayette, MO 65248-1198

tunities for engaging students in historical analysis and interpretation.

ENHANCING STUDENTS' ACHIEVEMENT IN HISTORY

Many educators and researchers have proposed curricular and instructional changes that would enhance the quality and quantity of history education in our schools. Among these ideas are several fundamental (and controversial) proposals that would dramatically change the nature of history education. One key issue is whether historical studies should focus on breadth of coverage or depth of understanding. Typically we have settled for a broad, sweeping coverage across the entire timeline (or as much as can be crammed into the time limits of the course). This coverage often emphasizes political events and world and national leaders. The opposing view is that a more in-depth approach would allow for more interdisciplinary content and encourage the development of more critical thinking skills as students grew to understand the complex causes of events. An in-depth approach would also facilitate the use of primary source documents and the exploration of social, political, economic, and cultural aspects of events and issues.

When should the study of history begin? Many educators think that the youngest children can study history, if it is presented in developmentally appropriate ways, using concrete representations and historical narratives. We can enhance the relevance of history to children by making people the center of the history curriculum and by linking its study to students' own lives and communities.

Historians and history educators can provide valuable resources for classroom use, and they should assist schools in developing a vital history curriculum. Historical thinking skills and historical understanding should be a primary focus across the span of schooling. Students should build their abilities to differentiate past, present, and future time; raise questions; seek and evaluate evidence; compare and analyze historical stories and records; interpret historical data; and construct historical narratives of their own. Doing all this will take inspired teachers, who are excited about the study of history and see the relevance and importance of these studies for today's students.

THE STATE OF THE ART OF HISTORY INSTRUCTION

U.S. students continue to exhibit low levels of proficiency in U.S. history, according to the 1994 NAEP assess-

ments. Based on their answers to a mixture of multiple-choice and constructed-response items, students were rated at three levels: Basic, indicating partial mastery of prerequisite knowledge and skills; Proficient, demonstrating competence in content knowledge, application of historical knowledge to real-world situations, and use of analytical skills; and Advanced, signifying superior performance.

The bad news is that approximately 57 percent of 12th graders did not reach even the Basic level of *partial* mastery. The scores of 4th and 8th graders were slightly better, with 35 to 40 percent of students below the Basic level. Fifty percent of 12th-grade white students scored below the Basic level of proficiency, compared with 83 percent of black students and 78 percent of Hispanic students. Fifty-five percent of males, compared with 60 percent of females, did not reach the Basic level. Forty-four percent of children whose parents are college graduates scored below basic proficiency; the percentage below Basic proficiency for children whose parents had only a high school diploma was 71 percent, and 85 percent for children whose parents did not graduate from high school.

The NAEP data may give us cause for alarm, but the larger worry is an equity issue: Are all students able to access adequate instruction in history? What is the quality of teaching, resources, and enthusiasm for historical inquiry in the nation's schools, and are these social, physical, and educational resources available to all children? If the answer is no, *then the data reflect the state of the profession,* not only the state of student knowledge and historical skills.

Standards for history education now exist; many states have adapted them and are emphasizing history instruction throughout the grade levels. The standards call for greater emphasis on historical thinking and analytical skills, as well as on the stronger integration of U.S. with world history content. Raising the level of expected achievement is a necessary but insufficient goal. We must also ensure that all students have access to competent history teachers and outstanding instruction.

ASSESSING STUDENT ACHIEVEMENT IN HISTORY

Three basic principles should govern the authentic assessment of history learning: (1) assessment should be ongoing and constructive, formative as well as summative; (2) assessment should have real-world applicability and meaning beyond the classroom; (3) assessment should offer students alternative ways to indicate their competence, and should pay attention to multiple modes of learning.

It is important that we use assessment of learning as a tool to shape instruction. Final tests—whether given at the end of the unit or the end of the year—can help to assess the general level of learning in any group of students. However, if part of the goal of history education is to better match instruction to students' current knowledge, conceptions, and misconceptions, then formative evaluation becomes especially valuable to educators, students, and parents. Students need to learn that assessment has value; they deserve to receive useful feedback on the products of their labors. Once this cycle of feedback and rethinking of certain materials or skills is established, students are more apt to take assessment seriously.

The actual form and content of assessment must make sense to students. Since problem solving, creativity, analysis, and developing informed judgments help adults succeed in both their work and personal lives, it seems natural that those same skills—as well as a mastery of factual information, of course—should be a major focus of history assessments. Moreover, assessments can have real-world meaning if students communicate what they have learned to an audience beyond the teacher. As adults already know, real-world applicability involves more than the search for a single correct answer. History assessments should require students to use multiple kinds of sources to construct their products and multiple forms of communication to present them.

Authentic assessment gives students alternative ways to demonstrate their knowledge and historical thinking skills. Giving students choices can motivate and empower them as learners. Although this practice makes the teacher's work more complex (both in designing assessment and interpreting student responses), such alternative means of assessment can give a more complete, in-depth picture of the nature of student learning. Multiple-choice items and traditional paper-and-pencil assessments can go just so far in uncovering the nature of a student's thinking, in analyzing primary source documents, for example. Individual or group history projects, role-plays, essays, visual interpretation of data sources, research projects, or the creation of a portfolio of one's best work might supplement more traditional forms of classroom assessment.

STRATEGIES THAT PROMOTE ACHIEVEMENT IN HISTORY

The following strategies for effective history teaching and learning are supported by experience in the field as substantiated and analyzed through research. Several principles provide the foundation for these strategies:

- Create a classroom environment that facilitates authentic historical thinking.
- Use inclusive curricular approaches that give attention to multiple perspectives and to social as well as political history.
- Provide chronological, spatial, and causal frameworks for the study of history.
- Facilitate students' active construction of their understanding of history.
- Develop visual and verbal historical literacy.
- Build bridges to home and community cultures based on respect for diversity and human dignity.
- Cultivate students' historical empathy, curiosity, and interest in the past and present.

● **STRATEGY 6.1:** CREATE A CLASSROOM CLIMATE THAT FOSTERS HISTORICAL THINKING. AUTHENTIC HISTORICAL THINKING REQUIRES A CLASSROOM ENVIRONMENT THAT ENCOURAGES THOUGHTFULNESS, COOPERATION AS WELL AS COMPETITION, OPPORTUNITIES FOR STUDENTS TO CONSTRUCT THEIR OWN UNDERSTANDINGS, AND RESPECT FOR ALTERNATE VIEWPOINTS.

DISCUSSION

A firm foundation of factual and conceptual knowledge lies at the base of sound historical thinking. Building on that base, students can formulate historical problems, locate relevant information, grapple with evidence, weigh alternative explanations, and form conclusions that follow logically from the evidence. Before students can thoughtfully and reflectively comprehend and interpret historical data, and make informed decisions, they must work within a classroom context that encourages such investigation and thinking.

Teachers must respect the study of history and the objective investigation of data sources; this leads naturally to their fostering these same attitudes in their students. The classroom can cultivate an attitude of inquiry. Engagement is more likely to occur and be sustained by tasks that students see as meaningful, valuable, and significant. Teachers must take the time to make the relevance of historical tasks obvious to students. They can facilitate historical thinking by presenting history as alive, unfinished, and in flux.

Authentic historical thinking takes place within a community of learners, not in isolation; so the classroom climate must promote cooperation. Cooperative learning is equally effective in urban, rural, and suburban settings. The cooperative history classroom gives all students an equal opportunity to learn. Teachers in successful cooperative classrooms emphasize personal and social responsibility.

Effective history teachers view history as a constructive activity that allows students many opportunities to develop their own meanings. Students learn when they seek answers to questions that *matter* to them; their understanding changes only when they become dissatisfied with what they know. To facilitate this kind of historical investigation, teachers must provide support for student endeavors by initiating their interest, breaking investigative tasks into manageable components, modeling procedures and behaviors, and giving feedback on student performance.

When students construct individual historical interpretations, they will not all arrive at one correct answer. Teachers model historical thinking for students by asking difficult and open-ended questions, seeking evidence from multiple sources with divergent viewpoints, and wrestling with conflicting interpretations. Data sources can reflect multiple perspectives on any issue or event; in studying the past, students can see themselves and their communities. Support of this community of history learners requires a classroom in which students can express differing and potentially unpopular opinions in a psychologically safe environment.

CLASSROOM EXAMPLES

Teachers can present opportunities for students to learn content in depth but also explicitly teach the skills needed for higher-order thinking in history. These skills include how to detect bias, create a well-reasoned argument, distinguish relevant from irrelevant information, respond to opposing viewpoints, and clearly and persuasively state one's views. Activities that allow students to compare and contrast viewpoints of people in history or of historical interpretations can lead to higher-order historical thinking. Likewise, making judgments about historical problems or current issues requires critical thinking. Teachers can use analogies and historical narratives to help students grapple with issues of historical significance and connect aspects of their understanding of their own lives to the past.

If a classroom is to be a community of historical learners, a cooperative approach is crucial. The teacher moves toward a cooperative classroom by creating the

appropriate climate. Establish ground rules that emphasize mutual respect. Form groups to examine historical events and issues that are heterogeneous in gender, ethnicity, learning style, knowledge level, and ability level.

Two key elements enable cooperative learning to be effective: group goals and individual accountability. First, groups must be working to achieve some common preset goals or to earn rewards or recognition. Second, the success of each group must depend on *the individual learning of each group member,* not on a single group product. Use procedural roles that encourage students to talk and work together, not merely roles that divide up the work. Creating tasks that draw on multiple abilities and multiple intelligences is another key to success.

Students make sense of history as they establish connections between new information and their prior knowledge and conceptions. Teachers help forge such links by posing open-ended historical questions—questions without simple or single answers—then providing opportunities for students to gather and consider appropriate data. It is important to begin with the prior historical knowledge students bring from family and community experiences. Historical narratives can link people to the study of history in an engaging way. Children need opportunities to create historical narratives after studying their community or an important event or person. Teachers can emphasize the "authored" nature of history by asking such questions as, Whose voice is heard? Whose is left out? How can we locate additional data on this issue that would allow us to understand it more completely?

RESOURCES

Aronson, Blaney, Stephan, Sikes, & Snapp, 1978; Barton, 1997a, 1997b; Beyer, 1971; Braun, 1992; Cohen, 1986; Ehman, 1977; Gay, 1991; Gezi & Johnson, 1979; Harmin, 1994; Johnson & Johnson, 1979; Johnson, Johnson, Holubec, & Roy 1984; Kagan, 1989; Lampe & Rooze, 1994; Levstik & Barton, 1997; Newmann, 1990, 1992; Sexias, 1994; Slavin, 1990; Spoehr & Spoehr, 1994; Stahl, 1992; Stahl & VanSickle, 1992; Teachers' Curriculum Institute, 1994; Thornton, 1987; VanSledright, 1997.

● **STRATEGY 6.2: TEACH A BALANCED, ACCURATE, AND INCLUSIVE HISTORY CURRICULUM. AN INCLUSIVE CURRICULUM LOOKS AT HISTORICAL EVENTS AND ISSUES FROM MANY POINTS OF VIEW; THE VALUES OF SUCH A CURRICULAR APPROACH INCLUDE HISTORICAL ACCURACY, GREATER DEPTH OF UNDERSTANDING, AND REINFORCEMENT OF OUR COMMITMENT TO DEMOCRATIC IDEALS.**

DISCUSSION

Even as we try to convince students that the United States is a country "of the people, by the people, and for the people," should we not also recognize that the people need to see themselves reflected in the country, in the country's history, and in the history curriculum in the schools? A truly inclusive curriculum presents a more honest, accurate, and complete set of data sources so that students can better grasp history's complexities, multiple perspectives, and subtleties.

An authentic, inclusive history curriculum would explore the roles played by all groups in society, not only the great heroes. It would include relevant groups and individuals not in featured and isolated parts of the curriculum, but rather as integrated members of society. African Americans, for example, often appear in the curriculum in any depth only during times of slavery, Reconstruction, and the civil rights movement. Japanese Americans appear during their World War II internment, and Mexicans are often portrayed merely as losers of the Mexican War and as migrant farm workers.

It is important to emphasize the power of these groups even as they were being oppressed: how they maintained a vibrant culture, how they worked for their own empowerment, and how they contributed to the broader culture and society. At the same time, teachers can help students see an accurate picture of the purposes and uses of power by dominant groups. Overattentiveness to a group's cultural self-determination can obscure the fact of economic and political dominance by a superordinate group. Accuracy and intellectual honesty are the guideposts to the meaningful study of history.

An inclusive approach to history reinforces the national commitment to a democratic society, concepts of social justice, and the belief in a representative democracy. A pluralistic, democratic society works best when its diverse groups believe they are part of its institutions and social structure. Alienation and ethnic polarization can occur when individuals feel excluded. Any classroom is a microcosm of our society and its democratic institutions. Students who see themselves portrayed positively in the daily life of their classes and curriculum are more apt to be engaged and motivated to participate and achieve, not only in the classroom, but in the community.

CLASSROOM EXAMPLES

It is important to build on students' prior knowledge and the historical understandings they bring to school. Students often have misconceptions and stereotypical views about other groups. Primary source documents can help students hear the voices of people as they have expressed themselves through diaries, letters, legal documents, poems, songs, paintings, photographs, and other means. Students can begin to realize that history has been made by everyday people, not only political leaders. The attention paid to underrepresented groups over the past 30 years has produced a wealth of curriculum materials for student research.

The notion that culture and ethnicity influence historical understanding presents a powerful challenge. Teachers can find ways to engage students in dialogues about their beliefs regarding historical authority. Small-group explorations comparing the text version of an event with other secondary accounts and first-person narratives raise valuable issues of interpretation, even for very young students. Older students are able to read historical fiction and investigate questions of historical accuracy. Such analysis can be difficult for students, and purposeful instruction in critical thinking skills is often necessary to enable students to ask questions about the source of the data, author's point of view, clues about the author's bias, nature of conflicting data, and possible reasons why two individuals might see the same event quite differently.

Above all, students need to hear multiple voices from the past reflected in their history curriculum. Students should learn to ask, Who else would have been involved? How did this event look to them? How can we find out? What difference does it make?

RESOURCES

Appleby, Hunt, & Jacob, 1994; Armento, 1994; Banks, 1991, 1994; Chakrabarty, 1997; Cohen, 1994; Crocco, 1997; Egger-Bovet & Smith-Baranzin, 1994; Elshtain, 1981; Epstein, 1997; Espeland, 1991; Gagnon, 1989; Gates, 1992; Gezi & Johnson, 1979; Gordon, 1990; Levstik, 1997; Levstik & Barton, 1997; Limerick, 1997; Loewen, 1995; Romanowski, 1996; Sleeter & Grant 1987, 1991; Tatum 1992; Thornton 1987; Tunnel & Ammon 1996; White 1982; Yeager 1997; Zinn 1990.

STRATEGY 6.3: EMPHASIZE SOCIAL AND POLITICAL HISTORY. FOCUS ON THE MULTI-DIMENSIONALITY OF LIFE. A FOCUS ON THE ROLE OF PEOPLE IN HISTORY MORE FULLY ENGAGES STUDENTS IN HISTORICAL STUDY AND PROVIDES A MORE ACCURATE ACCOUNT OF THE PAST.

DISCUSSION

Many students think that the study of history revolves around wars and international politics. The study of great men and women is indeed important, as is the study of the reasons for events and issues, and the underlying social, cultural, and economic aspects of life as lived by "ordinary" people.

Consider this sentence from a world history textbook: "Whenever, within a feudal system, towns and trade begin to grow, . . . then feudalism gives way to capitalism" (Levstik & Barton, 1997, p 92). This type of language removes the actions of people from the process of change. It also reinforces the notion of the inevitability of certain events and minimizes the alternative choices and actions of real people. Before students can imagine themselves in a certain time and place, they must first realize that *history is about humans.*

The traditional emphasis on abstract political and diplomatic institutions, warn Levstik and Barton, leads students to understand history "as separate from ordinary life, divorced from the puzzles of culture and change that absorb us on a daily basis" (1997, p. 2). A balanced approach that includes social history would be a major step in reinvigorating the study of history in the classroom.

Since human life is an interaction of social, political, economic, religious, cultural, aesthetic, geographical, psychological, and other factors, the study of history should reflect the true multidimensionality of life. History should center on the lives of the people who lived it, so it must include an examination of the role of ideas, religion, family, work, and the arts in shaping individual and group behavior.

CLASSROOM EXAMPLES

Open historical studies by using the art, music, dance, or architecture of the people of the time and place being studied. Ask students to make inferences about life during this time by studying such data as well as primary source narrative documents. Historical fiction can evoke the humanity of the past. In-depth studies can come from such initial hypotheses, as students search for the answers to their own questions.

Social history can be a magnet for attracting student interest. Relate experiences of people in the past to students' own lives. Focus on enduring human dilemmas, emphasizing their historical roots. Facilitate student examination of human empowerment: the ways people bowed to, ignored, or acted against oppression and injustice, as well as how people of every group and in all times worked to build the futures they desired. Associate historical perspectives with current issues in the classroom, the school, and the larger community.

Use study about religion and the arts to create a more complete and *interesting* picture of human experience. Students can consider the roles of religious belief, tolerance, and intolerance in history, and how they have influenced and continue to influence change. Provide opportunities for students to examine historical records, secondary accounts, sacred texts, and religious art and architecture to identify and categorize religious beliefs and institutions and how they have affected individual and group actions. Bring many examples of painting, sculpture, music, and dance into the classroom so students can analyze their significance for various cultures and in particular historical eras.

RESOURCES

American Historical Association, 1998; Appleby, Hunt, & Jacob, 1994; Barton, 1997a; Bradley Commission, 1988; Crabtree, 1989; Elshtain, 1981; Gordon, 1990; Levstik & Barton, 1997; Sexias, 1994; Spoehr & Spoehr, 1994; Tuchman, 1981; Zinn, 1990.

STRATEGY 6.4: FRAME HISTORICAL TOPICS WITHIN TEMPORAL, SPATIAL, AND CAUSAL PATTERNS. AUTHENTIC HISTORICAL THINKING REQUIRES AN UNDERSTANDING OF TIME RELATIONSHIPS, EXAMINING THE INTERACTION BETWEEN HISTORY AND GEOGRAPHY AND THE ANALYSIS OF CHANGE OVER TIME WITH CONSIDERATION OF CAUSE-AND-EFFECT FACTORS.

DISCUSSION

When did it happen? Where did it happen? Why did it happen? All historical studies should reflect the temporal, spatial, and causal context of events and issues. Two aspects relate to understanding historical time: the ability to place historical moments in order and the ability to match historical moments to specific dates. Both of these skills are often difficult for students who study historical events in isolation, and who do not understand the causal linkages between one event and another.

Young children have difficulty comprehending how long ago the 1940s were, much less the 1200s. When teachers use concrete and developmentally appropriate methods, however, even young children can begin building the essential concepts of time, space, and causality. Comparative approaches help students place historical events and eras in relation to one another. As students build timelines, they reinforce the temporal and causal relationship of one event to another. In the early elementary grades, children can focus on material culture and how it changes over time. The focus for older students can include changes in social relations and the reasons for change.

Students also need an understanding of the *place* where historical events occur. Students can examine the relationships among place, resources, technology, and human movement, including motivations behind movement. Historical moments can be presented within a spatial framework relevant to students: Where is that place in relation to here? How is that place similar to and different from here? Creating a concrete representation of an abstract historical place is particularly important for younger children and for visual and kinesthetic learners.

Authentic historical thinking must include the analysis of change over time, with consideration of cause and effect. Students need to understand that historical outcomes were *not* preordained. Students' ability to establish relationships among historical phenomena and ultimately to themselves in the present is crucial to the learning of history. Causal frameworks help students evaluate the significance of historical moments and analyze the reliability and importance of historical evidence—crucial skills in authentic historical thinking. Students should be able to trace back events to uncover prior and causal factors; they should be able to explain increasingly more complex issues in their own words.

CLASSROOM EXAMPLES

Important and fundamental aspects of understanding chronology include building sequencing skills, placing things in order, and being able to explain what happened between one event and another. Young children can begin by building timelines of their day in school, then progress to plotting key events in the current year and in their lifetime.

Tracing back objects, such as the fruit eaten for breakfast, is a concrete activity that can be visually represented on timelines and on maps. Ask students to create visual timelines. Use classroom walls, or string a line on which pictures and artifacts can be displayed next to the appropriate dates. Students can use research skills to locate photographs and materials related to specific historical eras.

The timeline should also be comparative, representing different groups of people and different places in the world during particular time periods. Students can represent the passage of time by using foam blocks to represent one decade, then linking decades to represent centuries. A show and tell focused on history allows students to bring in "old" family artifacts and explain their origin and significance. Placing these family artifacts on the timeline or representing them with the decade blocks can make the abstract concept of historical time more concrete; it also links the student's personal history to the larger sweep of events.

Explore spatial concepts through the use of maps, globes, charts, and graphs related to the geography of the place being studied. Visual representations help make places *real* to students. Use video footage, photographs, and paintings to allow students to analyze similarities to (and differences from) the present and other historical places and times. Use primary accounts and historical narratives that give rich descriptions of the historical setting. Ask students to relate themes such as human and environmental interaction and movement to their personal histories, to local history, and to previously studied historical contexts.

Students can explore the interrelationships between and among related events, places, people, and issues. Use historical narratives that give students a rich context, then explore particular dramatic moments in depth, focusing on why and how these moments came to be and what resulted from them.

Students can investigate the notion of change over time, including an analysis of how and why the meanings of such abstractions as "democracy" change over time. They should be able to explain major international trends over several time periods, plotting events on maps and timelines. In discussions, students can explain the social, cultural, economic, technological, and political components of events and trace contemporary aspects of past events and issues. The ability not only to comprehend but to critique data is not easily attained; however, a sound, interesting history curriculum that is interdisciplinary, promotes in-depth study, relies on primary data sources, and is developmentally appropriate can accomplish this task.

RESOURCES

Ashby, Lee, & Dickinson, 1997; Barton, 1997a, 1997b; Bradley Commission, 1988; Crabtree, 1989; Downey & Levstik, 1991; Levstik & Barton, 1997; Loewen, 1995; National Commission on Social Studies in the Schools, 1989; Sexias, 1994; Spoehr & Spoehr, 1994; Thornton, 1987.

● **STRATEGY 6.5**: ENCOURAGE AN INQUIRY-BASED APPROACH TO LEARNING HISTORY. STUDENTS LEARN AND UNDERSTAND HISTORY WHEN THEY CONSTRUCT THEIR OWN MEANINGS FROM PURPOSEFUL INVESTIGATIONS OF QUESTIONS WITH REAL-WORLD SIGNIFICANCE AND RELEVANCE.

DISCUSSION

Children learn by grappling with new information and reorganizing their previous networks of ideas in relation to the new knowledge. They learn when they seek answers to questions that matter to them; their understanding changes, in part, as they become dissatisfied with what they know.

All of this internal activity requires time for sustained attention and reflection. Researchers in the field, as well as the various history standards, emphasize that students should formulate historical problems, locate relevant information, wrestle with evidence, weigh alternative explanations, and form informed conclusions. In other words, students should do history through an inquiry-based approach.

Teachers can provide opportunities for disciplined inquiry, that is, for purposeful investigations taking place within a community that has established goals, standards, and procedures for study. Such study requires formulation of questions with real-world relevance, including looking at historical significance, comparing and contrasting events, and making historical judgments.

Historical questions should be open-ended, without single or simple answers; they should call for divergent thinking. The elements most foreign to traditional history learning, but critical to inquiry, are a willingness to suspend judgment and a tolerance for ambiguity. Students need to take time to locate enough sound evidence to support their answers; they have to avoid jumping to hasty conclusions.

In an inquiry approach, participants must be willing to deal with fragmentary and contradictory evidence. Inquiry leads to varied supportable conclusions, so students and teachers alike should be open to the possibility of many interpretations. All historical events and issues appear different from different perspectives, so interpretation becomes an inseparable part of historical understanding.

An inquiry approach to learning history can facilitate deeper student understanding. But it is not without drawbacks. For many large-scale investigations, teachers will have to be willing to dedicate days of their precious instructional time. In addition, parents (and colleagues, too) may resist the outcomes of inquiry that challenges traditional interpretations and enduring myths. Some parents, for example, may see some inquiry questions as a threat to patriotism, or they may not want their children investigating different religions or certain social controversies. Teachers must be prepared to answer such objections. Inquiry builds critical thinkers and engages students in serious historical study. Children who participate in historical inquiry are generally more enthusiastic about history and recognize the authored nature of history, and thus potentially are better prepared to become thoughtful citizens.

CLASSROOM EXAMPLES

Historical inquiry can start with what students already know, or teachers can introduce new information to pique student interest. Whichever approach is used, the students should then establish a common knowledge base. Students will need direct instruction and structure for doing historical research. The teacher's role is to support and encourage student efforts and to break the task into manageable parts.

From the very beginning, provide precise guidelines for scoring and grading, and use those guidelines for formative assessment, stressing student responsibility for making sure that the guidelines are met. Throughout the process, the teacher models procedures and behaviors and gives feedback on student performance. Students gather background information to use as baseline data. The class establishes a common terminology. These introductory activities are especially important when children have little prior knowledge. New information and ideas will then build on *and* challenge the database.

The teacher can structure activities to facilitate exposure to new data that reflect multiple perspectives and interpretations. This undertaking should create a cognitive dissonance with prior knowledge. Such questioning should lead students to generate questions and hypotheses for further study.

Students will need specific in-class help in selecting, gathering, and organizing data. Teachers can emphasize the importance of finding enough evidence to support conclusions and effectively using that evidence to build a convincing interpretation. Requiring students to keep research logs helps them organize and interpret their data.

Successful inquiry requires a significant amount of in-class time and much planning by the teacher. Some assignments can be completed outside of class, but much of the data gathering and analysis will be done in class. The teacher thus has the opportunity to monitor and refine student research skills, allowing all students equal access to resources.

One characteristic of authentic assessment is real-world applicability. Inquiry offers a forum for moving beyond the classroom. Students need to practice the skills involved in choosing what is important from their inquiry and organizing it for presentation to specific audiences. Possible outcomes can include books or museum displays to share with parents at an open house or with other classes at school. Students can participate in structured roundtable discussions to try to reach consensus on the inquiry question, then take some action related to their conclusions, such as writing letters to newspaper editors, politicians, corporations, organizations, or foreign governments. Students can use their research logs and the evidence they have analyzed to write position papers on how their ideas have evolved through the course of the inquiry.

RESOURCES

Agosta, 1991; American Historical Association, 1998; Barton, 1997a; Beyer, 1971; Bradley Commission, 1988; Brooks & Brooks, 1993; Cohen, 1994; Dow, 1993; Downey & Levstik, 1991; Duis, 1996; Field, Labbo, Wilhelm, & Garrett, 1996; Gagnon, 1989; Leigh & Reynolds, 1997; Levstik, 1997; Levstik & Barton, 1997; Loewen, 1995; National Commission on Social Studies in the Schools, 1989; Newmann, Secada, & Wehlage, 1995; Novick, 1988; Sexias, 1994; Spoehr & Spoehr, 1994; Teachers' Curriculum Institute, 1994; Thornton, 1987; VanSledright, 1997.

● **STRATEGY 6.6**: PROMOTE STUDENT CONSTRUCTION OF HISTORICAL UNDERSTANDING BY USING PRIMARY SOURCES. PRIMARY SOURCES ARE THE BUILDING BLOCKS OF HISTORY. STUDENTS CAN BUILD THEIR OWN UNDERSTANDING OF HISTORY THROUGH ANALYSIS AND INTERPRETATION OF A VARIETY OF PRIMARY SOURCES, INCLUDING DOCUMENTS, POETRY, STORIES, VISUAL IMAGES, MUSIC, DANCE, AND ARTIFACTS.

DISCUSSION

A primary documents-based approach to teaching history works with all levels of students. All students are capable of working authentically as student historians, analyzing primary source documents that are appropriate to their developmental levels. Complex analytical questions are more manageable when students work in collaborative groups and bring their diverse experiences and perspectives to bear on a problem.

Use the full range of primary sources when designing history activities. Students are particularly engaged when manipulating artifacts. Visual images are also compelling in constructing history. Paintings, poems, stories, songs, and dance can inject human qualities into the learning of history.

Including the arts gives a more complete depiction of history and culture. The arts provoke a markedly different type of historical thinking than do documents. They give expression to feelings and emotions and raise the question of what it was like to be in a particular historical era or experience. The arts provide a window into culture.

In fact, some students can convey deep understandings of history through artistic representations, even though their performance on traditional tests and written assignments may fall short. The arts are an excellent vehicle for authentic history assessment. At the end of a unit of study, students can convey something they learned in a story, poem, painting, collage, or song.

Clear assessment guidelines should reward historical accuracy, the complexity of representation of themes or concepts, and the expressiveness or extent to which a knowledgeable viewer could gain insight or empathy. Arts-based historical assessment can meet all three guidelines of authentic assessment: It is compatible with constructivist ways of learning. It has real-world applicability, particularly if the teacher shares student work outside the classroom. And it appeals to student choices and intelligences.

CLASSROOM EXAMPLES

Teachers can introduce the use of primary sources by raising the notion of the authored nature of history. Choose an event from the curriculum that would be interesting to students, and then ask students to read differing accounts of that event. Ask students if they are willing to accept only one perspective. What questions should be asked about a data source? How will we know if one interpretation is more accurate than another? The qualifications of the writer also are relevant—the more expert, generally the more reliable.

Students can look also at the time elapsed between the event and the source's reporting of it. In addition, students can look for clues about the bias of the source. Always require students to cite the specific evidence that supports their guesses and conclusions and their reasoning about the selection of primary source documents.

Teachers can use mystery artifacts to provoke curiosity. Ask students to guess the functions of artifacts and when they were used. Ask students to give names to artifacts that reflect their function and tell what we use today instead of the artifact. Raise issues of change over time by asking why some things become obsolete. Comparing postcards and photographs from different eras provides insight into social, geographic, and economic changes. Students can list what they see in the pictures, draw inferences based on their observations, and generate hypotheses and questions. Then they can use other primary and secondary sources to try to find answers.

Teachers using primary arts sources must teach students to analyze the form as well as the content; different inferences can be drawn from each. Use personal artistic representations, but also public art such as stamps, posters, murals, and statues. Ask students to consider how the artist uses content and form to manipulate people's emotions and make a point: Who was the audience? Why was the work created when it was? What was its effect? Students can analyze the source for historical accuracy, using other sources for verification. They can infer the artist's point of view, the artist's message, and the form of the work, and make guesses as to the political or social uses of the work.

Every teacher has easy access to historical archives, collections of documents, art and artifacts, and documents-based lessons through technology. There are CD-ROMs and software collections of primary sources. Most accessible, of course, are the databases available through the Internet. Historical societies, archival collections, and museums have digitized their collections and placed them within the reach of anyone with a networked computer.

As with all instructional resources on the World Wide Web, the teacher must be a critical consumer. Check out sites before asking students to investigate them. Carefully structure activities in which students explore archives or documents. Note that it may be more efficient for the teacher to do the searching, downloading appropriate primary sources for student use.

RESOURCES

Abel, Hauwiller, Vandeventer, 1989; Allen, 1981; American Historical Association, 1998; Barton, 1997a; Berson, 1996; Bodle, 1985; Bradley Commission, 1988; Brooks & Brooks, 1993; Dow, 1993; Downey & Levstik, 1991; Dunaway, 1984; Egger-Bovet & Smith-Baranzin, 1994; Epstein, 1994a, 1994b; Field, Labbo, Wilhelm, & Garrett, 1996; Fowler, 1984; Freeman, Bodle, & Burroughs, 1984; Gardner, 1988; Groth & Albert, 1997; Irvin, Lunstrum, Lynch-Brown, & Shepard, 1995; Kobrin, 1996; Leigh & Reynolds, 1997; Levstik & Barton, 1997; Percoco, 1994; Risinger, 1996; Schroder, 1976; Selwyn, 1995; Trachtenberg, 1989; Trinkle, 1997; Vockell, 1992.

● **STRATEGY 6.7:** USE LITERACY STRATEGIES TO PROMOTE HISTORICAL COMPREHENSION. HISTORICAL COMPREHENSION DEPENDS ON THE ABILITY TO CRITICALLY READ AND INTERPRET WRITTEN MATERIALS. LITERACY STRATEGIES CAN SHARPEN HISTORICAL THINKING SKILLS AND PROMOTE STUDENT ENGAGEMENT.

DISCUSSION

Using literacy strategies can help motivate students to read and write in history classrooms and can deepen their historical comprehension at the same time. Teaching new vocabulary and concepts through wide reading experiences is critical to historical understanding. Students need to have many opportunities to use context, structural analysis, and other strategies to guess the meaning of words.

A major goal of literacy—and historical instruction—is for students to become critical readers. Critical reading skills grow through practice in recognizing the purpose of the author; distinguishing relevant from irrelevant information; evaluating sources; noting special points of view or biases; distinguishing fact from opinion or fiction; recognizing and evaluating inferences; and identifying biased, slanted, or emotional language. A natural outcome of critical reading is greater expertise in writing. Students should be given many opportunities to organize their new learning and their responses to what they have read through a variety of written formats.

Historical narratives, both fiction and nonfiction, illuminate the everyday side of history and help children understand that people like themselves make history. Even reluctant readers are often drawn into historical stories that they see as relevant to their own lives. Students are interested in interpretation and moral issues—*why* humans in the past behaved as they did. Teachers must use narratives with caution, however. Young learners tend to believe the stories they read and accept them uncritically. Teachers must explicitly incorporate critical analysis when using historical narratives. Students can compare the events of the narrative with the textbook and other sources and analyze the points of divergence. The use of historical narratives requires a balance between students' search for historical truth and their recognition that people in other times saw the world differently from us and from each other.

CLASSROOM EXAMPLES

Vocabulary enrichment can happen within a meaningful historical context. Concept or word maps are an effective method of connecting new vocabulary to students' prior knowledge. In addition, conceptual organizers provide an overview of the main ideas of a lesson. Organizers are especially useful for visual and spatial learners, as word maps depict relationships between new concepts and previously learned vocabulary and ideas.

Authentic historical thinking requires skepticism with regard to sources of information. Provide opportunities for younger students to practice evaluating sources by asking them to match jumbled lists of topics and authorities. Ask, for example, if Thomas Jefferson or Frederick Douglass

would be a better source to ask about slavery, and require students to defend their choices. Older students can conduct research on authors' qualifications using *Who's Who*, other biographical dictionaries, encyclopedias, and almanacs. Give students readings from demagogues of the historical period under study, and ask them to evaluate both the author's purpose and qualifications.

Recognizing multiple perspectives is important to a deep understanding of history. Paired works of historical fiction can provide varying points of view on the same event. Teachers can also use divergent primary source accounts of the same event, asking students to identify point of view and analyze the reasons for the different accounts.

Young children need help in distinguishing between the real and the imagined. One way is to ask children to change a factual account into a fantasy. Older children can use newspaper editorials, history textbooks, primary sources, and advertising to identify opinion statements. Ask students to look for "loaded" words and identify those with positive or negative connotations.

All narratives are not appropriate for the history classroom, of course. Search for narratives that tell a good story, are accurate and authentic in historical detail, use language authentic to the period, incorporate sound historical interpretation, present multiple perspectives, and provide insight into current issues as well as those in the past.

Literature response groups combine students who either have all read the same book or who have read different books on related topics. In the groups, students might compare the narrative with the text and other sources, identifying similarities and differences. They could role-play one of the characters in the book, write letters to real historical figures of the era, write a sequel to the story, create murals and portraits of characters, or connect the story to historical and contemporary music.

RESOURCES

Anderson, Hiebert, Scott, & Wilkinson, 1985; Armbruster & Anderson, 1985; Armento, 1994; Au, 1993; Barton, 1997a; Beck & McKeown, 1988; Beck, McKeown, & Worthy, 1993; Davis, Rooze, & Runnels, 1992; Dimmit & Van Cleaf, 1992; Downey, 1993; Downey & Levstik, 1991; Epstein, 1993; Estes & Vaughn, 1985; Franklin & Roach, 1992; Gagnon, 1989; Irvin, Lunstrum, Lynch-Brown, & Shepard, 1995; Klein, 1988; Koeller, 1992, 1996; Kornfield, 1994; Levstik, 1995; Levstik & Barton, 1997; Loewen, 1995; Lynch-Brown & Tomlinson, 1993; Pappas, Keifer, & Levstik, 1990; Perez-Stable & Cordier, 1994; Romanowski, 1996; Smith, Monson, & Dobson, 1992; Teachers' Curriculum Institute, 1994; Tunnel & Ammon, 1993, 1996.

● **STRATEGY 6.8**: USE THE COMMUNITY AS A HISTORICAL RESOURCE. APPROACHES TO LEARNING HISTORY, SUCH AS FAMILY AND LOCAL HISTORY AND FIELD EXPERIENCES, BUILD BRIDGES TO STUDENTS' HOME AND COMMUNITY CULTURES AND MAKE THE LEARNING OF HISTORY MORE RELEVANT AND MEANINGFUL.

DISCUSSION

Students must see history as relevant and meaningful in their lives to be engaged in its study. The easiest way to build that relevance is to start with students' personal histories. Teachers can use the local community as a living laboratory for creating family and local histories and for structuring out-of-school learning activities. Many students will be able to see connections to the larger world that are not apparent in the sometimes isolated, artificial classroom environment.

Structured investigations into family and community histories can nurture intergenerational communication as students gather, reflect on, and interpret data at home and in their neighborhoods. Families turn into contributors to the learning agenda in nonthreatening and rewarding ways. Teachers should continually connect the local to the global, emphasizing student analysis of how their findings fit into or conflict with larger themes and concepts in history.

The local community provides opportunities for field experiences that use historic places to bring history alive. A historic place evokes a kind of knowing different from other primary sources. Real places provide a powerful temporal and spatial frame of reference and give history a human scale, fostering student empathy with the past. A historic place can also make universal cultural archetypes more concrete. Students can analyze features of the natural and built environments to form generalizations in conjunction with prior knowledge and data from other sources. Historical concepts—shelter, work, kinship, spirituality, and change over time—are no longer abstract. Children discover the effect of human events on their community and see the environment as a reflection of themselves.

CLASSROOM EXAMPLES

History can become personal for students through the creation of autobiographies. Even very young children can create timelines of the most important events in their lives, or time capsules of personal artifacts. Students soon find that their own memories are inadequate, so they seek evidence from their families, thus reinforcing the importance of examining data from multiple sources. Sometimes family members remember things differently, raising issues of multiple perspectives and the reconciliation of conflicting accounts. Students can use their own data for launching studies of other cultures and communities through primary and secondary sources or Internet activities such as e-mail pen pals.

Family and community histories constructed from oral interviews expand the notion of personal history beyond the individual student. Oral history projects make students active participants in the creation of histories that have meaning beyond the classroom. The teacher can use oral history to focus on an individual's story within a purely local setting, document cultural heritages, or link individuals to larger events and themes.

Products of oral history projects can include a variety of authentic assessments, including research papers, multimedia presentations, dramatic performances, or journal articles. Students can present their work to the entire school, to the PTA, to community groups, at libraries or shopping malls, to senior citizen centers, to professional organizations, to local media, to local heritage groups, or as social science fair or History Day projects.

Every community holds the potential for field experiences. Historic places are more than important buildings; they include battlefields, bridges, business districts, neighborhoods, Native American sites, or natural places such as rivers or mountain passes.

Preparation is the key to successful field experiences. The teacher must consider carefully how the historic place enriches and extends the curriculum. The teacher needs to visit the site prior to the field trip to gather information and instructional materials and to plan activities. Classroom preparation can focus on exploring the historical context using the full range of historical data. At the site, students can analyze spatial and temporal relationships, as well as focusing on interactions between humans and the environment.

After visiting the site, structure activities that require students to ground the story of the place in larger historical themes and events. Student products can include written and oral reports on their research and conclusions, creative writing such as narratives or drama, or persuasive writing advocating some position or action.

RESOURCES

Alleman & Brophy, 1994; Allen, 1981; Banks, 1994; Banks & Joyce, 1971; Barton, 1997a; Dunaway, 1984; Fredericks & Rasinski, 1990; Gagnon, 1989; Gay, 1991; Gezi & Johnson, 1979; Irvine, 1990; Jarolimek, 1990; Lanman & Mehaffy, 1988; Leigh & Reynolds, 1997; Levstik & Barton, 1997; Metcalf & Downey, 1982; Proctor & Haas, 1993; Protheroe & Barsdate, 1991; Rogers, 1988; Sitton, Mehaffy, & Davis, 1983; Steinberg, 1993; Tatum, 1992; Teachers' Curriculum Institute, 1994; Wellhousen, 1994; White & Hunter.

● STRATEGY 6.9: FACILITATE STUDENTS' HISTORICAL EMPATHY THROUGH EXPERIENTIAL LEARNING. EXPERIENTIAL LEARNING BRINGS HISTORY ALIVE AS STUDENTS RECONSTRUCT AND PARTICIPATE IN HISTORICAL EXPERIENCES.

DISCUSSION

Authentic historical understanding opens a window to human character and motivation. It can evoke historical imagination within the limitations of available evidence. Empathy is important in understanding the why of history, and it can play a central role in facilitating children's engagement with history. True understanding must be based on analysis, reason, and the use of sound evidence.

The development of empathy in students is an active process involving several layers of understanding. Students must consider the role of human action in a historical event or experience. In addition, they must come to understand the historical context and chronology. Along the way, they need to analyze a variety of historical data and interpretations of the event or experience, and then construct a narrative framework through which they reach conclusions.

Authentic historical thinking requires students to project their own ideas and feelings into a historical situation and recognize how the past is different from and similar to the present. Multiple sources beyond the textbook present differing points of view that allow students to construct authentic explanations grounded in the social, cultural, political, and economic context of past eras. When using empathetic approaches, take care not to focus on groups and individuals in the past only as victims, or to perpetuate students' commonly held stereotypes.

CLASSROOM EXAMPLES

After reading historical fiction or researching the event or era under study, even young children can create first-person narratives in which they place themselves in the historical experience. Students can write poems, journals, diaries, or letters describing an individual perspective on a historical experience, including vivid sensory descriptions that bring the account to life. Individually or in pairs, students can create an imagined dialogue between two historical figures who may or may not actually have met. Facilitate an exploration of how youngsters' contemporary feelings and experiences are similar to those of young people in past eras, but also how they differ across time and place.

Kinesthetic experiences that build empathy include dramatic role-playing, mock trials, creating living statues, and simulations. Students can create minidramas based on historical fiction, primary narratives, or visual images. Another type of role-playing would cast some students as historical figures who would be interviewed by student-reporters.

Simulations are recreations of historical events or situations such as the frantic pace of an assembly line, the discomfort and terror of trench warfare, or the inhumanity of a slave ship. Use care in emphasizing the complexity and multidimensionality of historical characters and contexts, avoiding oversimplification or appeals purely to emotion. It is important to fully debrief such activities, especially after powerful experiences, so that students can discuss how they felt during the experience and how their experience might have been similar to and different from historical reality.

Many students enjoy argument and debate; historical and contemporary controversies appeal to those interests and offer a stimulating avenue for teaching history. For some hot topics, students can gain distance by taking the perspective of a historian in the future—How would you explain the issue to people 50 years from now?—or the viewpoint of a person from another culture. Teachers can promote attention to multiple viewpoints by requiring students to argue from a position different from their own, or allowing them to debate the issue, then switch sides.

Despite the learning potential in using conflict to teach history, young people usually need practice in conflict resolution. Teachers must be prepared to treat controversy in a balanced and objective way, emphasizing the use of evidence drawn from current scholarship and the notion of student construction of their own understandings based on that evidence.

RESOURCES

Barton, 1997a; Bradley Commission, 1988; Chilcoat, 1988; Dewey, 1933; Evans, 1993; Gabella, 1994; Gagnon, 1989; Hickey, 1990; Hunt & Metcalf, 1968; Johnson & Johnson, 1979; Karjala & White, 1983;

Koeller, 1992; Kornfield, 1994; Levstik, 1995; Levstik & Barton, 1997; Loewen, 1995; Long & Long, 1975; National Commission for Social Studies in the Schools, 1989; Popenfus & Kimbrell, 1989; Portal, 1987; Selwyn, 1995; Spoeher & Spoeher, 1994; Tabor, 1986; Teachers' Curriculum Institute, 1994; Turner, 1989; VanSledright & Brophy, 1992; Yeager, Foster, Maley, Anderson, Morris, & Davis, 1997.

BIBLIOGRAPHY

Abel, F. J., Hauwiller, J. G., & Vandeventer, N. (1989). Using writing to teach social studies. *The Social Studies, 80*(1), 17–20.

Agosta, D. (1991). Presenting social issues with videotape. *Media and Methods, 12*(1), 19–20.

Alleman, J., & Brophy, J.. (1994). Taking advantage of out-of-school opportunities for meaningful social studies learning. *The Social Studies, 85*(6), 262–267.

Allen, B. (1981). *From memory to history: Using oral sources in local historical research.* Nashville: American Association for State and Local History.

American Historical Association. (1998). Criteria for standards in history/social studies/social sciences. *Perspectives, 36*(1), 29.

Anderson, R. C., Hiebert, E. H., Scott, J. A. & Wilkinson, I. A. G. (1985). *Becoming a nation of readers: The report of the commission on reading.* Urbana, IL: Center for the Study of Reading.

Appleby, J., Hunt, L., & Jacob, M. (1994). *Telling the truth about history.* New York: Norton.

Armbruster, B. B., & Anderson, T. H. (1985). Producing 'considerate' expository text: Or easy reading is damned hard writing. *Journal of Curriculum Studies, 17*(3), 247–263.

Armento, B. (1991). Changing conceptions of research on teaching social studies. In J .P. Shaver (Ed.), *Handbook of research on teaching and learning social studies.* New York: Macmillan.

Armento, B. (1994). *Research on children's learning of history: Issues and implications.* Paper presented at the annual meeting of the National Council for History Education, Westlake, OH.

Armstrong, T. (1994). *Multiple intelligences in the classroom.* Alexandria, VA: Association for Supervision and Curriculum Development.

Aronson, E., Blaney, N. T., Stephan, C., Sikes, J., & Snapp, M. (1978). *The jigsaw classroom.* Beverly Hills, CA: Sage.

Aronson, E., & Gonzalez, A. (1988). Desegregation, jigsaw, and the Mexican-American experience. In P. A. Katz & D. A. Taylor (Eds.), *Eliminating racism: Profiles in controversy.* New York: Plenum Press.

Ashby, R., Lee, P., & Dickinson, E. (1997). How children explain the 'why' of history: The *Chata* research project on teaching history. *Social Education, 61*(1), 17–21.

Au, K. H. (1993). *Literacy instruction in multicultural settings.* New York: Harcourt, Brace, Jovanovich.

Baker, E. L. (1994). Learning-based assessments of history understanding. *Educational Psychologist, 29*(2), 97–106.

Banks, J. A. (1991). Multicultural education: Its effects on students' racial and gender role attitudes. In J. P. Shaver (Ed.), *Handbook of research on social studies teaching and learning.* New York: Macmillan.

Banks, J. A. (1994). *Multiethnic education: Theory and practice* (3rd ed.). Boston: Allyn and Bacon.

Banks, J. A., & Joyce, W. W. (Eds.). (1971). *Teaching social studies to culturally different children.* Reading, MA: Addison-Wesley.

Barton, K. C. (1997a). History—it *can* be elementary: An overview of elementary students' understanding of history. *Social Education, 61*(4), 13–16.

Barton, K. C. (1997b). 'I just kinda know': Elementary students' ideas about historical evidence. *Theory and Research in Social Education, 24*(4), 407–430.

Beck, I. L., & McKeown, M. G. (1988). Toward meaningful accounts in history texts for young learners. *Educational Researcher, 17*(1), 31–39.

Beck, I. L., McKeown, M. G. & Worthy, M. J. (1993, April 12–16). *Questioning the author: An approach to enhancing students' engagement with text.* Paper presented at the annual meeting of the American Educational Research Association, Atlanta.

Berson, M. (1996). Effectiveness of computer technology in the social studies: A review of the literature. *Journal of Research on Computing in Education, 28*(4), 486–499.

Beyer, B. K. (1971). *Inquiry in the social studies classroom: A strategy for teaching.* Columbus, OH: Charles E. Merrill.

Bodle, W. (1985). The black soldier in World War I. *Social Education, 49*(2), 129–130.

Bradley Commission on History in the Schools. (1988). *Building a history curriculum: Guidelines for teaching history in schools.* Westlake, OH: National Council for History Education.

Braun, J. A., Jr. (1992). Social technology in the elementary social studies curriculum. *Social Education, 56*(7), 389–392.

Brooks, J., & Brooks, M. (1993). *In search of understanding: The case for constructivist classrooms.* Alexandria, VA: Association for Supervision and Curriculum Development.

Chakrabarty, D. (1997). Minorities' histories, subaltern pasts. *Perspectives, 35*(8), 37–43.

Chilcoat, G. W. (1988). The 'living newspaper' theatre as a teaching strategy. *Social Education, 52*(6), 439–440, 442–443.

Cohen, D. W. (1994). *The combing of history.* Chicago: University of Chicago Press.

Cohen, E. (1986). *Designing groupwork: Strategies for heterogeneous classrooms.* New York: Teachers College Press.

Cohen, E., & Lotan, R. A. (Eds.). (1997). *Working for equity in heterogeneous classrooms: Sociological theory in action.* New York: Teachers College Press.

Crabtree, C. (1989). Returning history to the elementary schools. In P. Gagnon (Ed.), *Historical literacy: The case for history in American education.* Boston: Houghton-Mifflin.

Crocco, M. S. (1997). Making time for women's history . . . when your survey course is already filled to overflowing. *Social Education, 61*(1), 32–37.

Davis, B. H., Rooze, G. E., & Runnels, M. K. T. (1992). Writing-to-learn in elementary social studies. *Social Education, 56*(7), 393–397.

Dewey, J. (1933). *How we think.* New York: Heath.

Dimmitt, J. P., & Van Cleaf, D. W. (1992). Integrating writing and social studies: Alternatives to the formal research paper. *Social Education, 56*(7), 382–384.

Dow, P. B. (1993). Teaching with objects: No fault learning? *The Social Studies, 84*(5), 230–231.

Downey, M. T. (1993, April 12–16). *Historical learning and the writing process: The writing to learn history project.* Paper presented at the annual meeting of the American Educational Research Association, Atlanta.

Downey, M. T., & Levstik, L. S. (1991). Teaching and learning history. In J. P. Shaver (Ed.), *Handbook of research on social studies teaching and learning.* New York: Macmillan.

Duis, M. (1996). Using schema theory to teach American history. *Social Education, 60*(3), 144–146.

Dunaway, D. (Ed.). (1984). *Oral history: An interdisciplinary anthology.* Nashville: American Association for State and Local History.

Egger-Bovet, H., & M. Smith-Baranzin. (1994). *U. S. kids' history: Book of the American revolution.* New York: Little, Brown.

Ehman, L. H. (1977, April). *Social studies instructional factors causing change in high school students' sociopolitical attitudes over a two-year period.* Paper presented at the annual meeting of the American Educational Research Association, New York.

Elshtain, J. B. (1981). *Public man, private woman: Woman in social and political thought.* Princeton, NJ: Princeton University Press.

Epstein, T. L. (1993). Why teach history to the young? In M. Tunnel & R. Ammon (Eds.), *The story of ourselves: Teaching history through children's literature.* Portsmouth, NH: Heinemann.

Epstein, T. L. (1994a). The arts of history: An analysis of secondary school students' interpretations of the arts in historical contexts. *Journal of Curriculum and Supervision, 9*(2), 174–194.

Epstein, T. L. (1994b). Sometimes a shining moment: High school students' representations of history through the arts. *Social Education, 58*(3), 136–141.

Epstein, T. L. (1997). Sociocultural approaches to young people's historical understanding. *Social Education, 61*(1), 28–31.

Espeland, P. (Ed.). (1991). *The kids' guide to social action.* Minneapolis: Free Spirit Publishing.

Estes, T. H., & Vaughn, J. L. (1985). *Reading and learning in the content classroom.* Boston: Allyn and Bacon.

Evans, M. D. (1993). Using classroom debates as a learning tool. *Social Education, 57*(7), 370.

Evans, R. W. (1988). Lessons from history: Teacher and student conceptions of the meaning of history. *Theory and Research in Social Education, 16*(3), 203–225.

Field, S. L., Labbo, L. D., Wilhelm, R. W., & Garrett, A. W. (1996). To touch, to see, to feel: Artifact inquiry in the social studies classroom. *Social Education, 60*(3), 141–143.

Fowler, C. B. (Ed.). (1984). *Arts in education, education in arts.* Washington, DC: National Endowment for the Arts.

Franklin, M. R., & Roach, P. B. (1992). Teaching reading strategies in social studies contexts. *Social Education, 56*(4), 385–388.

Fredericks, A. D., & Rasinski, T. V. (1990). Involving parents in the assessment process. *The Reading Teacher, 44*(4), 346–349.

Freeman, E. T., Bodle, W., & Burroughs, W. (1984). Eleanor Roosevelt resigns from the DAR: A study in conscience. *Social Education, 48*(9), 536–541.

Gabella, M. S. (1994). Beyond the looking glass: Bringing students into the conversation of historical inquiry. *Theory and Research in Social Education, 22*(3), 340–363.

Gagnon, P. (Ed.). (1989). *Historical literacy: The case for history in American education.* Boston: Houghton-Mifflin.

Gardner, H. (1983). *Frames of mind: The theory of multiple intelligences.* New York: Basic Books.

Gardner, H. (1988). Toward more effective arts education. *Journal of Aesthetic Education, 22*(1), 158–166.

Gardner, H. (1991). *The unschooled mind: How children think and how schools should teach.* New York: Basic Books.

Gates, H. L., Jr. (1992). The transforming of the American mind. *Social Education, 56*(6), 328–330.

Gay, G. (1991). Culturally diverse students and social studies. In J. P. Shaver (Ed.), *Handbook of research on social studies teaching and learning.* New York: Macmillan.

Gezi, K. I., & Johnson, B. (1979). Enhancing racial attitudes through the study of black heritage. *Childhood Education, 46*(4), 397–399.

Goodlad, J. (1984). *A place called school: Prospects for the future.* New York: McGraw-Hill.

Gordon, L. (1990). U. S. women's history. In E. Foner (Ed.), *The new American history.* Philadelphia: Temple University Press.

Groth, J. L., & Albert, M. (1997). Arts alive in the development of historical thinking. *Social Education, 61*(1), 42–44.

Hammack, D. C, Hartoonian, M., Howe, J., Jenkins, L. B., Levstik, L. S., McDonald, W. M., Mullis, I. V. S., & Owen, E. (1990). *The U.S. history report card: The achievement of fourth-, eighth-, and twelfth-grade students in 1988 and trends from 1986 to 1988 in the factual knowledge of high-school juniors.* Princeton, NJ: National Assessment of Educational Progress, Educational Testing Service.

Harmin, M. (1994). *Inspiring active learning: A handbook for teachers.* Alexandria, VA: Association for Supervision and Curriculum Development.

Hart, D. (1994). *Authentic assessment: A handbook for educators.* Menlo Park, CA: Addison-Wesley.

Hickey, M. G. (1990). Mock trials for children. *Social Education, 54*(1), 43–44.

Hiebert, E. H., & Hutchinson, T. A. (1991). Research directions: The current state of alternative assessments for policy and instructional uses. *Language Arts, 6*(8), 662–668.

Hunt, M. P., & Metcalf, L. (1968). *Teaching high school social studies.* New York: Harper & Row.

Irvin, J. L., Lunstrum, J. P., Lynch-Brown, C., & Shepard, M. F. (1995). *Enhancing social studies through literacy strategies.* Washington, DC: National Council for the Social Studies.

Irvine, J. J. (1990). *Black students and school failure.* New York: Greenwood Press.

Jarolimek, J. (1990). *Social studies in elementary education* (8th ed.). New York: Macmillan.

Johnson, D. W., & Johnson, R. T. (1979). Conflict in the classroom: Controversy and learning. *Review of Educational Research, 49*(1), 51–70.

Johnson, D. W., Johnson, R. T., Holubec, E. J., & Roy, P. (1984). *Circles of learning: Cooperation in the classroom.* Alexandria, VA: Association for Supervision and Curriculum Development.

Johnston, P. (1992). *Constructive evaluation of literate activity.* New York: Longman.

Kagan, S. (1989). *Cooperative learning resources for teachers.* San Juan Capistrano, CA: Resources for Teachers.

Karjala, H. E., & White, R. E. (1983). American history through music and role-play. *The History Teacher, 17*(1), 33–39.

Klein, M. L. (1988). *Teaching reading comprehension and vocabulary.* Englewood Cliffs, NJ: Prentice-Hall.

Kobrin, D. (1996). *Beyond the textbook: Teaching history using documents and primary sources.* Portsmouth, NH: Heinemann.

Koeller, S. (1992). Social studies research writing: Raising voices. *Social Education, 56*(6), 379–381.

Koeller, S. (1996). Multicultural understanding through literature. *Social Education, 60*(2), 99–103.

Kornfield, J. (1994). Using fiction to teach history. *Social Education, 58*(5), 281–286.

Kornhaber, M., & Gardner, H. (1993). *Varieties of excellence: Identifying and assessing children's talents* (Opinion Paper BBB12599). Pleasantville, NY: Aaron Diamond Foundation.

Lampe, J. R., & Rooze, G. E. (1994, April 4–8). *Enhancing social studies achievement among Hispanic students using cooperative learning techniques.* Paper presented at the annual meeting of the American Educational Research Association, New Orleans.

Lanman, B. A., & Mehaffy, G. L. (1988). *Oral history in the secondary school classroom.* Provo, UT: Oral History Association.

Lazear, D. (1992). *Teaching for multiple intelligences.* Bloomington, IN: Phi Delta Kappa Education Foundation.

Leigh, A. T., & Reynolds, T. O. (1997). Little windows to the past. *Social Education, 61*(1), 45–47.

Levstik, L. S. (1995). Narrative constructions: Cultural frames for history. *The Social Studies, 86*(3), 113–116.

Levstik, L. S. (1997). 'Any history is someone's history': Listening to multiple voices from the past. *Social Education, 61*(1), 48–51.

Levstik, L. S., & Barton, K. C. (1997). *Doing history: Investigating with children in elementary and middle school.* Mahwah, NJ: Lawrence Erlbaum Associates.

Limerick, P. N. (1997). Has 'minority' history transformed the historical discourse? *Perspectives, 35*(8), 1, 32–36.

Lockwood, A. T. (1993). Multiple intelligences theory in action. *Research and the Classroom, 4,* 1–12.

Loewen, J. W. (1995). *Lies my teacher told me: Everything your American history textbook got wrong.* New York: New Press.

Long, S., & Long, R. (1975). Controversy in the classroom: Student viewpoint and educational outcome. *Teaching Political Science, 2*(3), 275–299.

Lynch-Brown, C., & Tomlinson, C. M. (1993). *Essentials of children's literature.* Needham Heights, MA: Allyn and Bacon.

McNeil, L. M. (1986). *Contradictions of control: School structure and school knowledge.* New York: Routledge & Kegan Paul.

Metcalf, F., & Downey, M. T. (1982). *Using local history in the classroom.* Nashville, TN: American Association for State and Local History.

National Commission on Social Studies in the Schools. (1989). *Charting a course: Social studies for the 21st century.* Washington, DC: Author.

Newmann, F. M. (1990). Higher order thinking in teaching social studies: A rationale for the assessment of classroom thoughtfulness. *Journal of Curriculum Studies, 22*(1), 41–56.

Newmann, F. M. (1992). *Student engagement and achievement in American secondary schools.* New York: Teachers College Press.

Newmann, F. M., Secada, W. G., & Wehlage, G. G. (1995). *A guide to authentic instruction and assessment: Vision, standards, and scoring.* Madison: Wisconsin Center for Education Research.

Nickell, P. (1992). Doing the stuff of social studies: A conversation with Grant Wiggins. *Social Education, 50*(2), 92–94.

Novick, P. (1988). *That noble dream: The 'objectivity question' and the American historical profession.* New York: Cambridge University Press.

Pappas, C. C., Kiefer, B. Z., & Levstik, L. (1990). *An integrated language perspective in the elementary school: Theory into action.* New York: Longman.

Percoco, J. A. (1994). History in the making: The development of a high school applied history program. *History News, 49*(1), 8–12.

Perez-Stable, M. A., & Cordier, M. H. (1994). *Understanding American history through children's literature: Instructional units and activities for grades K–8.* Phoenix: Oryx Press.

Popenfus, J. R., & Kimbrell, M. (1989). The mock trial as an activity in high school. *The History and Social Science Teacher, 25*(1), 35–37.

Portal, C. (1987). Empathy as an objective for history teaching. In C. Portal (Ed.), *The history curriculum for teachers*. London: Falmer Press.

Proctor, D. R., & Haas, M. E. (1993). Social studies and school-based community service programs: Teaching the role of cooperation and legitimate power. *Social Education, 57*(7), 381–383.

Protheroe, N. J., & Barsdate, K. J. (1991). *Culturally sensitive instruction and student learning*. Arlington, VA: Educational Research Service.

Ravitch, D., &. Finn, Jr., C. E (1987). *What do our 17-year-olds know? A report on the first national assessment of history and literature*. New York: Harper & Row.

Reiff, J. C. (1997). Multiple intelligences, culture, and equitable learning. *Childhood Education, 73*(5), 301–305.

Risinger, C. F. (1996). Webbing the social studies: Using Internet and World Wide Web resources in social studies instruction. *Social Education, 60*(2), 111–112.

Rogers, K. L. (1988). Oral history and the history of the civil rights movement. *Journal of American History, 75*(2), 567–576.

Romanowski, M. (1996). Problems of bias in history textbooks. *Social Education, 60*(3), 170–173.

Schroder, F. (1976). Designing your exhibits: Seven ways to look at an artifact. *History News, 31*(11), 1–16.

Selwyn, D. (1995). *Arts and humanities in the social studies*. Washington, DC: National Council for the Social Studies.

Sexias, P. (1994). Students' understanding of historical significance. *Theory and Research in Social Education, 22*(3), 281–304.

Sheperd, L. A. (1991). Negative policies for dealing with diversity: When does assessment and diagnosis turn into sorting and segregation? In E. H. Hiebert (Ed.), *Literacy for a diverse society: Perspectives, practices, and policies*. New York: Teachers College Press.

Sitton, T., Mehaffy, G. L., & Davis, Jr., O. L. (1983). *Oral history: A guide for teachers (and others)*. Austin: University of Texas Press.

Sizer, T. (1991). *Horace's school: Redesigning the American high school*. Boston: Houghton Mifflin.

Slavin, R. E. (1990). *Cooperative learning: Theory, research, and practice*. Needham Heights, MA: Allyn & Bacon.

Sleeter, C. E., & Grant, C. A. (1987). An analysis of multicultural education in the United States. *Harvard Educational Review, 57*(4), 421–444.

Sleeter, C. E., & Grant, C.A. (1991). Race, class, gender, and disability in current textbooks. In M. W. Apple & L. K. Christian-Smith (Eds.), *The politics of the textbook*. New York: Routledge.

Smith, J. A., Monson, J. A., & Dobson, D. (1992). A case study on integrating history and reading instruction through literature. *Social Education, 56*(7), 370–375.

Spoehr, K. T., & Spoehr, L. W. (1994). Learning to think historically. *Educational Psychologist, 29*(2), 71–77.

Stahl, R. J. (Ed.). (1992). *Cooperative learning in the social studies classroom: A handbook for teachers*. Menlo Park, CA: Addison-Wesley.

Stahl, R. J., & VanSickle, R. L. (Eds.). (1992). *Cooperative learning in the social studies classroom: An introduction to social study*. Washington, DC: National Council for the Social Studies.

Steinberg, S. (1993). The world inside the classroom: Using oral history to explore racial and ethnic diversity. *The Social Studies, 84*(2), 71–73.

Tabor, J. L. (1986). The trial of Susan B. Anthony. *Social Education, 50*(4), 311–313.

Tatum, B. D. (1992). African-American identity development, academic achievement, and missing history. *Social Education, 56*(6), 331–333.

Teachers' Curriculum Institute. (1994). *History alive! Engaging all learners in the diverse classroom*. Menlo Park, CA: Addison-Wesley.

Thornton, S. J. (1987). What can children learn from history? *Childhood Education, 63*(4), 247–251.

Trachtenberg, A. (1989). *Reading American photographs: Images as history, Mathew Brady to Walker Evans*. New York: Hill & Wang.

Trinkle, D. A. (1997). *The history highway: A guide to Internet resources*. Armonk, NY: M.E. Sharpe.

Tuchman, B. (1981). *Practicing history*. New York: Ballantine.

Tunnel, M. O., & Ammon, R. (1993). *The story of ourselves: Teaching history through children's literature*. Portsmouth, NH: Heinemann.

Tunnel, M. O., & Ammon, R. (1996). The story of ourselves: Fostering multiple historical perspectives. *Social Education, 60*(4), 212–215.

Turner, T. N. (1989). Interactional drama: Where the long ago and far away meet the here and now. *The Social Studies, 80*(1), 30–33.

VanSledright, B. A. (1997). Can more be less? The depth-breadth dilemma in teaching American history. *Social Education, 61*(1), 38–41.

VanSledright, B. A., & Brophy, J. (1992). Storytelling, imagination, and fanciful elaboration in children's historical reconstructions. *American Educational Research Journal, 29*(4), 837–859.

Vockell, E. L. (1992). Computers and social studies skills. *Social Education, 56*(7), 366–369.

Wellhousen, K. (1994). Using the 1930's 'here and now' curriculum to teach cultural diversity in the '90s. *Social Studies and the Young Learner, 6*(3), 9–11.

Wexler-Sherman, G., Gardner, H., & Feldman, D. H. (1988). A pluralistic view of early assessment: The project spectrum approach. *Theory Into Practice, 27*(1), 77–83.

White, C. S., & Hunter, K. A. (n.d.). *Teaching with historic places: A curriculum framework*. Washington, DC: National Trust for Historic Places.

White, H. (1982). The politics of historical interpretation: Discipline and de-sublimination. *Critical Inquiry, 9*(1), 113–137.

Wiggins, G. (1989). A true test: Toward authentic and equitable forms of assessment. *Phi Delta Kappan, 70*(9), 703–713.

Yeager, E. (1997). Now is your time! A middle school history unit. *Social Education, 61*(4), 207–209.

Yeager, E. A., Foster, S. J., Maley, S. D., Anderson, T., Morris III, J. W., & Davis, Jr., O. L. (1997, March 24–28). *The role of empathy in the development of historical understanding.* Paper presented at the annual conference of the American Educational Research Association, Chicago.

Zinn, H. (1990). *Declarations of independence: Cross-examining American ideology.* New York: HarperCollins.

7

STRATEGIES FOR INCREASING ACHIEVEMENT IN SCIENCE

CHARLES WATSON, ALVIN PETTUS, AND STEVEN FAIRCHILD

Education has no higher purpose than preparing people to lead personally fulfilling and responsible lives. For its part, science education . . . should help students to develop the understandings and habits of mind they need to become compassionate human beings able to think for themselves and to face life head on.

—American Association for the Advancement of Science, 1990

Our media—both the popular media and the education literature—decry the inadequacies of science instruction in U.S. schools. For a variety of reasons, a great many students consider the study of science to be beyond their grasp. In recent years, students from the United States have been compared with students from many other nations; in general, those comparisons have not been flattering. On the most recent NAEP assessments, only about 60 percent of high school seniors and about 70 percent of 8th graders met the Basic performance levels in science.

Consider, too, that the NAEP assessments required students to plan investigations, interpret data and charts, solve problems, and form conclusions—activities that are often absent in science classrooms. The relatively poor scores may be grounded in the ways in which we teach science in schools. Teachers and programs tend to place too much emphasis on memorizing facts rather than applying and understanding concepts through inquiry and active involvement (Lawton, 1997).

Cultural and traditional factors may also be involved. Fort (1993) suggests that most people in U.S. culture—both students and adults—are science shy; that is, most students fear being involved in science and do not receive the support needed to become engaged in science and scientific activities. If U.S. students are to become "science savvy," they need (and most adults also need) to be more confident about science and have more positive experiences with science.

Teachers must rid *themselves* of science shyness so that they can better help their students. Science and science education need to become less mysterious, clearer, less abstract, and more accessible; when these conditions exist in classrooms, children experience the joy of being engaged in science.

Over the past decade, many highly regarded organizations—including the National Research Council (NRC), the National Science Teachers Association (NSTA), and the American Association for the Advancement of Science (AAAS)—have set forth standards and guidelines "calling for improvement in teacher qualifications and the learning environment, and setting levels of expectation for student achievement. The standards reinforce the notion that the pursuit of excellence must be open to all students, regardless of their sex, race, or the community in which they live" (Division of Research, Evaluation and Communication, Directorate for Education and Human Resources, 1996, p. 3).

In general, the standards call for the following:

• Expect all students to attain a high level of scientific competence.

• Expose all students to the full range of educational opportunities and demands of an appropriate science curriculum.

• Expect young people to learn science as an active process while focusing on a limited number of concepts.

• Ensure instruction and assessment that stress understanding, reasoning, and problem solving rather than memorization of facts and terminology.

• Create learning environments that involve students actively through discussion, problem solving, hands-on activities, and small-group work.

• Require teachers to act as facilitators of learning through proper management of the learning environment (Division of Research, Evaluation and Communication, Directorate for Education and Human Resources, 1996, pp. 4–5).

In addition, in *Science for All Americans* (1990, pp. 200–207), the AAAS states that science teaching should

• Be consistent with the nature of scientific inquiry.
• Reflect scientific values.
• Aim to counteract learning anxieties.
• Extend beyond the school.
• Involve students in activities to produce learning of lasting benefit.

The challenge ahead is clear, for both policy leaders and science teachers. Before students can become science savvy and actively engaged in learning science, both the instructional processes and the ways in which we view science must change. The summary in Figure 7.1 compares the traditional with the new forms of curriculum, instruction, and assessment.

ENHANCING STUDENTS' ACHIEVEMENT IN SCIENCE

Children learn best when they construct their own knowledge through interaction with the objects and people in their environment. This approach to learning—known as constructivist (Piaget, 1951), sense-making (McIntyre, 1984), or project (Katz & Chard, 1989)—is driven by student questions rather than textbooks or curriculums. To enhance their natural understandings of science, students need to explore the physical properties of a wide variety of objects; they must have time to think about their investigations; and they need to share their experiences with others

(Gega, 1994). Science teaching extends *beyond* the school; high achievement requires teachers, families, and the community to work together.

The following recommendations, which grew out of the AAAS report, suggest ways of increasing students' proficiency in science:

• Begin investigations with questions students ask themselves, possibly questions about nature.

• Engage students actively, giving them real items to observe, weigh, measure, compare, count, and categorize.

• Concentrate on collecting and using evidence; integrate science with other forms of expression.

• Use a team approach to learning.

• Deemphasize memorizing technical vocabulary; focus on contextual understanding, adding vocabulary for communication purposes.

• Welcome curiosity, creativity, and a healthy spirit of questioning.

Let us also consider the relationship between success in school and young people's motivation and self-confidence. For many students, science involves feelings of anxiety and fear of failure. Find strategies that enhance students' self-esteem. Build on their successes, maintain equal expectations for boys and girls, and support the roles of women and minorities in science.

THE STATE OF THE ART IN SCIENCE INSTRUCTION

Science education in the United States has changed significantly over the last several decades. The most visible change is the coordination of the work of associations, agencies, and institutions of science, education, and government toward the common goal of scientific literacy for all.

In a world filled with the products of scientific inquiry, scientific literacy is a necessity. Everyone needs to use scientific information to make choices that arise everyday. Everyone needs to be able to engage intelligently in public discourse and debate vital issues involving science and technology. And everyone deserves to share the excitement and personal fulfillment that come from understanding and learning about the natural world (National Research Council, 1996, p. 1).

With the publication of Benchmarks for Scientific Literacy (AAAS, 1993) and the National Science Education

FIGURE 7.1
Summary of Strategies That Promote Achievement in Science

CURRICULUM

Traditional Emphasis

- Memorization of facts
- Science disciplines as separate entities

- Science as a separate and unique human endeavor

- Science for high-ability students and those with high aptitudes for science
- Science as a body of information to be learned

- Science teachers as technicians and transmitters of science knowledge and skills

New Emphasis

- Understanding of concepts, skills, and principles
- Interrelationships of biology, chemistry, earth science, physics, technology, and mathematics
- Science as it relates to society, other subject areas, and everyday life
- Science for all students at all grade levels, regardless of ability or background
- Science as a human endeavor involving the application of knowledge, processes, and values
- Science teachers as leaders and reflective practitioners in communities of learners

INSTRUCTION

Traditional Emphasis

- Textbook driven
- Science facts

- Lectures and demonstrations
- Passive accumulation of facts

- Individual student achievement and competition
- Uniform instruction

New Emphasis

- Textbook as one of many resources
- Studying principles and concepts in depth and toward relevance
- Active involvement in scientific inquiry and exploration
- Examining ideas, sharing information, exploring, and discovering
- Cooperation and collaboration for achievement of all
- Flexibility and variety in approaches

ASSESSMENT

Traditional Emphasis

- Assessing what is easily measured
- Assessing for factual information

- Teacher assesses
- Grades given for remembering facts

- Teacher-made and standardized tests used exclusively

New Emphasis

- Assessing what is considered important
- Assessing student performances in applying knowledge and skills, solving problems
- Students and teachers assess
- Realistic contexts used to determine achievement, knowledge, understanding, and progress
- Variety of assessment strategies, including performance tasks, problem simulations, and demonstrations

Some information adapted from Kahle (1996).

Standards (NRC, 1996), coordinating this enormously important effort became easier, as if maps to the territory had been provided. Participants received guidelines separately directed toward their individual areas of concern (e.g., assessment, teacher education, or professional development of teachers) that also meshed together in pursuit of the overarching goal.

In fall 1997, the NAEP released the results of the 1996 assessment of science education. Just 29 percent of 4th and 8th graders were found to have proficiency in challenging subject matter. Among 12th graders, just 21 percent reached the Proficient or Advanced level in science. Moreover, 33 percent of 4th graders, 39 percent of 8th graders, and 43 percent of 12th graders failed to demonstrate even Basic achievement, that is, even partial mastery of prerequisite knowledge and skills. The administration of these tests came too early to have been affected by the Benchmarks (1993) and Standards (1996); the scores, however, will serve as a baseline.

THE CHARACTERISTICS OF SCIENTIFICALLY LITERATE PERSONS

A science-literate person, as identified in *Science for All Americans* (AAAS, 1990, p. xvii) is aware that science, math, and technology are interdependent human enterprises; understands key concepts and principles of science; is familiar with the natural world; and uses scientific knowledge and scientific ways of thinking for individual and social purposes. A companion definition of "scientific literacy," found in the *National Science Education Standards* (National Research Council, 1996, p. 22), includes the following abilities:

• A person can ask, find, or determine answers to questions derived from curiosity about everyday experiences.
• A person can read and understand articles about science in the popular press and converse about the validity of the conclusions therein.
• A person can identify scientific issues underlying national and local decisions and express positions that are scientifically and technologically informed.
• A person can evaluate the quality of scientific information on the basis of its source and the method used to generate it.
• A person can pose and evaluate arguments based on evidence and apply conclusions from such arguments appropriately.

We can attain the goal of scientific literacy for everyone. We now have a clear statement of what it means to be scientifically literate. When teachers, parents, and citizens work together, we can improve the state of science education of today's children for tomorrow's world.

ASSESSING STUDENT ACHIEVEMENT IN SCIENCE

Student assessment and evaluation in science, as in other subjects, typically involves administering teacher-made and standardized achievement tests, composed primarily of multiple-choice, true or false, short-answer, and completion questions. Given the focus of recent standards and directions, however, other assessment strategies and formats need to be included. All the recent reports—including the AAAS, NRC, and NSTA reports—suggest implementing varied approaches to assessment. Those strategies should, of course, be consistent with the learning objectives and desired outcomes identified with the content and principles being studied.

Any form of evaluation or assessment should focus clearly on the desired objectives and outcomes. That is, teachers should be able to answer the question, What do I want students to know or be able to do at the end of this lesson that they didn't know or couldn't do before? And once the learning outcomes are stated, teachers should also be able to answer this question: How will I know my students learned . . . ?

For example, if problem solving and critical thinking are desired outcomes (and they need to be, if students are to achieve scientific literacy), then assessments should focus on those same outcomes by providing students with stimuli and tasks that allow them to demonstrate their skills in these areas. The host of guidelines and standards advocated by national organizations and professional societies demand strategies that go far beyond the multiple-choice, pencil-and-paper testing used almost exclusively until now. Today's teachers must be skilled in designing and using such strategies as these:

• Performance-based assessments that depend on observing students demonstrate skills and apply knowledge, and evaluating a variety of student products.
• Portfolio assessments based on judging changes or progress in student performance, maximum or best performance by students, attainment of specific goals and objec-

tives, and other measures of the quality and value of science experiences.

• Test-based assessments that require students to construct responses indicating their ability to apply learning to new contexts.

Specific assessment tasks for science may require students to perform in the following ways:

• Perform various operations to display the proper use of equipment or technology.
• Perform experiments and investigations requiring application of learned skills and information.
• Present oral and written reports concerning observations and findings from experiments and investigations.
• Keep collections of work and products over time to depict accomplishments and progress.
• Reflect on failures, successes, experiences, and progress.
• Perform self-assessments concerning performances, accomplishments, and products.
• Complete projects and prescribe tasks.
• Design plans for solving practical problems.
• Respond to essay and other constructed-response test items requiring application, synthesis, and other higher-order mental processes.
• Perform library, online, or other research.
• Give oral responses to questions and make oral presentations concerning ideas, work, and discoveries.
• React to the work of classmates and others.
• Create devices and tools applying science knowledge and understanding.
• Describe observed phenomena, events, and sequences of events.

Student performance on these sorts of tasks may best be assessed by observing students while they are actually doing the tasks or by carefully looking at and judging student products and results. Performance assessment implies that the process (the behaviors the students demonstrate) is an important part of what is being assessed. Other assessments primarily examine the product resulting from the student's performance. Whether the emphasis is on the process, the product, or both, performance assessment needs to be based on specific criteria and standards established prior to the assessment.

Unlike conventional paper-and-pencil tests, performance assessment tasks usually do not have easily identi-

fied, single correct answers. Therefore, they are not usually scored by a machine or by persons unfamiliar with the content. The most valid results occur when scoring guides containing specific criteria, or rubrics, are developed prior to the performance. Rubrics serve the important function of providing clear performance targets and standards toward which students can strive; rubrics should be shared with students early in the instructional and evaluative process.

Of course, the design, content, and requirements of performance tasks should be consistent with the teacher's own objectives. The assessment rubrics (with criteria and standards for content and demonstrated performance levels) should be consistent with the identified tasks. Rubrics can be designed to allow the scorer to simply check whether or not each performance criterion has been met, or to rate performances or products along a numeric continuum. In other words, ratings can easily be designed that are similar to the scales used in more traditional grading. Regardless of the evaluative format, scoring rubrics should be shared with (and *understood* by) every student. Therefore, the content and design of rubrics and other assessment devices must be appropriate for students' background and developmental level (Perrone, 1991).

It is important to distinguish between instructional (or teaching) activities and assessment activities or tasks. The activities for both instruction and assessment can be similar, but assessment activities should be designed to determine if the instruction was effective; they should take place *after* the instruction has been provided, rather than during the instructional activities. Students must have opportunities to learn the desired science information and skills before being assessed in a summative manner. In addition, it is usually important to choose tasks for the assessment activities composed of different examples and conditions than those used in the teaching activities. Providing different examples and situations enables assessment of abilities beyond mere rote memorization (see Figure 7.2).

SCIENCE STRATEGIES THAT PROMOTE ACHIEVEMENT

The following instructional approaches and strategies are based on sound research and instructional principles that have yielded very positive results in students' science

FIGURE 7.2
Assessment Scheme for Animal Study

A. Objectives or Learning Targets

After a lesson on studying and recording information on the characteristics and natural behaviors of animals that emphasizes the difference between observations and inferences, the student is expected to be able to

1. Record the physical and behavioral characteristics and changes displayed by an animal over a period of time, based on critical observations.
2. Distinguish between an observation and an inference.
3. Provide a detailed, written description of an animal.
4. Design an investigation or plan a reasonably scientific approach to determine how an animal obtains food and water in its natural environment.

B. Instruction

Instruction is provided to help the student gain the knowledge, concepts, and skills needed to meet the objectives. Activities, examples of observations and inferences, and representative animals that are different from those that will be used in the assessment tasks will be used for the instruction.

C. Assessment Tasks

Directions for the student (after being assigned or allowed to identify a different animal for the task) are as follows:

1. Observe an animal (perhaps a cricket) during the time allotted and record as many observations as you can about its physical and behavioral characteristics.
2. List any inferences you can make about the animal based on your observations and indicate how the observations and inferences differ.
3. Write a report that provides a detailed description of the animal.
4. Describe in writing, as clearly as you can, the procedures and materials you would use to determine how the animal obtains food and water in its natural environment.

Rubric for Scoring the Animal Study

0 = Not attempted or not done
1 = Attempted or done to some extent
2 = Done to a satisfactory level
3 = Done at a high level (very good)
4 = Outstanding performance

Score	Accomplishments
0 1 2 3 4	Observations were recorded that included physical and behavioral characteristics that the animal displayed during the observation period. (The number and type are important.)
0 1 2 3 4	Inferences were identified well enough to demonstrate a clear understanding of the difference between an observation and an inference.
0 1 2 3 4	A written report was provided that conformed to prescribed guidelines and presented a detailed description of the animal.
0 1 2 3 4	A reasonable and clear plan was presented in writing for doing an investigation to determine how the animal obtains water and food in its natural environment.

achievement and understanding of scientific principles. Briefly, the strategies point toward

- Using hands-on activities, process skills, and strategies that allow young people to investigate, explore, discover, and reach conclusions about scientific phenomena.
- Using a learning cycle or discrepant event lessons to challenge students' perceptions about science, scientific principles, and the natural world.
- Using collaborative, cooperative methods so students can discuss scientific principles with others.
- Using activities and content that are naturally motivating for students and that include science and scientific discoveries from different cultural perspectives.
- Using content and principles that naturally link and integrate subjects so students can better understand how science is relevant to their lives.
- Using the available wealth of technology and network services to help students investigate and examine science and scientific principles.

● STRATEGY 7.1: USE A PROCESS SKILLS APPROACH TO TEACHING SCIENCE. TEACHERS USE PROCESS SKILLS SUCH AS OBSERVING, CLASSIFYING, MEASURING, INFERRING, COMMUNICATING, PREDICTING, AND EXPERIMENTING TO HELP STUDENTS UNDERSTAND THE NATURE OF SCIENCE.

DISCUSSION

Students need opportunities to *think;* indeed, they should see science as a way to understand their world. Regardless of grade level, students bring their own experiences and knowledge to classrooms each day, and with those experiences they bring natural curiosity and wonder. Good science teachers take advantage of this by providing well-designed learning experiences that allow students to make sense of their experiences, and in many cases, help them understand basic science principles that affect our daily lives.

Certain important process skills—observing, classifying, measuring, inferring, communicating, predicting, and experimenting—allow children to experience science. (Note that these terms imply action.) *Observing* involves using the

primary senses to examine a phenomenon; *classifying* involves sorting, arranging, and identifying relationships; *measuring* involves gathering information about relative size; *inferring* involves making judgments or conjectures on the basis of gathered information or experiences; *communicating* involves sharing or disseminating information; *predicting* involves using information to foretell what may take place based on what is known; and *experimenting* involves developing a hypothesis and then testing it. When students, regardless of their cultural or socioeconomic background, are actively immersed in process skills, the notion of science as a set of facts disappears and they come to understand science facts as they should: as building blocks for understanding their world.

CLASSROOM EXAMPLES

In recent weeks, Juanita Mendoza's students had been actively involved in examining several life science concepts and principles. Ms. Mendoza provided many different seeds that the students germinated, planted, and grew in the classroom. Each student maintained a daily journal of observations for a plant, keeping careful records of the plant's measurements, colors, development, and growth, and written predictions about what the plant might do next, based on previous observations. Each student was also required to identify the plant by its proper name; as the plants grew, the students identified their respective plants and classified them properly.

In addition, cellular examinations involved taking small samples of each plant's leaves and examining them under a microscope, looking for various cellular structures and examples of cell division. Results of these examinations were included in the journals and shared by creating posters and drawings.

Students also used their plants to pose experimental questions, mostly about how the plants would react to external stimuli and other environmental factors. The students then set up experiments that would help them answer their research questions.

Throughout the unit, Ms. Mendoza guided the students in their investigations and provided direct instruction about botanical processes, cellular structure, and related biological information.

RESOURCES

Fredericks & Cheesebrough, 1993; Hassard, 1992.

● Strategy 7.2: Encourage Exploration, Investigation, and Hands-On Approaches. Teachers use content-rich, active exploration and discovery methods that help students confront scientific misperceptions and understand scientific truths.

Discussion

Students of all ages hold many misperceptions about science and scientific concepts. When young people are confronted with and interact with materials and activities that allow them to reformulate their original ideas and gain new understanding, science concepts become real, constructing a sound foundation for acquiring additional science content and concepts.

Paper-and-pencil tasks and textbook assignments rarely offer students either a complete picture of a concept or an understanding of a concept's basic principles. Hands-on, active participation and manipulation of materials help students comprehend concepts and learn how to learn. That is, students learn to think about concepts creatively and critically when they engage in physically manipulating materials related to science.

Teachers should keep two things in mind as they set out to do science in their classrooms. First, science activities demand well-organized, thoughtful plans intended to assess students' prior knowledge of a concept, a carefully sequenced set of learning activities and student assignments, a method to evaluate whether students have learned the concept, and ways to link the activities and concepts to students' lives. Such activities are much more successful if the teacher is well organized—possessing not only the necessary materials and equipment, but other text-based materials as well. In short, the room should be full to bursting with materials to support lessons or units!

Second, for these types of lessons to be fully effective, teachers must have a clear and deep understanding of the concepts to be taught. Often, through no fault of their own, teachers have had little recent experience with some of the science concepts they try to teach; after all, it may have been some time since the teacher took a science class, and what was once learned may have faded in the face of other responsibilities. Therefore, teachers who intend to use hands-on approaches often spend considerable time refamiliarizing themselves with the appropriate concepts, using college and high school texts, association and conference materials, and the Internet to bring them up to speed.

Classroom Examples

Arlene Washington's classroom walls are decorated with charts, diagrams, and pictures of electrical appliances, generators, batteries, and other visual representations of electricity and its uses. Her lessons incorporate a variety of different approaches, but they have one thing in common: During every lesson, students manipulate materials and equipment, exploring not only the uses of electricity, but also how it is generated and transmitted.

One lesson asked students to examine static electricity. In addition to balloons and other objects commonly used to demonstrate the properties of static electricity, Ms. Washington introduced an electrophorus, which she had made from a pizza pan, a large dowel, and a section of plastic pipe. With these materials, she led the students toward understanding static electricity, as well as the difference between voltage and amperage.

Ms. Washington also used a neon wand and a small fluorescent bulb to further demonstrate how the various atoms within these tubes give off colored light when barraged by electrons. She used a wide variety of other materials (including magnets, iron filings, batteries, bulbs, wires, switches, and electric bells) to explore types of current and circuits, as well as more sophisticated principles such as resistance. She helped students overcome their misperceptions of how electricity works by setting up rows of marbles in a tray to show how electrical energy appears to move instantly along a conductor. Ms. Washington served as an expert guide through an exciting array of activities and experiences, including building small electric motors.

Parents of Ms. Washington's students are consistently very happy with their children's progress in learning science; they often remark that in her class, the children nearly always seem to be doing science.

Resources

Barba, 1998; Fredericks & Cheesebrough, 1993; Friedl, 1991; Martin, Sexton, Wagner, & Gerlovich, 1997; Ostlund, 1992.

● STRATEGY 7.3: USE A LEARNING CYCLE STRATEGY OF INSTRUCTION. TEACHERS USE THE THREE-PHASE LEARNING CYCLE MODEL OF INSTRUCTION TO HELP STUDENTS ENGAGE IN AND APPLY SCIENTIFIC PRINCIPLES.

DISCUSSION

Since the 1960s, the learning cycle has evolved into an instructional model that is easy to use, extremely effective, and very engaging. The learning cycle uses exploration, discovery, experiences, questions, and examples to help students understand scientific principles and apply them to new situations or problems, thus constructing knowledge.

The learning cycle includes three phases: exploration, concept introduction, and application. During the *exploration* phase, students explore various phenomena, principles, concepts, and problems, using materials and concrete objects to discover how the concepts are related or interact. They often form hypotheses regarding the principles, and explore various perceptions and misperceptions about the concept.

The second phase, *concept introduction*, involves a more direct form of instruction, as the teacher presents explanations and additional examples. This brief but critical portion of the lesson helps students understand how the activities and concrete materials relate to a scientific principle. Here, too, the teacher explains how the principle is related to students' lives.

The last phase of the learning cycle is *application*. After they have explored a scientific principle and heard the teacher's explanation and examples, students use what they have learned to solve an additional problem or apply the principle to a new situation. This final phase can allow students additional time to manipulate materials, or it can employ more traditional paper-and-pencil methods. This phase of the cycle not only reinforces students' understanding of a principle, but can also serve as a form of assessment.

The learning cycle can be used with nearly all ages, ability levels, and cultures. Both young children and older students benefit from this model because the format resembles the discipline of science itself: That is, students learn to construct knowledge from a series of explorations that lead to discoveries, predictions, and new knowledge. The model is especially effective in helping older students replace inaccurate thinking or erroneous knowledge with new, more authentic understandings.

CLASSROOM EXAMPLES

Maryann Watson's 6th grade students enter the room to find tables set up with a birthday candle, a canning jar, a Styrofoam plate, and a container of water. Using a small piece of clay to affix the candle to the jar's lid, they place the candle and jar in the center of the Styrofoam plate. After pouring a few milliliters of water into the plate, they predict what will happen to a lighted candle when the jar is placed over the candle. Most predict that the candle will go out, and some even suggest that lack of oxygen is the reason. The 6th graders seldom predict, however, the movement of the water upward into the jar as the candle goes out. Several attempts and explorations (using several more candles) reveal some discrepancies in the students' predictions.

After listing the various hypotheses on the board, Ms. Watson (concept introduction) explains briefly the phenomenon the class has just witnessed, using information about air, heat energy, air pressure, and molecular movement. She then presents another problem—perhaps using a hard-boiled egg, a glass milk bottle, and heat—to draw out predictions of what will happen if the egg is placed on the open top of the bottle after heat has been introduced into the bottle. Following this demonstration, she uses the appropriate textbook selection or a handout to reinforce students' learning.

RESOURCES

Beisenherz & Dantonio, 1996; Marek & Cavallo, 1997; Martin, Sexton, Wagner, & Gerlovich, 1997.

● STRATEGY 7.4: USE UNEXPECTED, DISCREPANT EVENTS TO FACILITATE SCIENCE PROCESS SKILLS AND EXPLAIN MISUNDERSTOOD SCIENCE PRINCIPLES. TEACHERS USE A VARIETY OF DISCREPANT EVENTS AND UNEXPECTED, SURPRISING OUTCOMES TO ASSESS STUDENT KNOWLEDGE, POINT OUT SCIENCE CONCEPTS, AND EMPHASIZE SCIENCE PROCESS SKILLS IN THE CLASSROOM.

DISCUSSION

Discrepant events can be especially effective, particularly when they are planned and executed in a thoughtful, engaging manner. Discrepant events are simply events and activities that appear to happen in a way that is counter to expectations; they create strong emotions in students and provide strong motivation for students of all ages, cultures, and abilities to solve the problem associated with the event.

Carefully planned lessons using discrepant events can prove to be very important learning experiences for students; indeed, many older students describe such classroom incidents as some of their most memorable school experiences. More important, they can lead students to true understandings of the scientific principles associated with them.

CLASSROOM EXAMPLES

Janet Greenberg has given her students beakers filled with ice, a thermometer, and a container of water. She displays a large chart on the overhead projector with spaces for pairs or small groups of students to predict the temperature in their respective beakers of ice water. Ms. Greenberg listens carefully, gathering and recording the students' predictions. Most pairs or small groups of students predict that the temperature of their ice water will be at or near zero.

Having recorded the predictions, Ms. Greenberg distributes small paper cups containing a few grams of common table salt. She then asks students to predict the temperature of their ice water after they add 15 to 20 grams of salt. Having seen salt used to melt ice on sidewalks, most students predict that the temperatures of their little systems will rise significantly after the introduction of the salt into the beakers. A few students may predict that the temperature will drop. Ms. Greenberg carefully records all the predictions and then asks the students to add the salt in the beakers and record their observations. Most are quite surprised to see the temperature drop.

Ms. Greenberg leads a discussion about melting and freezing points, heat of fusion, heat of vaporization, and other grade- and age-appropriate science concepts. Finally, she leads the class in a variety of activities and discussion about additional examples and how this phenomenon relates to their everyday lives.

RESOURCES
Friedl, 1991; Martin, Sexton, Wagner, & Gerlovich, 1998.

● **STRATEGY 7.5:** USE COOPERATIVE LEARNING STRATEGIES. TEACHERS USE A VARIETY OF GROUPING PRACTICES TO ENGAGE ALL STUDENTS, ESPECIALLY CULTURALLY DIVERSE STUDENTS, IN THE SOCIAL PROCESSES OF LEARNING SCIENCE.

DISCUSSION

When planned and implemented carefully and thoughtfully, cooperative learning brings about improved understanding of science concepts for nearly all students. Moreover, cooperative learning appears to improve concept and information retention, problem-solving skills, attitudes toward science (and toward teachers!), self-concept, and relations among different cultures and races. Students from different cultures consistently prefer group activities to competitive, individual classroom tasks—but they also prefer reporting on their respective group work individually. Well-organized and well-structured cooperative learning activities can blend group learning with individual accountability and group interdependence.

Cooperative learning needs to be distinguished from merely using small groups. Cooperative learning groups should be carefully formed, with group membership based on a combination of individual student strengths, weaknesses, behavior, and the teacher's learning goals. Cooperative learning groups seem to work best when students are given specific roles and responsibilities that combine learning the material with such roles as recording data, presenting data and information, managing materials, and managing cleanup.

Teachers proficient in cooperative learning strategies test and retest different arrangements and types of activities, given their changing student population and the science content being taught at any given time. Doing cooperative learning is not easy, nor is it something teachers are likely to master quickly; rather, it may take time, careful attention to detail, and many rehearsals and trials before teachers grow comfortable with this valuable approach.

CLASSROOM EXAMPLES

Introducing a lesson on animal adaptation using a six-minute video, Mrs. Martin asks her class to move into their prearranged cooperative groups. She has previously examined the students' prior knowledge of adaptation; their reading, listening, and writing skills; and their abilities to work together. Today's groupings represent her best thinking with regard to all of these factors. She reminds students that everyone has a designated role, that it is important to work together, and of the group work rules and procedures.

The materials manager in each group gathers the needed equipment and materials, and the recorder prepares to record the day's events using an observation worksheet the teacher has prepared. Once everything is place, Mrs. Martin gives a five-minute lecture covering some of the content in the video; she then directs the students' attention to a sheet of directions for the work ahead, reading over the sheet as the students follow along. Mrs. Martin reminds the class that they must depend on each other for ideas, and that a group score will be given for the group's work, which will be entered into a cooperative science learning gradebook. She also reminds them that they will be required to complete additional work on their own, but that for them to be able to do the individual work, they will need to pay careful attention to their own group's work.

As the lesson proceeds, the students examine a variety of texts, pictures, and real animals, discussing and listing the ways in which certain parts of the animals are adaptations, and then following the teacher's written and oral instructions. The members of each group work together to arrive at conclusions that they then present to the whole class. One student presents the group's conclusions; another displays the work on a bulletin board.

Near the end of the lesson, Mrs. Martin again presents some direct instruction that pulls together the lesson's major points and helps students relate the adaptations to their own lives. She finishes by assigning homework and reviewing what the class learned.

RESOURCES

Barba, 1998; Johnson & Johnson, 1986, 1987; Martin, Sexton, Wagner, & Gerlovich, 1998; Okebukola, 1985; Tobin, 1990; Watson, 1991.

● **STRATEGY 7.6: USE MOTIVATING ACTIVITIES. TEACHERS PLAN FOR AND USE MOTIVATING TECHNIQUES, ACTIVITIES, AND ATTITUDES WITH STUDENTS OF ALL CULTURES AND BACKGROUNDS.**

DISCUSSION

Teachers generally possess a bag of techniques they use regularly to motivate their students. In addition, how-

ever, there are positive ways in which teachers can motivate students' interest in science and science learning.

Students of all ages and cultures are naturally curious about the world in which they live; they can be encouraged to act on their natural curiosity in classrooms that link science with life outside the school. Motivating, too, are those classrooms blessed with a positive feeling tone; that is, the class reflects students' prior knowledge, regardless of their background or neighborhood, and it contains culturally familiar references, role models, analogies, and experiences.

Motivation also relates directly to the level of success students find in a classroom. The more students experience success, the more likely they are to expect success in the future. In turn, student success relates directly to the length of time students will keep trying to solve a problem or complete a task. Students who experience success in science class are less likely to misbehave; in fact, often they will help the teacher keep other students on task.

The reverse is also true, of course. Students who consistently experience failure are more likely to cause problems in class, less likely to attempt new tasks or assignments, less likely to participate fully in cooperative groups and other learning activities, and less likely to set personal goals.

Therefore, in addition to providing thoughtfully planned and delivered classroom experiences, science teachers need to be aware of students' cultural backgrounds, histories, and neighborhoods. Science teachers (and indeed all teachers) need to plan and implement lessons and activities that build on and encourage consistent student success.

CLASSROOM EXAMPLES

Gerald Foster's students are obviously a diverse group; looking around the classroom it is easy to spot black, Hispanic, Asian American, and Caucasian students. Mr. Foster's lessons consistently refer to common cultural items and articles, and he uses culturally related artifacts and analogies to emphasize his lessons. For example, he uses origami paper to demonstrate chemical relationships, automobile parts and functions to illustrate systems and principles of chemical and physical science, tortillas and bagels to illustrate types of chemical reactions, and local environmental problems to show chemical and physical changes.

Mr. Foster's classes are known for their absence of behavioral disruptions and for an obviously high level of motivation. He is flexible and accommodating with his use of cooperative learning and small-group work, realizing that some students' cultural backgrounds make it hard for them to answer questions in a large-group setting. And some of his students are made more comfortable by being allowed simply to observe a demonstration rather than to work with materials.

Mr. Foster favors short problem-solving segments that break a task or an assignment into small, student-centered objectives, as well as breaking complex content and science principles into small, logical, easy-to-understand pieces. His lessons are consistently positive; he avoids focusing on students' mistakes, instead highlighting the positive aspects of any given response while helping class members move toward proper understanding of each principle. His emphasis: A big part of science uses failed experiments, errors, and other disappointments to gain understanding and solve problems.

Gerald Foster is also known for his ability and commitment to differentiating assignments and allowing students to make informed and guided choices in their assignments and tasks. He uses assignment forms that give students choices without diluting the need for high-quality work. Often he allows students to demonstrate their understanding by performing culturally interesting, student-centered presentations; his classroom walls display rap songs, drawings, posters, or poetry demonstrating scientific principles.

RESOURCES
Atkinson, 1964; Barba, 1998; Gay, 1988; McClelland, 1965; Ogbu, 1992; Suzuki, 1984.

● STRATEGY 7.7: USE MULTICULTURAL PERSPECTIVES. TEACHERS GO BEYOND THE MALE, EUROCENTRIC POINT OF VIEW WHEN TEACHING SCIENCE, USING EXAMPLES OF SCIENCE AND SCIENTISTS FROM OTHER CULTURES AS WELL AS WOMEN'S SCIENTIFIC CONTRIBUTIONS.

DISCUSSION

Traditionally, U.S. schools have presented science from a white, male, Eurocentric point of view. The teaching of science has been grounded in scientists, scientific theory, and scientific methods that were generated primarily in Europe. Regardless of the origins of this pervasive Eurocentrism, this perspective results in the omission from the curriculum of many important scientists, scientific discoveries, and scientific methods.

U.S. classrooms increasingly contain students from diverse backgrounds and cultures. Global population shifts are affecting not only the methods teachers use, but also how their students understand content. Young people will be more interested in science content when they see how persons from their own cultures viewed the scientific principles, or how those principles are now better understood because of a variety of multicultural contributions.

Perhaps one of the most important reasons to include a more diverse approach to teaching science is the fact that minorities and women are significantly underrepresented in most fields of scientific endeavor. Including the many contributions and accomplishments that have been systematically omitted for so long can send students of all nationalities and cultures a strong message that everyone can do science and become a scientist.

CLASSROOM EXAMPLES

Ms. Wilkins's diverse class of 9th graders is beginning a short unit on space exploration and astronomy. Several students have limited proficiency in English, so Ms. Wilkins carefully selects small groups of students for work teams. She is determined to include a wide range of activities and assignments that will allow her students to investigate how 20th-century space exploration benefitted from the scientific contributions of many cultures, including a number of contributions from women astronomers and scientists.

After several short discussions about some of the scientists included in the textbook, she plans and constructs a bulletin board displaying brief biographies of several better-known, culturally diverse scientists. Another bulletin board includes areas in which students can post biographies and create short displays highlighting other, less-known female, Asian, South American, and Eastern European scientists and astronomers. Her students may use the Internet and a host of other resources to gather data about these scientists. By the end of the unit, the bulletin board highlights the contributions of scientists from all over the world and from many periods of history.

In addition, Ms. Wilkins assigns several groups the task of developing an electronic database and making computer-generated presentations about these scientists; the groups will present their findings to several other middle school science classes. The database includes such astronomers as Caroline Herschel, an American who discovered eight comets during the 19th century; Williamina Fleming, a Scot who discovered a way to classify stars; Arzachel, an 11th-century Spaniard who discovered the elliptical nature of planetary orbits; Subrahmanyan Chandrasekhar, a Pakistani who contributed much to the field of stellar evolution; Yusuke Hagihara, a Japanese man who was instrumental in the development of satellite systems; and Henrietta Leavitt, an American who discovered variable stars in the late 1800s.

Three times during the unit, Ms. Wilkins invites several women and culturally diverse scientists from local laboratories, hospitals, and businesses to speak about their work.

The successes of Ms. Wilkins's efforts are evident throughout the year; she has observed improved attitudes about science and a higher quality of student work. She also makes good use of student research: At the end of the year, she finds herself far more knowledgeable about the scientific contributions of other cultures and of women!

RESOURCES

Banks & McGee, 1993; Barba, 1998; Fathman, Quinn, & Kessler, 1992; NSTA, 1991.

● STRATEGY 7.8: USE TECHNIQUES THAT NATURALLY INTEGRATE OTHER CONTENT AREAS. TEACHERS USE NATURALLY FITTING, COMPLEMENTARY, INTEGRATED CONCEPTS AND CONTENT TO HELP STUDENTS UNDERSTAND HOW SCIENCE RELATES TO THEIR OWN INTERESTS AND LIVES.

DISCUSSION

No area of the curriculum is more suitable to integration or to an interdisciplinary approach than science. Indeed, teachers are finding that integrating curriculum results in deeper and more meaningful understanding of content and concepts, as well as better scores on standardized tests. When students have a realistic context within which to view scientific principles, they tend to remember them more clearly. In addition, students who successfully and regularly participate in interdisciplinary units generally have better attitudes about a subject and better relationships with teachers, and are better able to work in cooperative groups.

Use caution, however, in developing interdisciplinary approaches to science. Teachers need to be certain that an integrated approach actually is better than a more traditional approach; too often, science content taught in this manner can take too much time to present and lose its integrity and meaning for students. Teachers need to plan this type of instruction in a manner that ensures that students will learn more than they would using a more traditional approach.

Evaluation and assessment are one dependable means of being certain of the depth and breadth of student learning. Students' products and assignments should be assessed thoroughly, using a well-developed set of grading guides and rubrics that focus clearly on the content and objectives.

Furthermore, interdisciplinary, thematic, or integrated approaches need to be planned very carefully—whenever possible, with other teachers. When departments are not able to work together to integrate, individual science teachers can carefully incorporate other content areas into their lessons—especially mathematics and social studies, which often fit naturally. Science teachers can also weave English and language arts throughout a given topic, using a variety of trade books or supplemental texts. Whatever the process, careful planning is essential if integration is to work.

CLASSROOM EXAMPLES

Mathew Chang, a science teacher, and Louise Richards, a history teacher, are fortunate to share most of the same classes; they have a stable group of students throughout their respective block schedules, and they are able to periodically link their two disciplines in fairly concrete ways. For example, when Ms. Richards was teaching the period covering the early to mid 20th century, including World War II, Mr. Chang developed several lessons about some of the scientific inventions that occurred as a result of the war.

In discussing their content objectives for the remainder of the year, the two teachers realized they could link or connect naturally several different content areas. With a month of joint planning after school, they created a series of lessons to help their students understand how scientific advancement, especially in space exploration and astronomy, connected with the events that took place following World War II, commonly called the Cold War period.

Mr. Chang created lessons on propulsion, gravity, inertia, energy transfer, ascending cones, Newton's laws, and other principles related to exploring space; Ms. Richards, on the other hand, linked political events, national budgets, changes in education, and other historical topics to the space race and current space exploration efforts. Both teachers report that students' progress and test scores on these topics are much higher than they had been in the past.

RESOURCES
Beane, 1996; Friedl, 1991; George, 1996; Jacobs, 1989.

● STRATEGY 7.9: USE A THEMATIC APPROACH TO TEACH BROAD SCIENTIFIC CONCEPTS. TEACHERS USE THEMES TO CONNECT SCIENTIFIC BIG IDEAS, UNIFYING THEORIES, OR OTHER PRINCIPLES WITH BROAD IMPLICATIONS OR IDEAS ON WHICH THE PRINCIPLES ARE FOUNDED.

DISCUSSION

Themes should be a key component of the science curriculum. Themes are especially important if teachers are to avoid teaching science simply as a set of isolated facts to be memorized; themes allow teachers and students to see the larger framework or foundation of science. Most students are familiar with themes, since they often study the themes of various kinds of literature, themes that give structure to music, or themes that provide guidance in understanding mathematical concepts.

Common themes used in many science classrooms at all levels include energy, as an underlying concept for physical, biological, and geological science; *systems,* as a way to look at patterns, interactions, and boundaries of science areas; *evolution,* as it applies to patterns, processes, and changes throughout time; *change,* as a way of examining systems, trends, cycles, ecology, and adaptation; and *structures,* as a way to view the natural world and its tremendous diversity.

CLASSROOM EXAMPLES

The six-week theme the science department selected was "Change—The Earth in Its Universe." By using a wide variety of exploratory and direct instructional strategies, the science teachers expected students to come to understand how the Earth, as part of a changing universe, changes constantly as it speeds through time. They used the Sun as a central part of the unit, examining atmospheric effects and weather, the effects of the Sun and Moon on the Earth, the Earth's place in the Solar System and the Solar System's

place in the galaxy, and how galaxies form a tiny portion of the universe. Finally, they introduced students to the idea of chaos theory and how it is related to change.

Teachers continued to emphasize the interrelationships of many different but connected systems, the evolutionary processes inherent in our ever-changing Earth, and how humankind has effected changes on the Earth. They used the subtheme of cycles to help students understand the changing nature of life processes, the planets and the Solar System, plate tectonics, and ecosystems.

RESOURCES
Barba, 1998; Fredericks & Cheesebrough, 1993; Friedl, 1991; Gallagher, 1993; Hassard, 1992.

● STRATEGY 7.10: USE TECHNOLOGY, NETWORK SERVICES, AND MULTIMEDIA. TEACHERS USE A VARIETY OF ELECTRONIC MEDIA AND COMPUTERS FOR STUDENT WORK AS WELL AS TOPICAL RESEARCH, EXPLORATION, AND INSTRUCTION.

DISCUSSION

Teachers are gaining significantly more access to (and proficiency in the use of) various types of electronic media and computers. More schools are connected to the Internet each day, and the educational market is flooded with instructional software of varying quality and usefulness. Though teachers are growing more comfortable with technology, the speed with which new materials are introduced is staggering. CD-ROMs, high-speed modems, and digital video technologies enable teachers to demonstrate simulations, experiments, and scientific concepts and principles that were once far too complex for classroom use.

Students who use technology in a meaningful, well-planned, systematic manner appear to demonstrate improved attitudes toward science and higher achievement. Their retention of factual knowledge and basic skills also appears to improve when traditional instruction is accompanied by short, effective, computer-based exercises. Some research suggests that the time needed to learn a concept is shortened when standard instruction is supplemented with computer-based activities. However, science teachers should also be aware that higher-order thinking and problem solving are best achieved by using lessons based on active, hands-on, experimental, real-life activities.

Much of the software commonly found in school classrooms is multipurpose, containing programs for word processing, graphics and graphing, statistical computation, spreadsheets, and database management. Most of these software packages have become much easier to use; elementary students are often quite proficient in their use. The Internet holds much promise for young science students in the area of interaction and mentoring. By using listservers and newsgroups, teachers can connect students with working scientists, who can assist students with projects, research, and the investigation of scientific concepts.

In this area, too, good planning is crucial—not only in knowing how to use technology in the science classroom, but also in being able to evaluate the quality of the software and the uses to which computers are put. It takes time for teachers to become comfortable with computer software and hardware; though most applications are far easier to use than they were just a few years ago, lesson rehearsal and debugging are still necessary.

CLASSROOM EXAMPLES

Diane Rubin, an earth science teacher, planned and developed a sequence of topics to complement the state's mandated curriculum guidelines; the lessons featured outcomes she felt would prove to be both engaging and productive. Using a set of geology projects, each small group of students posed a question of interest to them and set out to investigate various geological processes and events.

Besides using an assortment of texts and trade books, Ms. Rubin arranged for her students to contact a number of scientists and graduate students working in the field. She also found several Web sites containing information and links to other sites in the general area of geology and geological processes. Her planning paid off as the students began to generate well-developed, focused questions.

Throughout the series of lessons, Ms. Rubin guided the students toward her predetermined set of objectives by having them present their findings to the rest of the class. In addition to the extensive list of resources the students gathered, they became familiar with how to use a database to sort and categorize data and bibliographic information; their presentations made use of an LCD overhead projector. Woven into the presentations were photographs and graphic and video clips of various geologic phenomena. Student peers, using a well-crafted set of evaluation items based on the teacher's learning objectives, evaluated each presentation. By e-mail, the students thanked their scientist mentors and electronically sent them copies of their projects and results.

These sorts of activities and strategies require extensive preparation and planning. Many such activities and assignments evolve over a period of time as teachers implement additional activities, ideas, and content—but they all begin with good planning.

RESOURCES

Barba, 1998; O'Neill, Wagner, & Gomez, 1996.

BIBLIOGRAPHY

American Association for the Advancement of Science. (1990). *Science for all Americans.* New York: Oxford University Press.

American Association for the Advancement of Science. (1993). *Benchmarks for scientific literacy.* New York: Oxford University Press.

Atkinson, J. W. (1964). *An introduction to motivation.* Princeton, NJ: Van Nostrand.

Banks, C. A., & McGee, J. A. (1993). Social studies teacher education, ethnic diversity, and academic achievement. *International Journal of Social Education, 7*(3), 24–25.

Banks, J. A., & Banks, C. A. (1993). *Multicultural education: Issues and perspectives* (2nd ed.). Boston: Allyn and Bacon.

Barba, R. H. (1998). *Science in the multicultural classroom: A guide to teaching and learning* (2nd ed.). Boston: Allyn and Bacon.

Beane, J. (1996). On the shoulders of giants! The case for curriculum integration. *Middle School Journal, 28*(1), 6–11.

Beisenherz, P., & Dantonio, M. (1996). *Using the learning cycle to teach physical science.* Portsmouth, NH: Heinemann.

Division of Research, Evaluation and Communication, Directorate for Education and Human Resources (1996). In L. E. Suter (Ed.), *The learning curve: What we are discovering about U. S. science and mathematics education.* Washington, DC: National Science Foundation (NSF 96–53).

Fathman, A. K., Quinn, M. E., & Kessler, C. (1992) Teaching science to English learners, grades 4–8, pp. 1–27. *NCBE Program Informational Guide Series,* Vol. 11, Washington, DC: NCBE.

Fensham, P., Gunstone, R., & White, R. (Eds.). (1994). *The content of science: A constructivist approach to its teaching and learning.* Washington, DC: Falmer Press.

Fort, D. C. (1993). Science shy, science savvy, science smart. *Phi Delta Kappan, 79*(9), 674–683.

Fredericks, A. D., & Cheesebrough, D. L. (1993). *Science for all children.* New York: HarperCollins.

Friedl, A. E. (1991). *Teaching science to children: An integrated approach* (2nd ed.). New York: McGraw-Hill.

Gallagher, J. J. (1993). Ability grouping: A tool for educational excellence. *College Board Review, 168,* 21–27.

Gay, G. (1988). Designing relevant curricula for diverse students. *Education and Urban Society, 20*(4), 327–40.

Gega, P. C. (1994). *Science in elementary education.* New York: Macmillan.

George, P. S. (1996). The integrated curriculum: A reality check. *Middle School Journal, 28*(1), 12–19.

Hassard, J. (1992). *Minds on science.* New York: HarperCollins.

Jacobs, H. H. (Ed.). (1989). *Interdisciplinary curriculum: Design and implementation.* Alexandria, VA: Association for Supervision and Curriculum Development.

Johnson, R. T., & Johnson, D. W. (1991). So what's new about cooperative learning in science? *Cooperative Learning, 11*(3), 2–3.

Johnson, R. T., & Johnson, D. W. (1987). How can we put cooperative learning into practice? *Science Teacher, 54*(6), 46–48, 50.

Johnson, R. T., & Johnson, D. W. (1986). Action research: Cooperative learning in the science classroom. *Science and Children, 24*(2), 31–32.

Lawton, M. (1997). Science proves a big mystery to U.S. pupils. *Education Week, 17,* 9.

Kahle, J. B. (1996). Highlights of the National Research Council's National Science Education Standards. *School Science and Mathematics, 96*(5), 274–275.

Katz, L. G., & Chard, S. C. (1989). *Engaging children's minds: The project approach.* Norwood, NJ: Ablex Publishing.

Mareck, E. A. & Cavallo, A. M. L. (1997). *The learning cycle: Elementary school science and beyond.* Portsmouth, N.H.: Heinemann.

Marek, E. A., & Methvan, S. B. (1991). Effects of the learning cycle upon student and classroom teacher performance. *Journal of Research in Science Teaching, 28*(1), 41–53.

Martin, R., Sexton, C., Wagner, K., & Gerlovich, J. (1997). *Teaching science for all children* (2nd ed.). Boston: Allyn and Bacon.

Martin, R., Sexton, C., Wagner, K., & Gerlovich, J. (1998). *Science for all children: Methods for constructing understanding.* Boston: Allyn and Bacon.

McClelland, D. C. (1965). Toward a theory of motive acquisition. *American Psychologist, 20,* 321–333.

McIntyre, M. (1984). *Early childhood and science.* Washington, DC: National Science Teachers Association.

National Research Council. (1996). *The national science education standards.* Washington, DC: National Academy Press.

National Science Teachers Association. (1991). *An NSTA position statement: Multicultural science education.* Washington, DC: Author.

Ogbu, J. U. (1992). Understanding cultural diversity and learning. *Educational Researcher, 21*(8), 5–14.

Okebukola, P. A. (1985). The relative effectiveness of cooperative and competitive interaction techniques in strengthening students' performance in science classes. *Science Education, 69,* 501–509.

O'Neill, D. K., Wagner, R., & Gomez, L. M. (1996). Online mentoring: Experimenting in science class. *Educational Leadership, 54*(3), 39–43.

Ostlund, K. L. (1992). *Science process skills: Assessing hands-on student performance.* New York: Addison-Wesley.

Perrone, V. (Ed.). (1991). *Expanding student assessment.* Alexandria, VA: Association for Supervision and Curriculum Development.

Piaget, J. (1951). *The child's conception of the world.* New York: Humanities Press.

Suzuki, B. H. (1984). Curriculum transformation for multicultural education. *Education and Urban Society, 16*(3), 294–322.

Tobin, K. (Ed.). (1993). *The practice of constructivism in science education.* Washington, DC: AAAS Press.

Watson, C. R. (1991). Common sense tips for cooperative learning. *NCLMLS Journal, 13*(1), pp. 24–25.

Wiggins, G. P. (1993). *Assessing student performance.* San Francisco: Jossey-Bass.

8

ASCD TALKS BACK

In this final chapter of *More Strategies for Educating Everybody's Children*, as in the original volume, we have provided an opportunity for forward-looking educators who are closely involved with ASCD affiliates worldwide to respond to the ideas presented in the book. We selected a wide variety of respondents who work in many different kinds of educational settings, from classroom teachers to university professors. Each respondent was asked two questions:

1. Where do we start instructionally tomorrow with the recommendations of this publication?

2. What are the barriers to effective instruction that prevent practitioners from implementing these recommendations? How can we best eliminate the barriers to effective instruction?

We believe that the responses in this chapter add an extremely useful dimension—straight from the real world of the ASCD member—to the findings and recommendations in this publication.

DENRICK T. RICHARDSON, PRINCIPAL, DENINOO SCHOOL, FORT RESOLUTION, NORTHWEST TERRITORIES, CANADA

Where do we start?

This book provides a clear beginning point for instruction. The best educators truly wish for learners to become collaborative workers, responsible citizens, effective communicators, and creative performers. Many schools, how-

ever, are not providing environments that ensure the acquisition of life skills, nor are they encouraging students to achieve at their potential. Addressing these shortcomings will require a new focus for meeting learners' needs. Schools should establish a process that leads to the completion of graduation requirements and to a career.

Many educators agree that we need programs clearly designated with defined curricular goals and objectives—programs that are integrated, have market value, and have publicly stated exit requirements. Instruction should be driven by a career focus. It should end with career-related certification and include career-related experiences.

What are the barriers?

Many schools are plagued by unhealthy conditions that create barriers to learning. A recent review of secondary schools in Canada's Northwest Territories identified seven such symptoms, including irregular attendance and punctuality; lack of motivation; lack of respect for self and others; apathy; alcohol and drug abuse; physical and emotional abuse; and angry, often violent outbursts. Avoiding these obstacles should be a high priority. Educators need to develop partnerships with such wellness organizations as victim services, and with local drug and alcohol programs to assist school personnel in coping with student problems that arise outside the school.

School programs clearly affect every young person's life. Schools have a responsibility to require students to work closely with parents and teachers on career development and planning. If they are to promote and facilitate successful achievement, teachers need to be caring and process oriented; they (and their students) could benefit from some background in counseling and experience in all the core academic areas.

Matching teaching with school program choices is an urgent challenge for education today. Career development and planning should become an integral and important part of schooling.

GREGG DOWTY, PRESIDENT, MAINE ASCD, HINCKLEY, MAINE

Where do we start?

If we are truly interested in educating all children, we must recognize the needs of our at-risk youth. As identified by Evelyn Reed-Victor and James Stronge, studies of resiliency have great potential for our work with this neglected population. Research has identified the great importance of a significant adult relationship that can support at-risk children in their development.

At-risk youth view supportive adults as those people who accept them unconditionally, regardless of their temperaments, personalities, attractiveness, or intelligence (Werner & Smith, 1992). As educators dedicated to the education of all children, we must first recognize that we are significant adults in the lives of children and choose actions and behaviors that result in supportive relationships.

What are the barriers?

To remove the barriers to implementing the recommendations in this book, we must first commit ourselves to the education of *all* children as a matter of public policy. At all levels of governance, from statehouses to school boards, we must encourage discussions that lead to education reform and public support for our diverse population of learners. At the same time, we must stop advocating for any one group of learners at the expense of another. Any policymaking must address the needs of all children. Furthermore, every policy decision should in some way connect to classroom practice. Too often, public policy decisions do not translate to the classroom. If we can begin to make such connections, we will positively affect instruction for all our children.

RESOURCE

Werner, E. E., & Smith, R. S. (1992). *Overcoming the odds: High-risk children from birth to adulthood.* Ithaca, NY: Cornell University Press.

MARÍA LUISA GONZÁLEZ, DEPARTMENT HEAD, EDUCATIONAL MANAGEMENT, NEW MEXICO STATE UNIVERSITY

Where do we start?

Our starting point should be to acknowledge that as teachers we are or will be working with students who are not native speakers of English. We must then accept that (1) it is our collective responsibility to help these students succeed in their classes; (2) we can do this by making content comprehensible to them; and (3) we must learn and use instructional approaches that may be quite different from those we have learned in the past.

What are the barriers?

Barriers to effective instruction include inadequate university and inservice preparation for all school personnel; school structures that discourage school personnel from working collaboratively with each other and with the community; and a lack of support and leadership from administrators in working with linguistically and culturally diverse students and their families. We can begin to eliminate these barriers by rethinking the nature of schooling and promoting equal access to education and social justice for all students.

JAY R. WUCHER, FORMER PRESIDENT, GEORGIA ASCD

Where do we start?

Our country's greatest strength is often our greatest weakness. We were founded by peoples of diverse backgrounds who labored and learned together to create the United States of America. As time has passed, our country has become more diverse, with countless subcultures, yet our understanding of and appreciation for cultural differences have not kept pace with the pervasive changes that are reshaping the United States today.

What are the barriers?

The barriers posed by cultural differences, values, poverty, crime, and the like are not going away; simply knowing that problems exist is not enough. The more we know about and value who we are now, and the more we vary our instructional strategies for all students, the more effective we will become as educators. This needs to be a top priority both in teacher preparation programs and in programs of systemic, systematic professional development for all those involved with children.

Expecting less of any individual because of his background or culture only perpetuates misconceptions. The value of education can be the reason students choose to achieve. Mentors (e.g., teachers, parents, siblings, coaches, or any significant adults who influence a child to achieve) must convey to youngsters the importance of a high-quality education. Positive role models can make the difference by persistently, insistently inspiring achievement.

HARRIETT ARNOLD, ASSISTANT PROFESSOR, GLADYS L. BENERD SCHOOL OF EDUCATION, UNIVERSITY OF THE PACIFIC, STOCKTON, CALIFORNIA

Where do we start?

We must recognize some of the negative factors in our system of education. These include resistance, poor communication, confusion, and change. We must continue to insist on dialogue and action planning at the national and local levels in the hope of institutionalizing policy initiatives that focus on the vital importance of diversity.

What are the barriers?

Practitioners must acknowledge the presence of barriers and fight for their elimination. The hidden barriers of racism, fears of exploration and the unknown, exclusivity, and change are often artificial ones. Quiet tolerance is not the answer to eliminating barriers, both known and unknown.

There is no silver bullet that will eliminate barriers for effective instruction to all students. One recommendation might be simultaneous national, state, and local initiatives that focus on diversity. Such powerful initiatives would encourage practitioners to participate by providing ample resources, personnel, expertise, research, and evaluation.

MONICA MANN, PROGRAM SPECIALIST, PACIFIC RESOURCES FOR EDUCATION AND LEARNING, HONOLULU, HAWAII

Where do we start?

We need to start by believing that we *can* educate all children. If we believe that change is possible, and if we know what is necessary to make it occur, then we must also help our teachers develop their teaching strategies so that, individually and collectively, they have the capacity to bring about change.

What are the barriers?

Our barriers include systemic structures such as time, professional development activities, and schedules that do not allow teachers opportunities to learn, practice, and continuously refine their teaching practices. To eliminate barriers, we must work at all levels; preservice and inservice educators, policymakers, and decision makers share a responsibility to assist teachers in developing their craft and continuing to find ways to grow professionally.

This book, like *Educating Everybody's Children*, contains terrific ideas for classroom teachers—and for educators at all levels. Professional development opportunities to learn, share, discuss, and practice the strategies herein are needed to help disseminate this valuable information.

MAXINE A. WORTHAM, EXECUTIVE DIRECTOR, EARLY CHILDHOOD PROGRAMS, PEORIA (ILLINOIS) PUBLIC SCHOOLS

Where do we start?

We start with ourselves. We are the boards of education, the administrators, the teachers, and the school staff. We must adopt a philosophy that supports a belief that

- All children can learn.
- All children and their families are valued.
- All children must meet high expectations.

What are the barriers?

The barriers to effective instruction that prevent practitioners from implementing these recommendations include

- Inadequate staff development.
- Stereotypical thinking.
- Inadequate funding.

We can eliminate the barriers to effective instruction for all students by providing

• Ongoing staff development that emphasizes a more inclusive philosophy.

• Adequate resources for public education through federal, state, and local agencies.

• Preservice education programs that emphasize the recommendations in this publication.

KATHY GRIFFEY, ASSISTANT SUPERINTENDENT, ELWOOD COMMUNITY SCHOOL CORPORATION, ELWOOD, INDIANA

Where do we start?

For the practitioner, implementing this vast array of student-centered recommendations is a multifaceted task requiring drastic changes. We are becoming increasingly aware that cognitive development is closely tied to social and emotional development; therefore, it's necessary for each classroom to embody a healthy environment in a child's everyday life. No longer can we allow financial restrictions, narrow views of the school's role, and various social ills to serve as excuses for providing a substandard education to those children in greatest need. This book is a call to action for schools and communities.

What are the barriers?

Barriers to effective instruction include a lack of effective preservice and inservice professional development, a lack of necessary funding, and a lack of the public understanding that real change starts in the local school. The concept of a professional development school (discussed in Chapter 3) may be the foundation needed to achieve effective teacher training. The expansion of this model depends on the commitment of the public sector to improve education in the United States. To some degree, the public is satisfied to wring their hands in dismay over the decline of education, but unwilling to step forward to supply the basics needed to improve schools: teacher training and adequate funding.

CH. CEDRICK HODGE, PRINCIPAL, ST. MAARTEN, NETHERLANDS ANTILLES

Where do we start?

All of these strategies can help any students from diverse backgrounds. As such, this publication represents a valuable resource for all stakeholders and should be widely disseminated. A collaborative effort by school, government, and community is required to implement these strategies.

What are the barriers?

Financial constraints, the lack of a caring classroom culture, dysfunctional homes, low self-esteem, and feelings of alienation are but a few of the barriers to be overcome so that the education we offer to our children can be vastly improved. The foremost need is proper professional training and sensitivity on the part of practitioners in dealing with students of widely varying backgrounds. We must ensure that all students attain a minimum of a high school education and that school failure is kept in check.

JOE PIERCE, SENIOR FACULTY, GRADUATE SCHOOL OF EDUCATION, CITY UNIVERSITY, RENTON, WASHINGTON

Where do we start?

Many of the recommendations in this book focus on relevance and student strengths. We can take a similar, personalized approach to implementing them: Which strategies are most relevant to our students? Which do we already use? Which could we easily try tomorrow? We can also identify our own interests and talents in relation to these recommendations. Which strategies excite us? Which remind us of our strengths? With choices and confidence, we are more likely to take action right away.

What are the barriers?

Narrowly defined professional development requirements leave little time for a personalized approach. We can change this by putting student needs, teacher interests, and classroom action at the heart of our professional development efforts. Moreover, we can encourage teacher-initiated classroom research related to these recommendations. Through this process, teachers assess needs, make choices, implement strategies, study results, and discuss findings with their colleagues. Both teachers and students benefit. Let's support these activities and eliminate less relevant professional demands.

PETE MCFARLANE, ASSISTANT SUPERINTENDENT FOR CURRICULUM AND INSTRUCTION, McLEAN COUNTY UNIT SCHOOL DISTRICT #5, NORMAL, ILLINOIS

Where do we start?

As a profession, we have not been effective in finding and sharing solutions to significant problems at the level of the individual school. Our historical traditions of isolating and standardizing teaching and learning practices against a narrowly defined norm has militated against effective problem solving, particularly as this relates to meeting the needs of a more diverse population.

Our first steps in addressing the important issues illuminated in this book should be to incorporate the research information and practical ideas for instruction that are set forth in both this volume and its predecessor into comprehensive school improvement initiatives. These local initiatives must be informed and supported by state and national efforts—not through mandates but through the provision of timely, accurate information as well as monetary and logistical supports for structural and systemic changes related to the uses of time, space, assessment practices, communication, and professional development.

J. PETER PREST, ASSISTANT PRINCIPAL, JAMES FOWLER HIGH SCHOOL, CALGARY, ALBERTA, CANADA

Where do we start?

In March 1998, the ASCD Board of Governors selected "know the learner" as one of many issues deserving the association's full attention. The recommendations in this book are clearly intended to focus the attention of teachers, administrators, parents, board members, and legislators on the escalating issues of homelessness, literacy, immigration, and national and international standards. When the terms "runaways" and "throwaways" are used to describe large numbers of children in classrooms around the globe, "know the learner" takes on new and vital meaning.

Public education is facing its greatest test. *Educating Everybody's Children: Diverse Teaching Strategies for Diverse Learners* and this volume, *More Strategies for Educating Everybody's Children* are resources for the resourceful. Although the data and illustrations are drawn predominantly from the United States, this study will be of value to educators, and those interested in education, everywhere.

What are the barriers?

The barriers to effective instruction are those concerns that interfere with the teacher's knowing the learner. This statement may seem simplistic, but many pressing issues distract the teacher's attention from seeing each child as unique—with background experiences, interests, and abilities that are molded daily. These issues, no matter how important, detract from the teacher's effectiveness in positively influencing each child's growth.

In the last decade, educational theorists and others have, with the best of intentions, set education off on tangents that have had less and less to do with fostering the teaching and learning relationship. Issues such as site-based management, teacher leadership, and the back-to-basics movement all have their virtues, but have had the high cost of the individual teacher and student relationship. "Know the learner" needs to govern our thinking. These two volumes, *Educating Everybody's Children* and *More Strategies for Educating Everybody's Children* focus on important ways that classroom teachers, schools, and school districts can focus attention on every single child.

ARIANDA F. M. BLOEM, EDUCATIONALIST, CURACAO, NETHERLANDS ANTILLES AND INE HADDOCKS-DWARKASING, TEACHER IN SPECIAL EDUCATION, CURACAO, NETHERLANDS ANTILLES

Where do we start?

Ideally, creating a better education for everyone's children means that schools need to provide future workers with a flexible mix of analytic capabilities—not only basic skills in key subject areas. It's imperative to introduce social skills, character education, and moral education in all our schools. This book offers a forward-looking view on building an education system that will prepare our youth for life in the 21st century.

To create better performance in our education system means lowering repetition and dropout rates. Aside from costing billions of dollars, repetition contributes to high dropout rates, as students become too old for their grades, suffer the stigma of failure, become discouraged, and eventually quit school.

Education can play a much more critical role in the Netherlands Antilles if we strengthen the teaching profession. Education is too important to be left to "experts" and national governments, though both play an indispensable role in policy decisions and affect everything from school financing to national testing and curriculum standards. For reforms to take hold at the school level, diverse stakeholders—including local officials, businesses, school administrators, teachers, parents, and children themselves—need to be involved. Promoting democratic participation in the education of everyone's children means creating a norm for a more consistent, broad-based demand for universal quality education.

What are the barriers?

Barriers constitute the gap between education in our schools and the needs of our community. Our schools are no longer alive, and we are not effective in creating a personalized climate that motivates children. We are not giving children what they really need! A corollary to this is that we do not truly see children from all socioeconomic levels. Finally, we lack the funding to create a better school system.

We can eliminate these barriers by committing to and implementing concrete programs that require immediate action, strengthening the teaching profession, and focusing on higher standards and local community participation. By any definition, though, successfully reforming education is a long-term process.

SUSAN H. COPLEY, PRINCIPAL, PETERBOROUGH ELEMENTARY SCHOOL, PETERBOROUGH, NEW HAMPSHIRE

Where do we start?

If teachers are to implement the recommendations in this book, they need time to discuss these ideas and encouragement to incorporate them into the daily life of the classroom. A study group approach may support teachers who are interested and willing to experiment with new teaching strategies. Principals can provide support and articulate the links between effective instruction and improved student learning, especially for at-risk children.

What are the barriers?

The barriers to implementing these recommendations include lack of time and appropriate materials (e.g., high-quality children's literature featuring the struggles and courage of newly arrived immigrant families, non-Western cultural traditions, and the plight of homeless youngsters), some teachers' limited experiences in traveling or living in other places, and the lack of a collaborative approach to working with people and organizations in the larger community.

Eliminating these barriers requires a common belief that schools must be welcoming, nurturing, safe places for all children to learn; bold leadership; and a recognition that

crucial aspects of children's attitudes, values, and virtues may not be measured on state and national tests. For instance, service-learning projects may contribute to students' and staff members' understanding of the diverse needs in their community—and a lifelong commitment to improving the lives of others.

LINDA THORLAKSON, DIRECTOR OF CURRICULUM, ASSINIBOINE SOUTH SCHOOL DIVISION, WINNIPEG, MANITOBA, CANADA

Where do we start?

So many strategies outlined in these chapters represent good teaching for *all* children, but too many teachers are unfamiliar with them or unaccustomed to using them. For these strategies to begin to be used routinely in classrooms, teachers simply need to be *expose*d to them—and this must go well beyond reading about them in a book. Teachers must experience the usefulness of these strategies in ways that *engage* them personally. Such experiences may take the form of lunch-hour or after-school sessions that allow interested teachers to try out a K-W-L or a story map. Once a teacher has experienced success in using a strategy and talked with colleagues about how easily it can be incorporated into everyday lessons, he or she will be more likely to use it the next time—and to try still other new approaches to teaching. The next step—and one that a school in my district is planning—is to organize a school-wide plan for teaching these excellent learning strategies to the children; for example, in grade 1 all students will know how to use K-W-L.

What are the barriers?

Unfortunately, one of the biggest barriers to providing effective instruction for all students is grounded in the beliefs teachers hold, and their attitude toward children who are disadvantaged in their learning. If we do not believe we are responsible for the learning of *all* the children who come into our care, then we will never be successful. We must take ownership for creating the conditions (at least, those we can control) that will contribute to positive learning experiences, even for those students whose lives are out of control. This happens when a staff works together, with a leader who supports the vision of success for all. Teamwork, ownership, and a belief in the potential for success—that's what it takes!

DAVID HILL, PROFESSOR OF EDUCATION, KEENE STATE COLLEGE, KEENE, NEW HAMPSHIRE

Where do we start?

Each chapter in this book describes the school as an unwelcoming environment for diverse learners. We can change this *tomorrow* by meeting these learners halfway—by more effectively merging learners' personal needs with schools' curricular needs. Each school employee must take the time to identify each learner's personal needs. Good instruction begins with a comprehensive assessment.

What are the barriers?

Time is the largest barrier to effective instruction. Teachers must be given enough time to assess student needs; adapt and teach the curriculum for diverse learners; and improve instruction through reflection, training in methods described in this book, teaming, and becoming better acquainted with school and community resources. There is no way to increase the teacher time needed to accomplish these tasks short of increasing the staff, the school day, or the school year. Learner needs that remain unmet in today's schools require that we rethink how and why we conduct school the way we do.

PAULINE STASKI, LEAD TEACHER, ANTHONY ACHIEVEMENT CENTER, ANTHONY, NEW MEXICO

Where do we start?

Implementing the strategies in this book can begin at many different levels of our school organizations. Teachers can immediately implement class-based strategies by incorporating them into their lesson planning. Site-based committees and strategic planning can focus on those strategies that require broad-based cooperative effort. District management teams can promote and support ground-breaking efforts by individual schools. Finally, state and national organizations can recommend and support these strategies. Careful reading of the recommendations demonstrates that they support and strengthen one another, and can be implemented jointly.

What are the barriers?

The greatest barriers to implementation are the conservative nature and the bureaucratic requirements of public school organizations. Long-term, systemic commitment to implementation is necessary for changes of this nature to be sustained. In addition, many school procedures act against the less traditional student or curriculum. Increased administrative flexibility is a must.

MELINDA TRAVIS, DIRECTOR OF ELEMENTARY CURRICULUM, EAST CENTRAL INDEPENDENT SCHOOL DISTRICT, SAN ANTONIO, TEXAS

Where do we start?

This book addresses several key issues that could help all students become responsible, contributing members of society. To put these ideas into practice, teachers need training in diversity awareness; developing civics, geography, and history concepts regardless of their teaching assignment; successfully engaging all students in real-life applications; and performance-based and portfolio assessment. Teachers need support through scheduled time for training and study groups as well as time to observe one another put such practices into action.

What are the barriers?

Barriers include anything that impedes productive staff development. Since more teachers are receiving content-based degrees with little or no attention to teaching methodology, school districts must provide such training. Attrition makes ongoing training a necessity.

BRENDA R. HAWKINS, LITERACY RESOURCE TEACHER, CRANSTON-CALVERT SCHOOL, NEWPORT, RHODE ISLAND

Where do we start?

Traditional, one-size-fits-all programs that promote competition and center on school-specific artifacts—such as textbooks, workbooks, and worksheets—must be eliminated. Student interests related to issues of social justice, the environment, and the economy should drive an inquiry-based curriculum. Classrooms must become supportive, democratic communities where diversity is perceived as a strength and where autonomous learners develop critical perspectives and strong voices as they collaborate to make the world a better place.

What are the barriers?

The status quo is maintained by institutionalized racism, sexism, and elitism represented by inadequate funding, discriminatory policies, and educational practices such as centralized control of schools, homogeneous grouping, tracking, retention, standardized testing, and instructional programs that value Eurocentric knowledge.

Budget, staffing, and curriculum should be controlled by school-based teams through a process of participatory management. In addition, teachers must be empowered to control their own professional development, not trained to implement new programs.

INDEX

ABOUT THE AUTHORS

Beverly J. Armento is research professor of social studies education at Georgia State University, and is chair of the middle and secondary education and instructional technology department. In addition, she has taught middle school social studies and language arts in Florida, Maryland, and New Jersey. Armento is interested in meaningful learning and teaching, cultural diversity issues in education, and in the preparation of effective social studies educators. She may be contacted at Georgia State University, University Plaza, Atlanta, GA 30303. Phone: (404) 651-2520. E-mail: barmento@aol.com.

Mary Ellen Bafumo is an education consultant based in Boca Raton, Florida. Bafumo was National Director of the Basic School Network, an initiative of The Carnegie Foundation for the Advancement of Teaching, and an associate professor at James Madison University in Research and Program Innovation. She can be reached at bafumome@prodigy.net.

Virginia E. Causey is assistant professor of social science education in the Department of Curriculum and Instruction at Columbus State University, Columbus, Georgia. As a result of her experience as a high school history teacher for eleven years, Causey's research focuses on equitable and effective practices in social studies classrooms and on teacher beliefs about diversity. She has developed curriculum for teaching about African Americans, Native Americans, labor, and women. Her chapter, "Social Studies," in *Perfecting Educational Practice: Culturally*

Responsive Curricula for Elementary and Middle Grades (J. J. Irvine and B. J. Armento, eds.; McGraw-Hill, 2000) analyzes and gives examples of effective instruction for culturally diverse students. Causey may be reached at Department of Curriculum and Instruction, Columbus State University, Columbus, GA 31907-5645. Phone: (706) 568-2255. E-mail: causey_virginia@colstate.edu.

Burton Cohen is Director of Secondary Education in the Palo Alto Unified School District in Palo Alto, California. He also consults nationally and internationally on school improvement issues. Cohen can be reached at (650) 329-3993.

Robert W. Cole is a consulting writer and editor who has served as editor-in-chief of *Phi Delta Kappan* and is past president of the Educational Press Association of America. He is a book development editor for ASCD and a member of the Editorial Advisory Board of *Education Digest* and the Board of Advisors of the Basic School Network. Cole edited *Educating Everybody's Children: Diverse Teaching Strategies for Diverse Learners* (ASCD, 1995). He can be reached at 9716 Seatonville Road, Louisville, KY 40291. Phone and Fax: (502) 231-9568. E-mail: literacy@mindspring.com.

JoAnn (Jodi) Crandall is professor of education, codirector of the master's program in ESOL/Bilingual Education, and director of the interdisciplinary doctoral program in language, literacy, and culture at the University of Maryland, Baltimore County. For five years, Crandall directed Project WE TEACH, to improve the academic achievement and post secondary options of immigrant secondary school students. She holds a doctorate in applied linguistics from Georgetown University. She can be reached at UMBC, Education Department, 1000 Hilltop Circle, Baltimore, MD 21250. Phone: (410) 455-2465. E-mail: crandall@umbc.edu.

Steven Fairchild is a professor of education in early childhood education at James Madison University in Harrisonburg, Virginia. His work focuses on young children and science. Fairchild has authored and directed several projects funded by significant grants, including four SCHEV, Dwight D. Eisenhower Grants. He has given several conference presentations and has written several publications on young children and the teaching and learning of science.

Mary E. Haas is a professor of educational theory and practice at West Virginia University. She taught geography for many years in public schools in Indiana and at the university level in Mississippi. Haas has published in all of the major social studies journals and is the senior editor of *Social Education* for the elementary level. Recent publications include "Implications of New Research and Scholarship in Geography for K–12 Curriculum Development" in *Social Science on the Frontier: New Horizons in History and Geography* published by the Social Science Education Consortium. Haas may be reached at WVU, Box 6122, Morgantown, WV 26506-6122. Phone: (304) 293-3442, ext. 1328. E-mail: maryhaas@aol.com.

Helené Hodges, formerly with ASCD, is an independent education consultant. Hodges is widely recognized for her work in improving the performance outcomes of diverse learners, which has been her specialty for more than twenty years. Hodges may be reached at Urban Curriculum Consultants, Inc., 1752 Preston Road, Alexandria, VA 22302. Phone: (703) 379-2669. Fax: (703) 379-5572. E-mail: helenehodges@aol.com.

Ann Jaramillo is senior project associate at California Tomorrow in Oakland, California. She has been an ESL teacher since 1971 and worked on California Tomorrow's project in the program on immigrant education to create immigrant-responsive secondary schools. Jaramillo conducts professional development on sheltered content instruction and English Language Development strategies throughout California. She holds a bachelor's degree from Stanford University and a master's degree from San Jose State University. Jaramillo may be contacted at California Tomorrow, 436 14th St., Suite 820, Oakland, CA 94612. Phone: (510) 496-0220. E-mail: annj@californiatomorrow.org.

Sonja Siegrist Lutz has taught at Glades Central High School for the past thirty years. Her specialty is writing and English literature. Lutz has been named Palm Beach County teacher of the year twice, and has won other teaching awards. She is a member of the Palm Beach County Guild of teachers and The Florida League of Teachers. Recently, Lutz was featured in a book published by the Palm Beach Post which celebrated 100 individuals who "changed the way we live" in Palm Beach County, Florida, in the last century. She may be contacted at Glades Central High School, 1101 S. W. Ave. M, Belle Glade, FL 33430. Phone: (561) 993-4400. E-mail: lutz_s@popmail.firn.edu.

Laurie Olsen is executive director of California Tomorrow, a nonprofit research and technical assistance organization in Oakland, California. She has developed a national reputation as a researcher, speaker, and consultant to schools on issues of equity and achievement in public schools. Olsen is the author of several publications on immigrant education, including *Made in America: Immigrant Students in Public Schools* (1997, The New Press). For five years, she directed a successful demonstration project in restructuring secondary schools to respond to the needs of immigrant students. Olsen has a doctorate in social and cultural studies in education from the University of California at Berkeley. She may be contacted at California Tomorrow, 436 14th St., Suite 820, Oakland, CA 94612. Phone: (510) 496-0220. E-mail: laurieo@californiatomorrow.org.

Alvin M. Pettus taught high school biology and served as a science supervisor before becoming a college professor. He has taught science curriculum and educational evaluation courses for preservice and inservice teachers. Pettus has published articles concerning science instruction and teaching diverse student groups. He may be contacted at School of Education, James Madison University, Harrisonburg, VA 22807. Phone: (540) 568-3887. E-mail: pettusam@jmu.edu.

Joy Kreeft Peyton is a vice president at the Center for Applied Linguistics in Washington, D.C. She served as associate director of the program in immigrant education;

coeditor of the series, *Topics in Immigrant Education*; and has authored, coauthored, and edited a several publications on educational approaches for immigrant students. She may be reached at Center for Applied Linguistics, 4646 40th St., N.W., Washington, DC 20016-1859. Phone: (202) 362-0700, ext. 245. E-mail: joy@cal.org. Web site: www.cal.org.

Evelyn Reed-Victor is an assistant professor in Teacher Education at Virginia Commonwealth University in Richmond, Virginia. She is Principal Investigator of the Training and Technical Assistance Center at VCU for professional development of community and school personnel, and codirector of UpLink, an interdisciplinary personnel preparation program in Early Intervention. Reed-Victor's research about homeless children and youth incorporates a resilience framework, to address the risk and protective factors that contribute to positive school and life outcomes. With colleagues, she has presented this research at national conferences and in several publications, including *Promising Practices for Educating Homeless Students*. She can be reached at Box 842020, Richmond, VA 23284-2020.

James H. Stronge is Heritage Professor of Educational Policy, Planning, and Leadership at the College of William and Mary in Williamsburg, Virginia. One of his primary research interests is in policy issues related to educating homeless students. Stronge served as editor and as a contributing author of *Educating Homeless Children and Adolescents: Evaluating Policy and Practice*, (Sage Publications), which received a 1994 American Library Association Book of the Year Award. He also coedited the Eye on Education 2000 book, *Educating Homeless Students Promising Practices*. Additionally, Stronge has written on homeless education issues for the *Journal of Law and Education, Journal of Children and Poverty, Journal for a Just and Caring Education, Educational Policy,* and *Education and Urban Society*. Stronge serves as State Coordinator for the Stewart B. McKinney Homeless Education Program in Virginia. He can be reached at The College of William and Mary, School of Education, Box 8795, Williamsburg, VA 23187-8795.

Charles Watson has been a classroom science teacher, an administrator, and a teacher educator. He has published several articles and books about science education and middle-level education and is the Executive Director of the Virginia Middle School Association and Director of the James Madison University School of Education. He may be reached at (540) 568-2813 or by e-mail at watsoncr@jmu.edu.

Related ASCD Resources

The topics in this book are so diverse that the following resources may assist you in finding more information on several topics. ASCD stock numbers are noted in parentheses.

Audiotapes

Connecting Research to Practice: Improving Achievement for Diverse Learners by Vera Blake, Maria Montalvo (#200128)

Educating Everybody's Children by Helené Hodges (#298113)

Educating Everybody's Children: Diverse Teaching Strategies for Diverse Learners by Helené Hodges (#297077)

Language Minority Student Achievement and Program Effectiveness by Virginia Collier and Wayne Thomas (#297040)

Solutions for Educating Language Minority Students by Joel Gomez (#297041)

Teaching Thinking to Multiple Intelligences and Diverse Student Populations by Richard Strong (# 294022)

Valuing Diversity in Children's Learning: Making It Happen in Our Schools by Elizabeth Hebert (#296123)

Print Products

Creating an Inclusive School Richard A. Villa and Jacqueline S. Thousand, editors (#195210)

Educating Everybody's Children: Diverse Teaching Strategies for Diverse Learners, Robert W. Cole, editor (#195024)

Educating Culturally and Linguistically Diverse Students by Belinda Williams (#998060)

How to Respond to Your Culturally Diverse Student Population by Sarah LaBrec Wyman (#61193180)

Inclusion: A Fresh Look; Practical Strategies to Help All Students Succeed, Elementary Edition by Linda Tilton (#398037)

Snapshot Assessment System for Migrant, Language-Minority, and Mobile Students by Rich Rangel and Bill Bansberg (Grades 1–3, #197131) (Grades 4–6, #197132) (Grades 7–8 #399256)

Videotapes

Inclusion [2-tape series] (#495044)

What's New in School—A Parent's Guide to Inclusion (#496221)

For more information, visit us on the World Wide Web (http://www.ascd.org), send an e-mail message to member@ascd.org, call the ASCD Service Center (1-800-933-ASCD or 703-578-9600, then press 2), send a fax to 703-575-5400, or write to Information Services, ASCD, 1703 N. Beauregard St., Alexandria, VA 22311-1714 USA.